Praise for Dorothy Butler Gilliam

"Dorothy Gilliam lived a fascinating life and shares it with you in *Trailblazer*. She started out afraid to tell her editors that D.C. cabs wouldn't stop for her—a problem for a reporter who needed to get to stories on time. She wound up a member of a group of minority columnists who regularly interviewed presidents.

"Her book is a tribute to her generous spirit. No one made greater efforts to share her success with others, to teach school-age journalists, to open the ranks of newspaper management to minorities.

"So many people in journalism are grateful that they met Dorothy. Here's your chance."

—Donald Graham, former publisher of *The Washington Post*

"Dorothy Gilliam is that most rare of revolutionaries, one who not only climbs the barricades, but lets down a ladder to help others up, too. In her more than six decades at the centers of journalism in New York and Washington, she has often been the first African American woman and the best of everything. Her memoir shows us that a few can be both, but no one should have to. We will have no democracy until each of us can be our unique individual selves."

—Gloria Steinem, feminist activist and writer

"Dorothy Gilliam is a great reporter, a pioneer for all women in the news business, and African American women particularly. Her story is about a time in American journalism where courage and brilliance were called for in the white-male bastions that were American newsrooms. It's a story that has been waiting a long time to be told."

—Carl Bernstein, Pulitzer Prize–winning reporter
of Watergate fame

"Dorothy Butler Gilliam's inspirational life story is the journey of a daughter of the South who became a pioneering black woman journalist, an influential voice in the pages of *The Washington Post*, a national leader of the movement to foster diversity in the news media, and a dedicated mentor of countless aspiring young journalists. It is also the story of her role in a remarkable era of growth and influence of a leading American newspaper now evolving in the digital age. And it is a welcome gift for colleagues and readers who have benefitted from her work and presence in our lives."

—Leonard Downie Jr., former executive editor of
The Washington Post, Weil Family Professor, Walter Cronkite
School of Journalism and Mass Communications

"Dorothy Gilliam has contributed a rare and important history of the journey of a black reporter, who is also a woman, focusing on *The Washington Post*, but having implications for the entire industry, writ large. Such a book would have always been a great contribution to the canon, but it is even more relevant today as the industry, as well as the society grapples with diversity and the way forward. Dorothy Gilliam provides answers that give us a road map to successfully navigate that way forward."

—Charlayne Hunter-Gault, award-winning journalist, and
former foreign correspondent for National Public Radio and
the Public Broadcasting Service

"Dorothy Gilliam is a national treasure. Her groundbreaking career in journalism is a monument to triumph, inspiration, grace. She is admired by journalists of color everywhere—not only because of her pioneering body of work but because she cared about us so much."

—Kevin Merida, editor in chief of ESPN's *The Undefeated* and
former managing editor of *The Washington Post*

"For those in the forefront, those "Firsts" of black America, life was seldom a crystal stair to a glorious summit. Dorothy Butler Gilliam's memoir of her life and times chronicles such an ever-upward climb, step by step.

"Hers is the story of a woman ahead of her time, yet deeply involved in the critical issues of that time, and deeply concerned about younger ones in time yet to come.

"She succeeded at one of the premier American newspapers, charting a path of determination, commitment, and inspiration for others to discover and appreciate, and to follow as well."

—Milton Coleman, retired senior editor of *The Washington Post*

"Powerful voice, inextinguishable brilliance, quiet strength, elegant beauty, visionary leader, honored journalist: Dorothy Gilliam. First African American female journalist at *The Washington Post*, Dorothy Gilliam is a trailblazer who still is having an impact on journalists and journalism.

"It's my honor to know Dorothy, serve on the board of the Maynard Institute for Journalism Education, and be one of her many fans who credit Dorothy with being an early career role model."

—Paula Madison, first executive vice president
of diversity at NBC Universal, author

"Dorothy Gilliam didn't just shatter racial and gender barriers at *The Washington Post*, she shattered the journalistic view that white 'objectivity' was the only way of seeing the world. Gilliam pioneered a way of writing about African Americans that was accurate, balanced, and compassionate—principles that had only applied to the coverage of whites before she arrived. The courage and intellectual rigor that it took for her to become the first African American woman journalist at *The Post* makes her a revered elder among black journalists today. Transforming the practice of journalism and paving the way for others makes her a legend for all time."

—Courtland Milloy, fellow columnist at *The Washington Post*

"As a documentary filmmaker whose work focuses primarily on African American history, politics, and culture, I find Dorothy Gilliam's trailblazing career and body of work to be invaluable. I'm thrilled by the thought of having her memoirs as a reference, offering insight and wisdom to my understanding of those who paved the way for so many in the field of journalism."

—Phil Bertelsen, producer/director, *Hope & Fury: MLK, The Movement and The Media*

"Dorothy Gilliam offers a needed perspective as the news industry contemplates where it stands fifty years after the Kerner Commission declared that 'the journalistic profession has been shockingly backward in seeking out, hiring, training, and promoting Negroes.' Her experience grappling with this most intractable issue is without peer."

—Richard Prince, columnist, "Richard Prince's Journal-isms," reporting on diversity issues in the news media

"I would like to take this opportunity to support publication of Dorothy Gilliam's memoir, *Trailblazer: A Pioneering Journalist's Fight to Make the Media Look More Like America.*

I began researching Ms. Gilliam's background several years ago when researching a book about the reporters who were on the Ole Miss campus during the 1962 integration riot. Ms. Gilliam is one of twelve reporters featured in the book because of her experiences as a woman in journalism and as an African American reporter during the civil rights era. Her background speaks of a woman who faced challenges and did not let them stop her and as a woman who used her profile to lecture and encourage a generation of journalists to succeed no matter the barriers set in place. She has many stories to tell, the writing skills to do the job, and the eye for detail that should result in a stunning memoir."

—Dr. Kathleen Wickham, professor/journalism, School of Journalism and New Media, University of Mississippi

TRAILBLAZER

A Pioneering Journalist's Fight to Make the
Media Look More Like America

---◦◦◦---

DOROTHY
BUTLER GILLIAM

CENTER
STREET

Nashville New York

Center Street
Hachette Book Group
1290 Avenue of the Americas, New York, NY 10104
centerstreet.com
twitter.com/centerstreet

First Edition: January 2019

Center Street is a division of Hachette Book Group, Inc. The Center Street name and logo are trademarks of Hachette Book Group, Inc.

The publisher is not responsible for websites (or their content) that are not owned by the publisher.

The Hachette Speakers Bureau provides a wide range of authors for speaking events. To find out more, go to www.HachetteSpeakersBureau.com or call (866) 376-6591.

Featured *Washington Post* articles written by Dorothy Butler Gilliam courtesy of *The Washington Post*.

Featured *Washington Post* article entitled "The Loneliness of Being First," written by Joel Dreyfuss © 1974, The Washington Post.

Library of Congress Cataloging-in-Publication Data

Names: Gilliam, Dorothy Butler, author.
Title: Trailblazer : a pioneering journalist's fight to make the media look more like America / Dorothy Butler Gilliam.
Description: First edition. | Nashville : Center Street, 2019. | Includes bibliographical references and index.
Identifiers: LCCN 2018034533| ISBN 9781546083443 (hardcover) | ISBN 9781549171352 (audio download) | ISBN 9781546083436 (ebook)
Subjects: LCSH: Gilliam, Dorothy Butler, 1936– | Journalists—United States—Biography. | African American women journalists—Biography. | Women civil rights workers—United States—Biography.
Classification: LCC PN4874.G387 A3 2019 | DDC 070.92 [B] —dc23
LC record available at https://lccn.loc.gov/2018034533

ISBN: 978-1-5460-8344-3 (hardcover), 978-1-5460-8343-6 (ebook)

Printed in the United States of America

LSC-C

10 9 8 7 6 5 4 3 2 1

In memory of Robert C. Maynard and Dori J. Maynard, for their journalism diversity leadership and dedication to the goal of helping the news media accurately portray all segments of society. May this work inspire a diverse journalism workforce and help the next generation of journalists of all races and those who aspire to careers in journalism to understand the value of diversity.

Contents

Nelson Mandela with his wife, Winnie Mandela, on his first visit to Washington, D.C., in 1994. Pictured between them, I was honored to cover the visit. I wrote several columns about their trip. (Courtesy of the Dorothy Butler Gilliam personal collection)

My escort John Gamble, President Bill Clinton, and me at the White House State Dinner on October 4, 1994, while I was president of the National Association of Black Journalists. (Official White House Photo)

Pictured far right, I attended an Aspen Institute retreat for journalists in Aspen, Colorado, around 1993. (Ferenc Berko Photo)

Atop a camel in Egypt while en route to the International Women's Conference in Nairobi in 1995. (Courtesy of the Dorothy Butler Gilliam personal
collection)

Speaking in Washington, D.C., in 1998 at a community event, about my experience as a Knight teaching fellow. (Courtesy of the Dorothy Butler Gilliam personal collection)

Me, front center, with women members of my Columbia Journalism School Class of 1961 at the fiftieth-year reunion. Our class included only fifteen women, and I was the sole black woman. Seated to my right is Joan Konner, dean emerita of the J-school and who was for many years a producer for Bill Moyers. (Courtesy of the Dorothy Butler Gilliam personal collection)

Coming to *The Washington Post*, 1961

At my desk in the fall of 1961 or early in 1962, soon after I arrived at *The Washington Post*. (©*1962, Harry Naltchayan*, Washington Post)

When I arrived in Washington, D.C., in 1961, the city, the entire country, and the African continent were all on the threshold of change. The dashing, young John F. Kennedy had just begun his presidency promising "a new frontier." The Civil Rights Movement was kicking into high gear with Dr. Martin Luther King Jr. now urging young people like me to pursue professions we'd been excluded from and to excel. It was thrilling to be in the nation's capital to begin my career as a daily newspaper journalist in the white press.

I brought a pretty placid nature to that career. When I later looked back, I surprised myself. I was so conservative politically! For example, only six years earlier, when I wrote about school integration in the student newspaper while attending Lincoln University from 1955 to 1957 (the Negro college in Missouri that provided higher education for colored students, allowing the state to keep all its other colleges and universities white), I indicated reasons we should go *slowly* with integration. But reporting for *The Tri-State Defender* in Memphis as the Civil Rights Movement dawned had begun to change me. The bus boycott victories had begun to liberate my thinking. And added confidence came from my faith, strengthened my spirit, and pushed me to do things that other people in my family didn't do.

Just twenty-three years old, I was won over by the magnificence of official Washington's buildings and even the romanticism of the streetcars that daily clanged past the U.S. Capitol and on which I could choose a seat anywhere I wished, unlike in the Deep South, where I was born and the segregation was debilitating. The train my family had taken when we moved from Memphis to Louisville, in 1941, had had segregated seating. I don't recall much else about that train ride, but even though I was only five years old, it was apparent to me that train cars for colored people weren't as nice as those for whites. My mother had prepared our food at home to eat on the train, since African Americans had no dining car and could not use the one for whites. Despite the unsegregated streetcars in Washington, I soon realized, with deep disappointment, that D.C. was a deeply divided, segregated, Southern town, not unlike Louisville and Memphis.

In late September 1961, I went to work at *The Washington Post*. As I entered the huge building at 1513-21 L Street N.W. on my first day, the memory of my Columbia University professor John Hohenberg, who had told me, "You've got so many handicaps, you'll probably make it," prompted a tiny roar inside me. He had been referring to my race and gender. My very person—separate from my abilities—could hamper my probability of success. I pushed aside that thought as I pressed the button for the fifth-floor newsroom. My initial nervousness made me feel a bit like a lone soldier about to face an army, or a fledgling swimmer getting ready to dive into an ocean where she would have to learn to swim while the waves roared relentlessly toward the shore. I tried to appear cool and calm as I walked into the newsroom. It was no time to ponder handicaps. I was entering a new world—a complicated, fast-moving newsroom dominated by white men and where the sparse number of white women were mostly marooned on an island called For and About Women, a section of the newspaper filled with social froth about rich white women like Perle Mesta, the famed Washington hostess.

I put on my game face, walked past desks with typewriters and strewn with newspapers, books, phones, and six-ply paper (typing paper with multiple carbon sheets for copies), past men and an occasional woman, and made my way to the City Desk—a long, dark-brown desk situated in the Metropolitan section. I spotted the city editor, Ben Gilbert, who had interviewed me at Columbia and been largely responsible for hiring me. I walked over, smiled, and extended my hand, which he took cordially. He introduced me to the assistant editors and showed me to my desk.

In graduate school, journalists in training said *The Washington Post* was run like the Democratic Party and *The New York Times* like the International Ladies' Garment Workers' Union. This was because Washington was the world's political power center and the editorial pages of *The Washington Post* were seen as liberal and civil libertarian but as arbitrarily managed as the Democratic Party. (Liberal in those days did not mean Blacks and women were well represented in the newspaper's reporting and editing staffs.) *The New York Times* was in the nation's financial and cultural capital and some of its journalists were our teachers at Columbia University, but in its internal management, *The Times* was as rife with intrigue and drama as the cantankerous labor union.

The Washington Post historian Chalmers Roberts called *The Washington Post* of that era internationalist and liberal. It started in 1877 as "a Democratic Daily" and changed hands five times before Eugene Meyer, a visionary Republican, purchased it at a bankruptcy sale in 1933. In 1954, *The Washington Post* acquired and merged with the rival *Times-Herald* in a financial and circulation triumph that solidified *The Washington Post* as the leading newspaper in Washington. Its staff in 1961 numbered more than 850—including news–editorial, business, and production employees. As a business corporation, as well as a newspaper, it was on the upswing.

Ben and I had agreed that I would become a general assignment reporter as I simultaneously got my "sea legs" as a daily journalist. I had come to the newspaper with the same credentials as its white journalists, and I did not want to be stereotyped as qualified to cover only black stories. I thought it wise to be seen as a reporter who could handle any story I was assigned. I saw myself as one of the new-style, aggressive black Americans moving up in Washington and elsewhere and who represented the change in our people—not like the old-style conservative black appointees in government prepared to work for whites within the existing system of gradualism.

I immediately faced prejudice outside and inside the tension-filled newsroom, as one of only three black journalists and the first African American woman. (Two African American men, Luther P. Jackson Jr. and Wallace H. Terry, were already there.) When I showed up to cover some stories, people often didn't believe I was a reporter. One day, I was assigned to write about the one hundredth birthday of a white woman who lived in one of the high-rise apartment buildings in a swank northwest section west of Rock Creek Park, a dividing line between black and white Washington. Wearing a proper professional dress with a skirt below the knees and medium heels, I walked briskly past manicured lawns to the front door.

A black doorman in full uniform, including a plumed hat, looked at me coldly. "The maid's entrance is around the back," he said.

"I'm not a maid," I answered icily. "I'm a reporter for *The Washington Post* and here to do a story on a resident's one hundredth birthday party." I gave him the person's name and showed my *Washington Post* ID.

He looked shocked, almost disbelieving, but went inside and spoke to the white desk clerk. After a few minutes, he returned to where he'd left me standing outside the door and reluctantly let me inside the ornate lobby. I walked toward the equally surprised desk clerk, who knew about the party and telephoned the resident's apartment to let her know I was on my way up. The party-givers also looked surprised to see me. I ignored them as I did my reporting and left. The elderly lady liked the story I produced—which ran in the Metro section and *not* in For and About Women—and graciously called *The Washington Post* to thank me the next day. I felt gratified by her call, understanding that she was forced to see black Americans in a new and different way. Moments like that helped me deal with the many negatives I faced on a daily basis.

Going into white neighborhoods often amounted to an invitation to be abused. My editors would assign me a story for the next day's edition, and, like other reporters, I had only a few hours to get the story, return, and write it before deadline. The inherent segregation of D.C. made it difficult even to travel back and forth to report stories. Standing at the corner of 15th and L Streets a few steps from *The Washington Post* and six blocks from the White House, I would wave frantically for a taxicab, mostly driven by white men, but all would whiz past me. Some would slow down, until the drivers would see my dark-brown skin, when they would press down on their accelerators. By then, I would be fighting back tears, which occasionally broke through in my desperation, until one of those white male drivers would take mercy on me and finally stop. White taxi companies that worked downtown where *The Washington Post* was located didn't hire black drivers.

When I eventually got to my assignment, I did my reporting, and I would again try to flag a cab to get back to the paper to type my story. As time passed, deadlines neared and no taxi stopped, I would start writing my stories out in my reporter's notebook using the Gregg shorthand I had perfected at Ursuline College. I had been one of a group of the first eight African American girls invited to attend the Catholic women's college, as the faculty acknowledged that segregation did not reflect the values of their Catholic faith. Secretarial jobs were a high-reach profession for colored women when I attended Ursuline from 1953 to 1955; the nuns had encouraged me to develop those skills in the welcoming environment of sisters, priests, and fellow students. Now, thanks to them, when I finally secured a cab and got back to *The Washington Post* newsroom, I could quickly transcribe the Gregg symbols, type the story at eighty words per minute, and try to meet my deadline.

On rare occasions, if time permitted, I would call for a Black-owned Capitol Cab with a black driver to pick me up, especially if I was going into black neighborhoods far from downtown. Many black cabs worked only Negro neighborhoods, where they would be assured of passengers; black professionals working in down-town Washington were sparse in those days.

Because of segregation, I couldn't eat in many restaurants in the city. At lunchtime, the only place I could be guaranteed admission was Sholl's Colonial Cafeteria near *The Washington Post*. Some-times Luther and I would go there because we knew we would be welcome and comfortable.

I never told my editors about these snubs and slights because race was not discussed in the workplace. I felt that complain-ing would just give the editors a reason not to hire another black woman. I feared they would say, "You can't hire them because they can't get the job done. Cabs won't even pick them up. It's not our fault she didn't make it; the reality of the times just doesn't make it possible." It's hard for those who never experienced life during legal or de facto segregation to imagine it. It's difficult for me to think back to how I felt, not being able to eat in a restau-rant of my choice, or taking twice as long to get back and forth to assignments because taxis wouldn't pick me up.

One of the hardest problems for me was being ignored by white colleagues when I saw them on the street. White co-workers might speak to me inside the building but would act as if they didn't know me if we passed on the street or outside the newsroom because they didn't want to acknowledge me in front of other whites. The rejec-tion hurt, and I resented that I had to use valuable creative energy masking my emotions. As an accomplished woman with a gradu-ate degree to face such daily slights, I felt not only pained but "less than," "inferior," "not good enough"—not for what I did or did not do, but simply because of who I was. On the street, I tried to consciously avoid some people I worked with who had previously ignored me. I would jaywalk, risk being hit by a car, to avoid being humiliated. Inside *The Washington Post*, some white men, but not all, would let me exit the elevator first, as they did white women.

My lot wasn't as bad as that of my black male friends who were firsts in previously whites-only jobs. One told me white women who saw him on the elevator would refuse to enter it alone. When President Dwight D. Eisenhower's only black staff person, E. Frederic Morrow, finally got a job in the White House, women entered his office only in pairs to avoid talk of sexual misconduct.

The newsroom was not always a safe harbor either. My first city editor, Ben Gilbert, was supportive of me, as were several others. However, not everyone in the newsroom had Ben's progressive sense of racial justice. Luther reached out to me and helped me make connections, especially with other female reporters; some of whom were friendly and helpful and others less so. Luther, who specialized in housing and urban affairs, worked at *The Washington Post* from 1959 to 1963. He was the son of a college president, and in 1968, he became the first black faculty member at the Columbia Journalism School. I could talk to him about any problems I encountered in covering assignments, the racial slights, who might be a bigot, and the politics of the newsroom—such as who were considered the best writers or reporters and got the choice assignments.

Still, I was determined not to fail. I was fortunate to have landed a job at *The Washington Post*. It was my first experience working for a daily. I had, by then, worked for three black weekly publications, *The Louisville Defender* from 1953 to 1955, *The Tri-State Defender* in Memphis in 1957, and *JET* magazine in Chicago from late 1957 to mid-1959. However, it had been my ambition to be a daily newspaper journalist. That meant I would work for a white-owned publication. There was only one black daily newspaper in the country, *The Atlanta Daily World*, founded in 1932 by W. A. Scott. It was the first black daily in the U.S. in the twentieth century and the first successful black daily in all U.S. history. I respected *The Atlanta Daily World*, but I didn't want to go back to live in the South. Like so many in my generation, I was feeling the push by Martin Luther King and other leaders to seek places in white corporations that had been closed to those before us. Even at that early stage in my career, I believed in diversity and wanted to bring a black female sensibility to events and stories that a reached a broad audience. Those were the goals of civil rights activism, and I knew my landing a job at a white daily was a step forward for black women. Many young Blacks were eyeing potential careers in white corporations, although racism (and sexism) permeated every American industry. Few women—and far fewer African Americans—held jobs in the daily press anywhere in the nation in 1961.

Ben Gilbert wrote about the nation's capital as I experienced it in an article published in *The Washington Post* in 1967: "[The history of Blacks in Washington] is a story of adversity and a little progress, accompanied by a shocking indifference and some hostility from the mass of whites." Gilbert explained that any progress that had been made after Reconstruction was thwarted in the 1880s. "The segregation of government employment by race, begun at the turn of the century, became policy under Wilson, whose first wife was distressed to see Negroes and whites working together in the Post Office." Gilbert credits Harold Ickes, Franklin D. Roosevelt's secretary of the interior, with laying "the public foundation of today's integrated city by insisting that the facilities under his jurisdiction be used without discrimination." As a result, in the era before civil rights laws were enacted and before affirmative-action policies were in place, Washington was unique in that some Blacks worked in low-level government jobs that created a level of economic security. Across the nation, few Blacks or women worked in white-collar jobs. Black women, generally forced into the marketplace to help support their families, often worked in jobs beneath their abilities. In the 1950s, relatively few white women worked outside the home.

The place of Blacks in American society was undergoing radical change when I started working at *The Washington Post*, and I wanted to be part of telling the story of trials, trauma, and, I hoped, transformation. If black men and women could risk their lives to break the chains of fear and second-class citizenship in the land of our birth, I could try to integrate the white media industry and bring a black female perspective that was missing from daily newspapers. The Legal Defense and Educational Fund of the National Association for the Advancement of Colored People (NAACP) had pushed for years for an end to racial segregation in public education. In 1954, the Supreme Court outlawed school segregation, and black Southerners had been on the move, pushing against massive white resistance in the South. In December 1955, Rosa Parks had refused to move to the back of the bus in Montgomery, Alabama, and Dr. Martin Luther King Jr. had stepped reluctantly but boldly onto the stage of history. He had become a Moses to lead Blacks in nonviolent protest out of the bondage of Jim Crow that had kept white feet on their necks for nearly a century after slavery's end.

In 1957 after my graduation from Lincoln University, which had been started by black soldiers decades earlier, I became a rookie reporter for *The Tri-State Defender*, and traveled to Little Rock, Arkansas, after my boss, L. Alex Wilson, was brutally beaten when he covered the integration of Central High School. The black students would successfully integrate the all-white high school only after President Eisenhower reluctantly sent in federal troops to enforce the nation's laws in accordance with the 1954 Supreme Court decision outlawing school segregation. White Southerners were horrified when paratroopers formed a protective ring around the black children and walked them into the school, as soldiers stood at attention around the building. One white onlooker called this forced desegregation the darkest day in the South.

When my boss was severely beaten in Little Rock, the white mob didn't know he was a reporter. They thought he was the parent of one of the children. L. Alex Wilson died prematurely about four years after he was attacked by the white mob in Little Rock, and his death made the hate and the violence of whites personal to me. It almost sickened me to my stomach that a misunderstanding by white parents could bring premature death to someone I knew. I felt helpless. I felt angry. By the time of my first days at *The Washington Post*, I had probably started to turn that anger inward, in what would be an ongoing issue in my life, depression. At *The Washington Post*, I often reported on tough subjects. Anger at injustice and melancholy were a normal part of the work. But the case of Mr. Wilson was an aberration; I was such a young reporter, just twenty. Working for him in Memphis at *The Tri-State Defender* was my first civil rights reporting experience. I was not a yeller and a screamer. I felt a kind of helplessness to make change at that point.

On February 1, 1960, seven months before I entered Columbia University, four black men from North Carolina Agricultural and Technical College—Ezell Blair Jr., Franklin McCain, Joseph McNeil, and David Richmond—staged the first sit-in in a Woolworth's in Greensboro, North Carolina. Black college students began sitting in at segregated lunch counters. Old folks and children were soon fighting segregation by gasping for air against the pressure of water hoses and standing stoically as vicious dogs snapped at them, pulled against leashes held by hostile Southern police.

As I was beginning my final semester at Columbia University, before I came to *The Washington Post*, black activism was exploding in the South:

On January 6, 1961, after a two-year battle by the NAACP, a federal judge ordered Charlayne Hunter and Hamilton Holmes admitted to the University of Georgia. Georgia appealed to the U.S. Supreme Court, but two days later, the top court refused to hear the case. When Hunter and Holmes arrived on campus, white students jeered and taunted, "Two, four, six, eight. We don't want to integrate!" Five days later, after a sports event, a white mob attacked Charlayne Hunter's dormitory, and police with tear gas had to fend them off. Instead of punishing the white rioters, university officials suspended Holmes and Hunter "for their own safety and the safety of other students."

University and government officials reportedly hoped to repeat the tactic that had worked for the University of Alabama in Tuscaloosa, when it expelled Autherine Lucy. On February 3, 1956, Lucy enrolled as a graduate student in library science, becoming the first African American ever admitted to a white public school or university in the state. Autherine Lucy attended her first class on Friday, February 3, 1956. On Monday, February 6, 1956, riots broke out on the campus, and a mob of more than a thousand men pelted the car in which the dean of women drove Lucy between classes. Threats were made against Lucy's life, and the university president's home was stoned. The police were called to secure Lucy's attendance. These riots at the university were the most violent, post-*Brown*, anti-integration demonstration to date. After the riots, the University of Alabama suspended Lucy from school, citing her own safety as a concern. She never reenrolled in the university.

This time, with Charlayne Hunter and Hamilton Holmes, the suspension strategy backfired. A majority of the University of Georgia faculty members, all white, came to the rescue of the two black students. They denounced the violence and suspensions and called for Hunter's and Holmes's return.

On February 1, 1961—a year to the day after the Greensboro sit-in—ten young people were convicted of trespassing for sitting-in at the McCrory's lunch counter in Rock Hill, South Carolina, and sentenced to fines of $100 each or 30 days' hard labor on the county chain-gang. Using a new "Jail-No-Bail" tactic, they began serving their sentences on February 2. Four days later, leaders of the Student Nonviolent Coordinating Committee (SNCC)—J. Charles Jones, Diane Nash, Charles Sherrod, and Ruby Doris Smith—traveled to Rock Hill and staged a solidarity "Jail-No-Bail" sit-in that energized the Rock Hill sit-in movement and inspired similar protests in other Southern locations.

Late the following month, after careful planning and training, nine members of the NAACP Youth Council at Tougaloo (Mississippi) College attempted to use the white-only public library in nearby Jackson. They sat at different tables reading books not available in the city's colored library.

I could relate to the Tougaloo Nine because even though I had grown up with a substandard library, later a black librarian, Louvan Gearing, had helped open the doors to higher education for me. Black Louisvillians were better off than Blacks in most Southern cities because in 1921, Louisville became the nation's first city to have a public library for colored people. However, when compared with the beautiful downtown library for whites, it was clearly second-rate. As a child, I used the library in Louisville's all-black West End but felt outraged and second-class by comparison to those who used the white facility. They got new books; we got used ones. Blacks couldn't go to the white public library in most cities even if it was closer to their homes; Blacks had to travel to the colored library in historically black areas, if they had a library at all. Even in the North, some Blacks had to use the back door of the public library and were confined to a small back room. So I applauded when the nine students refused to leave the white library in Jackson, because they helped start a revolution in public libraries.

Arrested for disturbing the peace, the Tougaloo Nine languished in jail. Students at the segregated Jackson State College, including two sisters, Dorie and Joyce Ladner, organized a prayer vigil in their support—challenging Mississippi's ban on civil rights demonstrations and other activities at the school. Hundreds of black people attended the prayer vigil, which was broken up by Jackson State President Jacob Reddix, backed by a squad of cops. Although many presidents of historically black colleges and universities (HBCUs) were white in the earlier years, black presidents increasingly took charge; Reddix was a fair-skinned descendant of slaves.

Three students, the Ladner sisters and student body president Walter Williams, were expelled for their activity in support of the Tougaloo Nine. In response, Jackson State students boycotted classes, retaliated with a defiant rally, and marched toward the jail. They were met by policemen swinging clubs and using tear gas and dogs to disperse them. Simultaneously, Governor Ross Barnett was reviewing several thousand white marchers dressed in Confederate uniforms and waving rebel flags in celebration of the one hundredth anniversary of Mississippi's secession from the Union in 1861.

When the Tougaloo Nine arrived at the courthouse, they were met by a small crowd of black supporters who had been unable to squeeze into the colored section of the courtroom. As they began cheering the students enthusiastically, the policemen attacked them with clubs and dogs. That night, more than a thousand people—many of them adults—attended a rally in support of the Nine. Myrlie Evers later said: "The change of tide in Mississippi began with the Tougaloo Nine and the library sit-in." Although many activists challenged segregation laws through writings and individual action, it was not until the Civil Rights Movement of the 1950s and 1960s that segregated public libraries would be challenged through coordinated, nonviolent protest action.

On May 4 of that same year, 1961, the Freedom Riders emerged. James Farmer, director of the Congress of Racial Equality (CORE), led an interracial group of thirteen (seven Blacks, six whites) out of Washington, D.C., on Greyhound and Trailways buses. They planned to ride through Virginia, the Carolinas, Georgia, Alabama, and Mississippi to test national legislation outlawing segregation in interstate travel. Their destination was New Orleans. Most of the riders were from CORE—many in their forties and fifties—and a few were young students from the Student Nonviolent Coordinating Committee. As they traveled through Virginia and North Carolina, resistance was minimal. However, three riders, John Lewis, Al Bigelow, and Genevieve Hughes, were beaten in Rock Hill, South Carolina. Local police in Charlotte, North Carolina, and Winnsboro, South Carolina, defied the federal ban and arrested some of the riders.

On May 15 (Mother's Day), a mob of more than one hundred Klansmen ambushed a Greyhound bus in Anniston, Alabama, smashing windows and slashing tires. The bus driver tried to get the vehicle out of harm's way, but the attackers chased it, halted it outside town, and then set it on fire. When the mob held the door shut, trying to burn the riders alive, only the presence of an undercover cop from the Alabama Highway Patrol saved the protesters' lives.

SNCC had joined the freedom rides, and the buses moved deeper into the South, encountering more white mobs. White Citizens' Council members and Klansmen in Mississippi as well as black groups rejected calls for a "cooling off period" by President Kennedy and Attorney General Robert Kennedy, who condemned the riders as "unpatriotic" because they were embarrassing the nation on the world stage. CORE, SNCC, and the Southern Christian Leadership Conference formed a Freedom Riders Coordinating Committee to keep the rides rolling.

In June, July, and August, more than sixty freedom rides crisscrossed the South. Most of the rides converged on Jackson, Mississippi, where every rider was arrested. By the end of the summer of 1961, more than three hundred freedom riders had been jailed.

The Kennedys again called for a "cooling off period," and Robert Kennedy was quoted as saying he did not "feel that the Department of Justice can side with one group or the other in disputes over Constitutional rights." Civil rights supporters retorted that the federal department's job was to defend the Constitutional rights of American citizens.

It became increasingly clear that only a political movement and political power could force an end to racial and economic injustice. Student activists morphed into community organizers, building popular mass movements for justice.

I was finishing my journalism training at Columbia with thoughts of entering the work force, and I was inspired and energized by these young people, only a few years younger than me, who were challenging and changing the injustice around America.

I had grown up in the Jim Crow system and felt deeply angered by it. I was also encouraged by the emerging action of brave people in the South. But I knew that breaking the hold of segregation would be difficult. I was also saddened by white Americans who hated and feared Blacks even when they did not know any. While I was being trained to be an objective reporter telling both sides of the story, I thought my work for mainstream media, shining light on the history, culture, and activities of Blacks, could help open-minded white people begin to know and understand African Americans and replace some of their fears with facts. Journalism was giving me tools to combat segregation by changing the attitudes of whites. If I could wield reporting and writing tools well, I would no longer be helpless and could channel my anger into powerful print.

Objectivity in the media has become a big subject. On the one hand, people say there is no such thing as being an objective reporter; then on the other hand, readers clearly don't want to be subjected to the reporter's opinion. From the 1950s black press, I learned to translate that to: Tell both sides of the story and you wield the power of the media to make change. At Columbia Journalism School objectivity meant learning *how* to tell both sides of the story; how do you definitely not ignore certain aspects of the story? I could use that training, those same journalist tools, to tell the *whole* black story, the integration story. The goal was truth telling, to the extent that you could uncover the truth. Accuracy was the aim, learning who, what, when, where, how. Much of what I learned at Columbia was, of course, how to do everything more quickly and the importance of how *good* reporting and writing must be done. One professor would walk through the classroom and say, "Go with what you got." We couldn't get any more information. We had to go with as much as we could verify. We were taught to check out facts. One of my colleagues used to say, "If your mother says she loves you, check it out." I felt I could bring these tools of fair reporting to stories about the black community, educate Blacks about each other, and change the way white people perceived us.

Meanwhile, countries in Africa and Asia were freeing themselves from colonial rule, and sent diplomats to Washington and the United Nations in New York City. Dark-skinned ambassadors traveling between New York and D.C. through segregated Maryland were denied service and subjected to the same Jim Crow humiliations that African Americans were. The owner of one establishment explained after refusing to serve the ambassador from Chad and then physically assaulting him: "He looked just like an ordinary nigra to me." Such incidents embarrassed the U.S. government, damaging efforts of the State Department to attract the new nations to the West and reduce the possibility of their turning to the Soviet bloc.

U.S. 1 and U.S. 40 were the major highways used by travelers driving to and from Washington. Spurred by the actions of the Freedom Riders, the feds pressured restaurants on those routes to serve African diplomats, and gas stations to allow them to use the white restrooms, which were starkly different from the black ones. White restrooms had toilet tissue, working toilets, floors with covering like linoleum, clean sinks, working soap dispensers, and paper towels. Colored restrooms were often dirty, sometimes with toilets that did not work, bare floors that were smelly and damp with leaked water from damaged washbowls, and broken paper towel dispensers. I first encountered white and colored restrooms and water fountains in the train station in Louisville. The colored facilities were horrible and degrading.

The government did not want foreign dignitaries to be exposed to segregated facilities, and protesting students had a plan. To be taken for foreign dignitaries, students at nearby black colleges dressed as Africans and received service. CORE started its Route 40 Project, systematically protesting at highway restaurants up and down the state, demanding desegregation for all Blacks regardless of what they wore.

Those events foregrounded what life was like for many Blacks in America in 1961. Whether they experienced them firsthand or watched the confrontations and violent white resistance on TV or followed them with a black perspective in the Negro press, Blacks were aware of what was going on.

The black press has been an important factor in America for almost two hundred years, since the first Black-owned newspaper, *Freedom's Journal*, was started in 1827—nearly fifty years before slavery was abolished—with Samuel Cornish and John Russwurm as founding editors, declaring that they "wanted to plead our own cause." They challenged bigotry in white newspapers, spoke out against slavery, and appealed to the country's 500,000 freed Blacks.

In the years since, some five hundred black newspapers of varying importance began publication. Among the leading ones were *The Chicago Defender*, *The Pittsburgh Courier*, and *The Atlanta Daily World*. Black newspapers, most of them weeklies, have been an important vehicle for keeping African Americans informed, advocating for justice, and challenging the status quo, as they publicized pivotal events, such as the murder of Emmett Till.

Northern black papers that made their way to the South are even credited with fueling the Great Migration. In recent years, black papers' numbers and influence have waned. I am grateful that I got my start in the black press and for the experience I gained, since the atmosphere within *The Washington Post* felt unwelcoming to me at times. *The Washington Post* was like a factory; it included not only the press room but also the production facilities where the paper was printed, and some African Americans worked on those lower floors. But the fifth floor, where reporters worked, was a world apart—with only three black reporters on a floor of whites. I felt isolated, but my emotional pain was light years removed from the experiences many young Negroes my age were having in the Civil Rights Movement in the South.

In my first few weeks and months at *The Washington Post*, I met the legendary top boss, Philip L. Graham. A 1939 graduate of Harvard Law School, Graham came to Washington to clerk for Supreme Court Justice Felix Frankfurter, one of his mentors. In 1940, after a brief courtship, he married Katharine (Kay) Meyer, daughter of publisher Eugene Meyer. She had recently returned to the nation's capital after working as a reporter in San Francisco.

Philip Graham became publisher of the Meyer family paper in 1946 and assumed a major and highly effective role in crafting the paper's future. In 1954, after a merger with *The Times-Herald*, he made the cover of *Time* magazine, which called the newspaper "the...most influential paper...in the world's most influential city."

Graham and some of his top editors had access to the highest level of government, and they used it to help shape American politics and society. Graham had extraordinary access to the Kennedy White House, as *Post* historian Chalmers M. Roberts, a longtime diplomatic correspondent for the paper in the 1950s and 1960s, wrote in his book *"The Washington Post": The First 100 Years* (1977):

> For John F. Kennedy and his good friend Philip L. Graham inauguration day 1961 was a moment of triumph. Not since the days of Warren Harding and Ned McLean, 40 years earlier, had *The Washington Post* been so "in" at the White House. Once again, triumph turned into tragedy for President and publisher.

Graham had a manic-depressive illness, which manifested in cycles of frenetic activity and devastating despair. By the time I was hired in late 1961, Graham was said to be desperately ill. I met him a year and a half before his shocking suicide in August 1963.

During many of his periods of depression Katharine Graham spent weeks with him at their country estate, but when he felt better he made occasional visits to the office. He made a point of knowing everyone who worked at the paper, especially new employees. He couldn't miss me sitting at my typewriter on the west wall of the newsroom. Occasionally, when he made his rounds on the fifth floor, he would stop by my desk, sit on its edge, and ask how I was doing.

Graham looked to me like the quintessential wealthy WASP (White Anglo Saxon Protestant) I had seen in movies at the segregated Lyric Theater in Louisville. (While some Blacks in the South sat in segregated sections reserved for colored people in white theaters, in Louisville we had separate theaters, where I watched white movie stars—never people who looked like me.) Tall and slender, with pleasant features, Graham exuded confidence and was comfortable with power. His manner when he spoke to me gave no hint of his illness. I would later learn about the strong moral core he exhibited, and in these brief early visits to my desk, I felt he genuinely wanted me to thrive just as he had desired success for his newspaper's first African American hire—Simeon Booker. In his 2013 memoir, *Shocking the Conscience*, Booker said Graham had told him, "Don't hit anybody. If you get mad, just come up to my office and sit down and cool off."

Graham didn't give me such explicit advice, but his brief, sporadic chats provided helpful moral support in the daily trials of working in a segregated city and socially chilly newsroom.

Managing Editor Alfred E. (Al) Friendly, who had also been instrumental in the decision to hire me, was running the news and feature operations by the time I arrived. He was a slight man of medium height who was learned, sophisticated, and imaginative. I didn't have much daily interaction with him in my first year, but that changed at the start of my second year, when I received the assignment to cover James Meredith's integration of the University of Mississippi. Roberts said Friendly "gave both the news pages and the Sunday Outlook section a liberal tone and an intellectual cast with a new emphasis on analytical pieces." I later learned Friendly was a longtime close friend of Phil and Katharine Graham and part of the tight inner circle that helped make the paper the powerhouse it would later become.

The newsroom was divided into local desks covering the paper's circulation area—Washington, D.C., Maryland, and Virginia—and editors for each jurisdiction shared the big desk in the center of the room. I quickly took in the dress code of the deskmen—suits and ties—which they shed or loosened as they worked.

Ben Gilbert, the city editor, was a central figure in all issues at the newspaper involving Blacks, according to Roberts's history of *The Washington Post*. Roberts described Gilbert as a "bright, perceptive and conscientious city editor, tireless in his determination to build a great newspaper. However, he was humorless, abrasive, and without patience for error or incompetence. His city room enemies were numerous. Some couldn't 'take his pressure and quit. At least one squared things by threatening loudly to punch him in the nose.' He became city editor at 27 and held the post for 21 years, longer than anyone else."

Despite Ben's ferocious reputation as crotchety, I liked him from the start. He had been city editor a dozen years when I arrived at *The Washington Post*. One thing I learned from him was how social and business events merged completely. Editors gave cocktail parties and intimate dinners as occasions to meet leaders, those aspiring to move up the ladder as well as newsmakers. Social occasions were opportunities to get information for developing stories and dig out kernels of information that might lead to news stories. Ben Gilbert was the first editor to invite me to a cocktail party in his home on Grant Road N.W., west of Rock Creek Park. There, I met his personable wife, Maureen, and some of black Washington's movers and shakers. Among them were Walter Washington, director of the National Capital Housing Authority, his wife, Benetta Washington, principal of Cardozo High School, and Sterling Tucker, executive director of the Washington Urban League—all of whom would be leaders after the city gained a degree of political autonomy in 1967.

In the office, Gilbert anticipated some of the difficulties he sensed I'd face, and he tried to soften them. For example, he asked veteran reporter Elsie Carper to become a buddy and take me to lunch sometimes. Elsie had started at the paper during the war, was one of the few women on the national staff, and had covered some of the events of the Civil Rights Movement. I was relieved when the two of us would occasionally go to Sholl's Colonial Cafeteria or one of the few unsegregated restaurants because not many of my white colleagues asked me to lunch. She was warm and friendly and became an ally.

One of my favorite assistant city editors, whose job was to give out daily assignments and follow them to their completion, was Steve Isaacs. He was the son of a newspaperman and was the antithesis of the night city editor, John Riseling. A small, slight, old-school editor, Riseling was in his final years before retirement. I recall overhearing Riseling refusing to publish stories about murdered black persons because he did not believe black lives mattered. He called them cheap deaths. This made me so angry I wanted to lash out but I didn't. Controlling my temper, I made a mental note that I would someday find a way to fight against such arrogance, ignorance, and white supremacy. And later, as editor and columnist, I did.

By contrast, Isaacs was young, open-minded, and respectful of me as an African American woman, and he appeared to be sensitive to issues involving Blacks and women.

The nation's capital at that time was virtually a colony. Run by an appointed three-man board of commissioners, it had only gotten its first black commissioner when President Kennedy named former D.C. recorder of deeds John B. Duncan to the board in 1961. The commissioners were limited in what they could achieve because they ran the city under the hawkish, often cruel oversight of Southern lawmakers like Senator Robert C. Byrd, Democrat of West Virginia, a former Klansman. D.C. had no mayor, no city council, no member of Congress. But some local citizens were fighting segregation at every turn. A dozen years before I arrived, for example, Educator Mary Church Terrell had sued to desegregate Thompson's Restaurant, a cafeteria near the White House.

By the time I arrived, Washington, D.C., had a small but long-established black middle class—not as economists might define the term but as defined by such values as strong, intact families, home ownership, dedication to education, necessity of hard work, and individual enterprise. This had been made possible in part because in these families both parents usually worked in low-level government jobs that provided security, or they taught school or worked in black businesses.

Blacks were a majority of the city's citizens—53.9 percent of the total population, according to the 1960 census. The D.C. schools had been officially desegregated in the year before the 1954 Supreme Court ruling against segregated schools. But by 1961 the city's schools were predominantly black, as the dwindling white population continued its flight to the Maryland and Virginia suburbs, creating de facto school segregation. Dunbar High School, the nation's first public colored high school, had long graduated students who became distinguished black professionals, and many of its teachers had doctorates.

When school segregation officially ended, Dunbar students and faculty began scattering to different schools. Howard University was a venerated institution located in D.C. with highly regarded professors and the famous graduate of its law school Thurgood Marshall had made the winning argument in the Supreme Court case that legally ended segregated schools across the nation. Still, D.C. citizens were voteless and voiceless, although some progress had been made; many Blacks lived under harsh socioeconomic oppression rooted in slavery and then legalized in the Jim Crow era that followed. I knew firsthand the economic challenges they faced.

During my first year, under my byline then as Dorothy Butler, I enthusiastically wrote general assignment features. Later, I chose to write stories about poverty, welfare, juvenile courts, and youth crime. For variety, it was interesting to cover stories about routine activities of the president that didn't merit the attention of the White House correspondent. The first time I stood within a few feet of President Kennedy at the White House to cover a very routine story, I thought I would faint from the excitement of seeing the great man up close! Fortunately I didn't.

Later, I enjoyed covering a speech by President Kennedy in which he encouraged 3,500 American college students to pursue public-service careers. I shared the excitement of the students, which seemed to herald a new day, when young people were ready to do new and different things. JFK spoke to the students at Constitution Hall, and the speech reminded me of his inaugural address, when he had spoken his famous words, "Ask not what your country can do for you; ask what you can do for your country."

I covered a Walk for Peace demonstration in which marchers calling for world peace were arrested near the White House. Protests against the Vietnam War were growing.

I was also inspired when I went to the Lincoln statue in the Capitol rotunda for the second unveiling of the statue of Lincoln in honor of its newly restored Emancipation Proclamation scroll, which was placed in Lincoln's hand.

A few months into my first year at *The Washington Post*, I recognized that I was naive to want to be only a general assignment reporter. I had felt it would be limiting to write stories about the black community, but it turned out I was limiting myself. I had, at first, wanted to say I could cover any story and prove that. It was important to me to demonstrate that I could write, and although I wasn't the best writer in the room, I stayed in the room. Poverty was emerging as a national issue, and stories on welfare and poverty received front-page display, while my feature stories were carried in the Metropolitan section. So I asked for—and enthusiastically received—assignments to write those stories. I got the D.C. Juvenile Court beat and wrote stories almost daily. Some were, frankly, bizarre but reflected the poverty that permeated the city. One of the oddest stories I wrote appeared in the paper on November 1, 1962. Here's an excerpt:

An 11-year-old District boy who for several months this year traveled nights on all fours with a pack of dogs is scheduled to appear Friday in Juvenile Court.

The boy, who also barks like a dog, has been in a detention home for the past two months awaiting the court hearing. His parents told the court that he was beyond their control.

Because the District has no in-patient facility where an emotionally disturbed adolescent such as this can get long-term care, this boy will likely end up in a welfare institution with problem children, law violators or waifs.

I couldn't sleep thinking about this little black boy who was so emotionally disturbed. I was bothered that the city had no adequate placement for him. Running with dogs was shocking and strange, but he was just an extreme example of a more common problem I was encountering: the many poor black children living in the capital of the richest nation in the world, who were literally castoffs, segregated in poverty-stricken neighborhoods and housing projects. While I had grown up in a low-income neighborhood, my family was insulated from poverty because my father was the pastor. We lived in the parsonage and had food to share. When we lived in the country later, we experienced the full effects of rural poverty, but the boy's emotional disturbance and the fact that there were no facilities for his treatment were new to me. Maybe having so many handicaps of race that I had to endure growing up, gave me a lot of empathy and love for the African American community.

Welfare was a big story in the District when I arrived, and Eve Edstrom, an experienced and resourceful writer who was sympathetic to the black poor, was covering it. After a few months of general assignment, I wanted a part of it. Racial strife was rising in the city, and I wanted to write about these critical social issues because I hoped black residents would share deeply and openly with me. I asked the editors to let me cover and seek out these stories. My stories soon began to reflect the tension between the city's haves and the have-nots. I wrote about complaints that welfare recipients were buying luxury items—televisions, stereo phonographs, and radios—with their public assistance. I interviewed the people involved. Some insisted their welfare checks hadn't paid for the items. Others said the items kept their children off the streets or calmed their own nerves.

On October 8, 1961, a front-page article detailed welfare cuts. Another front-page article, on October 22, 1961, was headlined "Grownups Can Mask Hunger but Children Scream." It was about local activists' urging a delay in cutting welfare so children would not go hungry. District welfare authorities invoked the "man-in-the-house" rule, which denied aid to mothers who lived with employable men. Even if the man didn't have a job, the family was not eligible for aid. District commissioners wanted the rule changed to help poor children. Placement is based on what is well written and newsworthy, and although it was not uncommon for a news writer to get front-page stories, it made me feel good to get front-page stories so soon after being hired, because it demonstrated that I was an asset to the paper.

The excitement of the Kennedy era drew to Washington dynamic black trailblazers who had experience working as the lone Black in a white newsroom. I reached out to Carl Rowan, whom Kennedy appointed deputy assistant secretary of state in 1961. Rowan had been a reporter for *The Minneapolis Tribune* a few years earlier, when, as he later wrote in his autobiography, "no more than five Blacks could claim to be general assignment reporters, and few were writing anything serious about the American social, political or economic scene."

Rowan had covered the civil rights battles in the South, including the effect of the Supreme Court's decision requiring school desegregation in Little Rock. He wrote so passionately on race relations that he became one of the nation's most highly visible and vocal black men, and Kennedy tapped him to help integrate the State Department. Rowan would become a delegate to the United Nations during the Cuban missile crisis, ambassador to Finland in the Kennedy administration, and director of the United States Information Agency in the Johnson administration, which in 1964 made him the highest-ranking Black in American government.

Rowan and I sometimes spoke of Ted Poston who, as a reporter for *The New York Post*, a white-owned daily, had written riveting stories on the Little Rock Nine and other triumphs and tragedies of the Civil Rights Movement. Poston had impressed me greatly when I was a rookie working at *The Tri-State Defender* and had met him briefly. Orrin Evans, who worked for *The Philadelphia Bulletin*, which ceased publication in 1982, and Thomas Johnson, who was the first black reporter at *Newsday* and later joined *The New York Times*, had been the examples that encouraged me and other Blacks to apply to the white-owned dailies.

The black women journalists I admired were in the African American press. I met Ethel I. Payne of *The Chicago Defender*, known as "first lady of the black press," who was occupying what she called her box seat on history in Washington in the early 1960s. She had risen to prominence in a segregated America. While women in the white newspaper business often occupied inferior positions, the Negro press was less male dominated. For example, anti-lynching activist Ida B. Wells was a newspaper editor, and Era Bell Thompson was the editor of *Ebony* when I worked at *JET*.

Working with *The Defender* since 1951, Payne was its Washington correspondent and the second woman in the black press to be assigned to the White House press corps. I admired Alice Dunnigan, who was the first black woman to cover the White House. (Harry McAlpin had integrated the White House press corps in 1944 as a correspondent for the National Newspaper Publishers Association.) In 1948, Dunnigan, while working for the

Associated Negro Press, had traveled with Truman, covering his presidential election campaign. One of my first forays from *The Washington Post* to seek out other black journalists was to the Keith-Albee Building, where *JET* magazine's Washington bureau was located. The fast-growing news weekly had started a Washington bureau in 1956, and Simeon Booker, who had been *The Washington Post*'s first African American hire, was named to head it. Simeon had left *The Washington Post* in 1953 after only a year and a half because he was "becoming neurotic." He said "coldness and hostility replaced the support usually volunteered newcomers." Outside the newsroom, Booker encountered questioning of his credentials, cab drivers who would not pick him up, the overtly racist chief of police . . . who once physically threatened him, and a lack of welcoming eating places. Booker later said, "God knows I tried to succeed at *The Washington Post*. I struggled so hard that friends thought I was dying. I looked so fatigued after a year and a half, I had to give up. Trying to cover news in a city where even animal cemeteries were segregated overwhelmed me."

I certainly understood what he meant. D.C.'s bias against black business was so great that White House aide Max Rabb had to intervene so *JET* could rent the space in the Keith-Albee Building.

The community of black journalists helped sustain me. I was fortunate to have already been mentored by Frank Stanley of *The Louisville Defender* and L. Alex Wilson, editor of *The Tri-State Defender*, who was a veteran reporter of so much of the Civil Rights Movement. Many of the stories had not gotten wide attention from white society, but a lot of black Americans were paying attention. Wilson had opened the door for me to a very respected band of black reporters who shared what was a very dangerous beat in the South. This band included Clotye Murdock of *Ebony* magazine, Francis Mitchell and Mark Crawford at *JET* magazine, Simeon Booker and Larry Still of *JET*'s Washington bureau, and many others. These black reporters were true trailblazers. *JET* published the picture of Emmett Till in an open casket, and it was one of the seminal moments, one of the horrifying events, that ignited the Civil Rights Movement. I learned so much when I lived in Chicago from 1957 to 1959 and worked for John H. Johnson, the founder and owner of *JET* and *Ebony*. I also began to connect with Blacks in Africa and think beyond the black experience in America when, through *JET*, I met and became friends with Tom Mboya, the charismatic Kenyan labor leader and freedom fighter.

But my dream was to work for a daily newspaper and I took seriously Dr. King's urgings to young people to enter corporate America and make a difference. For the nearly one hundred years since Emancipation, Blacks had been so systematically and cruelly shut out from white corporations, that it took Dr. King's soul-stirring messaging to spark my faith that a career in daily newspapers was even remotely possible for a Negro woman. There were few Negro *or* women examples, role models, or mentors I could look to in the white media. The black press had nurtured my talent early, then provided me opportunity and moved me quickly up the ranks. It was a risk to choose the path Dr. King helped my generation dare to dream, although my choice to work for a white daily was made a bit less difficult by the fact that *The Atlanta Daily World* was the only black daily, and, once I had moved North, to Chicago, I had resolved not to live in the segregated South again. But, the position at *The Washington Post* had not come with community.

I would sometimes experience panic attacks when I was walking to work, fearing what was happening at the office, what I would encounter there, who would not speak to me as I was walking from the bus stop. I would feel humiliated by not being acknowledged by my co-workers. I felt rejected, helpless about my situation. My colleagues hurt me, and the self-pity and resentment I felt were horrible. Many years later, I discovered I had turned a lot of my anger inward in what became depression, and someone close to me at that time later told me, "you didn't know how much bondage you were in at *The Washington Post*." I felt I was battling against enormous odds, odds I couldn't conquer because it was a segregated city and a segregated world. Another black female reporter who came to *The Washington Post* much later, Jill Nelson, stayed only about three years and called her time there volunteer slavery.

What sustained me those first months and years in Washington and enabled me to stay the course and experience the gamut—from endurance to enjoyment—in thirty-three years at *The Washington Post* was the small group of journalists from the Negro press in the early years and the multiracial band of diversity warriors with whom I worked in later years.

Simeon Booker was welcoming and lively, but it was E. Fannie Granton, his reporter, office manager, and eventually associate editor who later became my mentor and friend, introducing me to key people. Middle-aged and a professed "old maid" with a huge heart and love of people, Fannie invited me several times to the home she shared with three other family members in the Anacostia section of southeast D.C. I enjoyed Sunday dinners of her signature cinnamon beef roast and other tasty foods. Fannie knew all the important black people in Washington because they frequented *JET*'s headquarters where they shared news in hopes of appearing in *JET*, attending holiday parties, or joining in some of Booker's evening poker games.

One tradition I enjoyed was the annual *JET* Christmas Party attended by my former boss John H. Johnson, publisher of *Ebony* and *JET*. Booker and Fannie also clued me in to U Street, the famous Howard Theater where leading entertainers such as singer

Jackie Wilson and the entire Motortown Revue—including the Miracles, the Supremes, Marvin Gaye, and Mary Wells—appeared in the fall of 1962. All were typical of black cultural life at the time.

Fannie helped me find housing—twice. First, she told me about a young black woman on Capitol Hill who worked as a secretary and was seeking a roommate. The arrangement worked well until I was the victim of a mugging one night when I was coming home from work. Soon I was looking for another home. I shared my plight with Fannie. She told me about a middle-aged couple, Mr. and Mrs. John Griffin, who lived at 1358 Jefferson Street N.W., a neighborhood of modest black middle-class homes known as Petworth, who wanted to rent a room and bath. My move to the Griffins' placed me in a community that provided a measure of comfort and distance from the high-pressured newsroom.

For seven years, I had kept in touch with Sam Gilliam Jr., an artist and college student I had met on a city bus in Louisville and begun dating when I was a seventeen-year-old student at Ursuline College. Sam, born in Tupelo, Mississippi, had spent most of his life in Louisville, but had done a stint in Japan in the U.S. Army, from 1956 to 1958. Already showing talent as an artist, he earned his master's degree in fine arts from the University of Louisville. The school was integrated and had a good art program. He lived at home while pursuing his degree, so he did not have to pay room and board. He visited me in Chicago while I was at *JET* and a couple of times in New York when I was at Columbia. In June 1961 when I was leaving the States for a postgraduate school trip to Africa, he had lent me a badly needed $100—a very large sum at that time. Although we had known each other for seven years, ours was a loose dating arrangement; we both saw other people.

Sam had been talking for a long time about the possibility of getting married. For me—a preacher's imperfect daughter—these were not days of casual sleeping around. In that era, a reputation for doing so would have been shocking. Birth control was neither reliable nor readily available, and an unintended pregnancy would have been the death knell of a young woman's education or career.

I turned twenty-four during my first year at *The Washington Post* and Sam turned twenty-seven, and I guess we both were ready to settle down. He had been asking me about marriage, and we had talked about it soon after we met. But I had said, "I'm not ready yet." We didn't fall in love a traditional way. We got to know each other over time and got to know other people and saw the value of each other. At Christmas 1961, I accepted his engagement ring, and we were married in Louisville on September 1, 1962, in Youngs Chapel A.M.E., the church my father had built.

I rented a wedding dress for $50 from a formal rental store in Washington. My brother Adee gave me away, and my sister Evelyn and my sister-in-law Margaret were bridesmaids. We had a reception at an upscale black club in Louisville. We loaded all the gifts into the back of Sam's Volkswagen Beetle for the trip back to D.C., stopping one night for a honeymoon stay at a hotel in Cincinnati.

Sam already had a job lined up to teach art at McKinley High School, a predominantly African American arts public high school, where he would work for the next five years. We started marriage in a one-bedroom apartment on Summit Place N.W. in Adams Morgan, the city's diverse, Bohemian section. I began my second year at *The Washington Post*, still one of only three black reporters, and still the sole black woman.

Assignment:
Mississippi, 1962

I posed wearing pearls in this portrait in the early 1960s. *(Courtesy of the Dorothy Butler Gilliam personal collection)*

Ernest Withers and me taken in 2005 when we were featured in a documentary by Syracuse University professor Richard Breyer: *Freedom's Call—A Story about Two Courageous Journalists Who Covered the Civil Rights Movement in the Turbulent '50's And '60's. (Photograph by Robert D. Short Jr. Courtesy of Richard Breyer)*

I am standing third from left, front row, with my graduating class of 1961 from the Graduate School of Journalism at Columbia University. Next to me, fourth from the left, is my friend Merle Goldberg. *(Used with permission of University Archives, Rare Book & Manuscript Library, Columbia University in the City of New York)*

Bankhead-Weems-Hodges Funeral Home in Oxford, Mississippi, where I lodged while covering the Civil Rights Movement. Even as a reporter for *The Washington Post*, I could not get a room in hotels, which were segregated. *(Used with permission of LaVera Hodges)*

James Meredith, as featured in a documentary by Syracuse University professor Richard Breyer: *Freedom's Call—A Story about Two Courageous Journalists Who Covered the Civil Rights Movement in the Turbulent '50's And '60's. (Courtesy of Richard Breyer)*

In early 1961, as I was in the final semester of work on my master's degree in journalism at Columbia University, James Meredith filed suit, with the help of the NAACP Legal Defense and Education Fund, against the University of Mississippi, charging racial discrimination and demanding admission.

Although I had been admitted to Columbia and was closing in on my graduate degree, Columbia was barely integrated. But my situation as a student in the North, in the most prestigious graduate program in journalism, was certainly enviable, compared to Meredith's experience of being denied entry to a Southern university, even after serving his country in the military for nine years.

I was one of fifteen women in my class at the Columbia Journalism School. We joked that the small number was a result of a quota. I was the only black female. The class included forty-five men, one of whom was African American. My most shocking experience at Columbia was realizing the huge gap in my life experiences and those of my classmates. Most of the white students had traveled across the U.S. and to cities in Europe on several occasions. Not only had I not traveled abroad, I had never even been to California or New England, although my work at *JET* had taken me as far away as Florida. Most of my classmates were products of Western society and Western triumphalism, were studying at the best school of journalism in America to prepare for an occupation where they hoped to wield the power of the pen to influence people and events at home and abroad.

If broad exposure to the world had been a seesaw, I would have been in the air, outweighed by most of my white classmates. But we all were expected to hit the ground running. At first, I was afraid I would never catch up or measure up. I was afraid of failure around the strutting men exuding confidence, experience, and whiteness. I had a lot to learn.

Although I could have lived on campus, I chose to live at nearby International House, at 500 Riverside Drive, with other graduate students because it was a perfect complement to my expanding world as it helped me meet students from around the world. I had never lived in a dorm or apartment building with white people before. My world broadened exponentially. International House provided my first cross-cultural living experience and my first interracial dating experience—with a German graduate student.

Fortunately, I met Merle Goldberg, a red-haired Jewish woman from Brooklyn who was filled with life and rebellion and became my bridge over troubled waters. She helped me understand how to maneuver the subways so I could more quickly cover assignments. She decoded New York's extraordinary cultural mix by taking me to ethnic restaurants. She even helped me in the newsroom. I taught her about African American life and culture. Merle revealed that she ironed her hair on an ironing board, and I shared with her the mysteries of the straightening comb my beautician used. We became lifelong friends. She shocked me with her bad talk about her parents. I cringed because respect for parents was a crucial part of the black tradition. Her words may partly have reflected youthful rebellion, but I nearly expected her parents to be devils before I met them at graduation. My only shame about my own family was that my mother and sister Evelyn could afford only the Greyhound Bus as transportation from Louisville for my graduation, whereas most students' parents came by plane. Merle's major focus became medical writing and women's health activism, and she became founder and president of the National Women's Health Coalition.

Another classmate was Nina Auchincloss Steers, a stepsister of Jacqueline Bouvier Kennedy and half-sister of the famed novelist Gore Vidal. Nina commuted from Washington, D.C., to New

York for school. Her rarified breeding was evident in her conversation. She was very smart, spoke with a kind of breathlessness,
and laughed easily. Nina and I were polar opposites—she rode
horses and I rode buses—but we liked each other and as a result
kept in touch after graduating.

Like many colleges and universities of that time, Columbia had
student protests against the war, and against segregation. These
were mild compared to the raging white mobs that so fiercely
objected to James Meredith's integration of Ole Miss. There it
took thirty-two thousand federal troops to enroll him, and two
people were killed on the campus in the insurrection that followed
his enrollment. I couldn't imagine Meredith's situation! I couldn't
even imagine being at Columbia without a good friend like Merle
or acquaintances like Nina. Beyond the fear for his life, I imag-
ined Meredith's loneliness, not having white friends to demystify
Ole Miss or black friends to sustain him and counter the white
supremacy he had come to fight.

I was thrilled that my people were ripping off the manacles of
segregation all over the South. The issue of black people's role in
American society had entered a new phase with the 1954 Supreme
Court decision in *Brown v. Board of Education* and the revolutionary
Montgomery, Alabama, bus boycott led by the Rev. Dr. Martin
Luther King Jr. Yet, when I heard the news of Meredith's suit, my
Southern upbringing made it hard for me to believe he was taking such a bold and dangerous course. I remarked to friends, "A
lone black man trying to integrate that bastion of white supremacy? Meredith must be very brave—or crazy!" When I later got
to know him, I learned he was shrewd, disciplined, independent-
minded and incredibly courageous. I did not know at the time
that Meredith filed suit that I would soon be covering a part of the
story about his hard-won integration of the university.

Meredith was a native Mississippian who had served nine years in the U.S. Air Force and studied a year and a half at Jackson State College, a black institution. He was born on an eighty-four-acre farm in Kosciusko, Mississippi, and lived there until he left to spend his senior year in high school in Florida and then serve in the U.S. Air Force, much of that time in Japan. He was twenty-six, married, and the father of a six-month-old son when he returned in 1960, in his own words, to "fight a war." He wanted to attack what he considered "the Negroes' worst enemy: the principles and doctrine of 'White Supremacy.'"

When Meredith enrolled in Jackson State College, he entered as an advanced junior. There he found a group of intellectuals who became his support group in his daring goal to get a degree from the University of Mississippi—the state's flagship university. He was encouraged by the way that President Eisenhower had intervened in Little Rock. Meredith said he felt the election of President Kennedy provided the proper atmosphere for the inevitable struggle between the state and the federal government that his application would prompt. He wrote the University of Mississippi seeking an application on January 21, 1961, the day after Kennedy's inauguration. The university twice denied him admission, but the veteran's action was destined to spark the greatest constitutional crisis since the Civil War.

For months, Meredith and his lawyers traveled across Mississippi, often followed by state government investigators, pursuing their legal fight, while state officials retaliated with a battle plan of obstruction, evasion, and delay. The case eventually went to the U.S. Supreme Court, which ruled in Meredith's favor on September 10, 1962.

Mississippi governor Ross Barnett led state officials in defying the courts and the U.S. government, fueling his state's rebellion in a stand that delighted most white Mississippians. On the afternoon of September 20, with Meredith en route to Oxford, the university's panic-stricken board of trustees voted to dodge the crisis by appointing Governor Barnett "temporary registrar" of the university. When Meredith and escorts from the U.S. Marshal's Office arrived for his first attempt to enroll, about two thousand protesters, some shouting, "Go home, nigger," greeted him. Governor Barnett personally denied him admittance.

The U.S. government bucked this direct challenge to its authority in federal court. Barnett issued a proclamation declaring the federal government's action a "direct usurpation" of state power— invoking the invalid doctrine of interposition. A closely watched contempt trial followed, and state education officials promised to permit Meredith to register.

On his second try, officials told Meredith he had to register in Jackson in the Woolfolk State Office Building with the university's board of trustees. When Meredith and federal officials arrived to register him, a crowd of some two thousand white people taunted him, and Meredith was again turned away. As Meredith departed, some in the crowd shouted that Ross, not Attorney General Robert F. Kennedy, was "the big boss." On September 26, when Meredith and the U.S. Marshal escorts traveled to the Oxford campus so he could try to enroll for the third time, Lieutenant Governor Paul Johnson turned him away from the entrance to the campus. Cited for contempt, top Mississippi officials refused to appear in the U.S. District Court in New Orleans for the trial. The frustrated judges responded that it was up to the U.S. government to act.

Robert Kennedy, who had been orchestrating events from Washington, D.C. as the nation's chief law enforcement officer, thought he had an agreement with Barnett to enroll Meredith the next day, September 27. However, as the motorcade bearing Meredith was making the ninety-mile drive from Meredith's safe house in Memphis to Oxford, the plan fell apart, and Meredith's caravan turned around—failing in his fourth attempt to enroll.

Meanwhile, Oxford was descending into anarchy as word spread that Meredith would soon be returning to the campus. Ku Klux Klansmen were relaying information to the imperial wizard at his Alabama headquarters. White Citizens' Council members mingled in the crowd. Some people brazenly walked the streets with their guns in plain sight. A mob numbering some 2,500 people gathered around the campus.

The fifth attempt to register Meredith would be on Monday, October 1. On the day before, Sunday, September 30, a hastily organized federal protection force made up of 123 deputy marshals led by Assistant Attorney General Nicholas Katzenbach, 316 border policemen, and 97 federal prison guards was deployed to the Ole Miss campus in anticipation of Meredith's arrival.

Wearing gas masks, helmets, and vests with pockets for tear gas canisters, the marshals lined up outside the Lyceum Building where Meredith would go to register that Monday. The crowd cursed the stoic marshals and called them nigger lovers. Oxford radio stations began announcing that the federal government had taken over the university, prompting hundreds more people to descend on the campus.

Robert Kennedy successfully worked out a secret plan with a reluctantly compliant Governor Barnett. As dusk fell that Sunday evening, Meredith slipped unnoticed with his escorts onto the campus through a side entrance and moved into his dormitory, Baxter Hall. The goal was for him to register the next day as the first African American student at Ole Miss. Twenty-four federal agents guarded the hallway outside his room with a standing order to kill anyone who threatened Meredith's safety.

As word spread that Meredith was on the campus, intense rioting by whites broke out on the circle in front of the Lyceum

Building, where marshals stood, and the usually staid campus became a battle scene. At one point, the mob started hurling bottles at the dormitory where Meredith was, and federal officials monitoring events from Washington panicked. "You don't want to have a lynching," JFK aide Kenneth O' Donnell was quoted as saying. The U.S. marshals and Mississippi National Guard held the bloodthirsty mob at bay into the wee hours. By morning, two people had been killed execution-style by the white mob, a French journalist, Paul Guillard, and a twenty-three-year-old white curiosity seeker, Ray Gunter. More than seventy others were injured. President Kennedy went on national television and announced to the nation he would send in federal troops, tens of thousands of troops in all, to make certain Meredith would be enrolled.

People often ask why black people in Mississippi didn't fight back when the white segregationists rioted on the campus of the university. Fear was a factor. The small black population in Oxford were mostly service workers at the university. While some doubtless owned guns to protect their families, even the bravest would be afraid to fight against such overwhelming odds. Members of the Klan walked about displaying guns. Black people had no power and no vote in Mississippi, nor in most other Southern states.

On October 1, Meredith successfully enrolled in the university, and shortly after the news reached Washington, Ben Gilbert, *The Washington Post*'s city editor, walked over to my desk and asked me to come with him to the office of Al Friendly, the managing editor, in another part of the newsroom. Al asked me to sit down, and Ben told me they wanted me to go to Oxford and other sites in Mississippi. They wanted me to interview black leaders across the state for their reactions and to write about the African American community's response to these historic events.

I had been working at *The Washington Post* for twelve months and married for one month. In the days before this assignment, I had watched with the rest of the world, feeling angry and helpless to do much about it. By going to Mississippi, I could at least write about it. Although I knew I would have to report objectively about what I found, I had felt a deep anger at Mississippi's rebellion and the way Meredith was being treated, and I rejoiced at the chance to report from the scene. I would write a major piece for *The Washington Post*'s weekly "think" section called Outlook, over which Friendly, as managing editor, presided. I would also contribute news stories from Oxford, depending on what my reporting uncovered.

It was encouraging that Ben realized I was a special resource for the paper—someone with whom black Mississippians would talk honestly and share deep feelings. However, I wasn't the first black reporter the newspaper had sent south. Wallace H. Terry had been hired in 1960 and traveled to the South often, one of the few Negroes working the civil rights beat for a mainstream daily. He later joined *Washington Post* reporter Robert E. Lee Baker in covering Alabama governor George Wallace's defiance against integration at the University of Alabama in 1963. I was nervous about going to Mississippi, where black life was considered cheap as dirt. White supremacy's legal and political framework was established at a Mississippi constitutional convention in 1890 that excluded Blacks from voting and that was maintained through violence and lynching. From 1882 to 1927, 517 Blacks were lynched in the state—the highest number in the nation for any state during that period.

I had always looked at Mississippi as a place apart. James Meredith was risking death. I was afraid but kept my fears to myself and accepted the assignment with a degree of confidence, because I would have a secret weapon—I intended to hire Ernest Withers, a freelance photographer, to take pictures for me. I knew he was experienced and savvy in dealing with the threats, dangers, and violence of Mississippi. .I had worked with Withers while at *The Tri-State Defender*, most notably traveling with him to Little Rock in 1957 during the integration crisis at Central High School. I had later used him as a photographer when I was an associate editor at *JET* magazine from late 1957 to August 1959. I knew he had seven sons and a daughter. He often joked with me that I had something in common with his wife. Her name was also Dorothy.

I was so excited about the opportunity to go to Oxford that it didn't occur to me to protest to Ben and Al that I didn't know where I would stay when I got there. I presumed the tiny town of 6,200 residents had no hotels or motels for Blacks, but I figured Withers would help me find sleeping arrangements somewhere. As a *Washington Post* reporter, I had a reasonable expense account and was happy to provide Withers with per diem pay and expenses, plus the cost of any photographs the paper used. I hadn't had those kinds of funds when Withers accompanied me to Little Rock.

Withers was a double asset because he knew his way around the South, including how to comport himself around white Southerners. He was a quick-talking former policeman who learned photography in the army and loved taking pictures. He took some of the most iconic photographs of the Civil Rights Movement. Some of his photographs hang in the National Civil Rights Museum in Memphis, and his work has appeared in many books about the movement. I felt privileged to work with him and protected from some of the dangers of covering the segregated South.

The Washington Post had been covering the daily breaking news about Ole Miss in detail. The newspaper had reorganized its staff to cover the Civil Rights Movement after the Supreme Court passed its unanimous decision to outlaw public school segregation across the nation. The executive editor, J. Russell Wiggins, and Al Friendly put the city editor in charge of school desegregation and civil rights coverage, even though it had national as well as local and regional impact.

Gilbert had hired Robert E. Lee Baker away from the Fredericksburg, Virginia, *Free Lance-Star*, and he had been covering the beat for several years by the fall of 1961, when I arrived at *The Washington Post*. According to Chalmers Roberts, Gilbert had given these instructions to Baker: "You've got to forget that you're white and are dealing with Negroes. Adopt a different skin color—have a green skin. Write so that both Negroes and whites will understand what you are talking about."

Baker's enterprise reporting on the news pages had yielded big results. He covered the Montgomery bus boycott and first introduced *Washington Post* readers to a "27-year-old Negro pastor of the Dexter Avenue Baptist Church and an active NAACP member"—Dr. King. Baker had covered some racial issues in Virginia as its legislature fought to preserve segregation. In 1958, Baker had reported from Dawson, Georgia, where white authorities and others were brutalizing and terrorizing Negro residents. Baker quoted Sheriff Z. T. (Zeke) Matthews: "You know, Cap', there's nothing like fear to keep the niggers in line.... I believe we ought to be strict about who votes."

As a Southerner, I knew Mississippi was a land of black death, but I went there anyway. When I received this possible last assignment one year into my job at *The Washington Post*, not only was I just twenty-four and newly married but, unbeknown to me, I was already pregnant. Sam, a native Mississippian although raised in Louisville from age seven, expressed concern for my safety because he knew the dangers firsthand. He was fearful, but he realized it was an assignment that I could not pass up, even if I had the choice. I knew it was dangerous, too, from my experience five years earlier, when I had covered the Little Rock Nine when I worked at *The Tri-State Defender*.

I flew to Memphis to meet Withers on October 2, 1962, the day after Meredith enrolled. I arrived in the late afternoon, and we soon set out in his car down U.S. 51 to drive the ninety miles to Oxford. Dusk was beginning to fall, and the roads felt eerie. Just before we got to Batesville, Mississippi, on a two-lane country road, I noticed that a pickup truck with gun racks on the roof was tailing us. The men in the truck signaled for us to pull over by waving their arms. They pulled in front of us. Withers pulled over. It was dark by then, and I wondered if they were stopping us not only because we were black but also because Withers's car had out-of-state (Tennessee) license plates. Two menacing-looking men walked slowly and threateningly to the driver's side. "Where y'all nigguhs going?" one asked. They weren't huge men, but they looked strong enough to do some harm. In the darkness, I couldn't see if they actually had guns. These white men, who were not connected with any law enforcement, knew any white could stop any Blacks for any reason.

"To Jackson, to see my cousin," answered Withers, who had packed his cameras away in the trunk where he always kept them when he drove south, so as not to arouse suspicion.

"Get goin' then, and make sure you steer clear of Oxford," the other one said.

Ernest said, "Yassuh," and drove away. My heart was in my mouth as Withers drove down several dark side roads, taking an alternate route to get to Oxford.

The radio had been reporting that unreconstructed rebels, White Citizens' Council hardliners and various other segregationists from across the nation had descended on Mississippi to help repel the federal takeover in an insurrection that some said was like a replay of the Civil War.

In his 2001 book, *An American Insurrection: The Battle of Oxford, Mississippi, 1962*, William Doyle reconstructed the fighting that had been raging earlier that day a few blocks from the campus even as Meredith was registering. Former army general Edwin Walker, a right-wing fanatic, had gone on the radio publicly pleading for volunteers to help repel the "Federals." Some of these volunteers had rioted at Ole Miss the previous night, and others kept arriving the next morning and setting up positions at Courthouse Square and beyond.

Even as some threatened to "burn nigger churches," Mississippi highway patrolmen stood by doing nothing, one saying their orders were "not to interfere." Federal officials intervened. A thousand men of the Second Infantry Division's Second Battle Group, wearing bulletproof flak jackets, had arrived from Fort Benning, Georgia, as I was preparing to fly out of Washington, D.C. It was an integrated group, almost one-third black, and as they marched to the Square, the furious rioters taunted the black and white soldiers and threw bottles at them. Meanwhile, more troops were pouring into Mississippi.

As we drove, Withers told me that he and Larry Still, a dogged reporter from *JET* magazine, had interviewed and photographed Meredith the first time he had tried to enroll. I knew Larry from my two-year employment at "the little magazine that could." Withers said Still and he had followed the caravan of marshals and state highway patrolmen in a rental car from Memphis and, when the motorcade stopped, got to take some pictures. Withers said the two of them followed the entourage all the way to Oxford but weren't permitted on campus. "We got the hell outa there!" said Withers, who took their being barred as a frightening harbinger of what might lie ahead.

Most of the black reporters and photographers, who with rare exceptions were still employed only by the black press, couldn't get into good positions to cover the story in Oxford.

Moses Newson of the Baltimore *Afro-American* and Jimmy

Hicks of *The New York Amsterdam News*, both of whom I had met covering Little Rock five years earlier, were denied access and proximity to the campus and covered most of the story from Memphis. A story buried deep in *The Afro* carried this disclosure, "Colored newspapermen on the scene are being kept away from the campus of the university." After Meredith registered on October 1 and thousands of troops were in place, black reporters could finally report from the campus.

By the time Withers and I arrived in Oxford on Tuesday, October 2, the smell of tear gas was still in the air as thousands of army troops were keeping peace on the campus. At night, soldiers slept in tents on a hillside behind the campus. The next day, it was safe for us to drive onto the campus that still bore the marks of the "Battle of Ole Miss" two nights before. We saw Molotov cocktails, dead squirrels (that had been overcome by tear gas), a smoldering vehicle, and bricks strewn about. I took special note of the Negro soldiers in the background. Initially black soldiers were on the front lines, but they were later pulled back when they became targets of the mobs.

I was in a battle zone and felt much tension.

I didn't attempt to interview James Meredith in Baxter Hall, the huge dormitory he occupied alone, except for his U.S. Marshal escorts and guards. Let the black and white reporters covering breaking news do that. I was focusing on the reaction of Blacks on the streets of Oxford and across the state to this breakthrough in civil rights. I wanted to know what difference Meredith's military-backed admission had made in the lives of other black Mississippians. My mission was out in the town, where the people lived, and I felt a wave of relief as we left the campus through the front entrance.

Harder than finding the story, however, would be locating a place to stay. I knew Mississippi's white hotels and motels wouldn't rent me a room, and I could risk my life by even trying them. Black reporters working the Southern beat for black newspapers had faced this problem for years. Black journalists shared all the problems of white reporters—as a largely Northern antagonistic press confronting fiercely hostile white populations—but in addition, we faced the actual circumstances of segregation: we could not check into a hotel, eat in restaurants, use public restrooms, or drink from water fountains as the white journalists did. At highly covered civil rights trials, such as that for the murder of Emmett Till, ample space was set up for white reporters, while the "Negro press table" was a folding card table not large enough to accommodate the black reporters. Describing it in his book *Shocking the Conscience*, Simeon Booker called it the Jim Crow table.

When I worked at *JET*, I admired reporters like Booker, Francis H. Mitchell, and Mark Crawford, who risked their lives for years to tell readers about the struggle for freedom in the South. Moses Newson of *The Afro-American* was fearless and dedicated as he traveled to Southern hot spots. He suffered burns when a bomb exploded on the bus he was on with the Freedom Riders. "You prepare to go south like you prepare to go to war," he once told me.

The racial obstacles would be no different for me or the handful of other Blacks working for the white press. When Carl Rowan covered the dramatic struggle to integrate Little Rock's Central High School for *The Minneapolis Tribune*, he sometimes stayed with Daisy Bates, the mentor of the Little Rock Nine, and her husband, L. C. Bates, as did the other black reporters. Rowan later said, "This was a pleasure and a great journalistic advantage—until the racists began shooting through the Bates' window and dropping an occasional homemade bomb. During my late-in-the-crisis visits, we would put lights around the house and sit up all night playing poker, utterly afraid to go to sleep." Rowan recalled these experiences in his book *Breaking Barriers*.

I had also stayed at the Bateses' house when I went to Little Rock. In later years, I realized that as a woman, I was even more vulnerable than the black men were when segregation forced me to stay in the home of strangers just to do my job. I often felt only divine protection kept me from being molested in those situations. Who knew what kind of "sleepwalkers" might be around these houses at night? I was afraid at times but had learned to be courageous when working in the Deep South war zone.

In Oxford, the white reporters could comfortably bed down in hotels, dine in the restaurants or order room service, and sit in the lobby trading stories with their peers. Not so for Withers and me. Our first night there, Withers suggested we find a black funeral home because he knew they were valuable sources of information and might suggest a home in which I might lodge. Every black community had one. It was late when we arrived at Oxford's only black funeral home and met the owner and director, G. W. Bankhead. Withers found other quarters, but I was grateful to stay at the mortuary—in a spare room in the family quarters upstairs from where bodies were received and prepared for burial. I was glad for a clean, safe place to lay my head and to have found a black establishment that would get me closer to my story. Black funeral directors were the go-to people for information for black reporters.

That night, I heard the noise of people's voices in the house, and in the morning I learned the body of a young black man had been brought in in the wee hours—not unusual at a funeral home. With whites engaging in bloody rioting on the campus, I suspected foul play—a fear that the funeral director did not corroborate, so I neither investigated nor reported it. Twenty-five years later when I repeated my suspicion at a forum for journalists at the twenty-fifth anniversary of the integration of Ole Miss, a white Mississippian told me that no killing of a young black man had occurred during the siege of "Ole Miss."

In the morning, Withers and I got directions to Freedman's Town, the neighborhood where most Blacks lived. I set out to survey some of Oxford's Blacks for their reaction to Meredith's heroic feat, and I easily found people to interview there. I introduced myself as a reporter from *The Washington Post*, but I'm not certain many knew it was the second-largest paper in the nation.

People were welcoming and talked openly even if they were surprised to see a young colored woman from a white newspaper. In fact, I found them eager to talk to me. Reporters from the white, rabidly segregationist Mississippi papers that Blacks saw as the enemy never interviewed them. Northern reporters were mainly interested in Governor Barnett and the Meredith drama on campus. Some black Oxford citizens said mobs attacked them as they tried to report to the university for their service jobs— as maids, janitors, drivers, servers, and cooks. Mobs pulled them from their cars, smashed their windows, and otherwise heaped a stream of violence on them.

In *An American Insurrection*, William Doyle quoted Bill Mayes, a member of the army's 503d Military Police Battalion, as saying that on the second and third days of the occupation, so much fear spread through the Freedman's Town area that he found black families up in the surrounding hills, huddled together, camping. "They had abandoned their homes and gone up to the forests with tents. . . . We found them in the woods," he said.

The black people I interviewed had *not* run for the hills. They were shocked and amazed by Meredith's courage and overjoyed by his determination to integrate the university.

I wrote my first story about the community when we left Oxford and arrived in Jackson, Mississippi, where I was able to check into a black motel. I felt safer there because Jackson was more urban, with black churches, businesses, and a significant black population. When I worked at *JET*, reporters on the Southern race beat had shared stories of how in the 1930s, reporters for black newspapers would steal into town by bus at night to avoid the Klansmen. Some reporters would wear overalls and muddy shoes to disguise themselves. They would carry their wobbly Royal portable typewriter wrapped in brown paper so it would look like a pack of clothes. Even in the 1950s and 1960s, black journalists carried Bibles to look like preachers or had false credentials in case local authorities became suspicious of their roles.

With a Jackson, Mississippi, dateline, the first story I wrote was headlined, "Mississippi Negroes Happily Stunned by Meredith," and appeared on the front page of *The Washington Post* on October 6:

> The hot sun glistened on the young Negro lawyer's face as he lolled in a seat by his office window. He was reminiscing about his first racial jolt—at age 6.
>
> "I went into a store to buy a coke and the storekeeper yelled at me. 'Put it back! We don't sell no Cokes to no niggers on Sunday!'"
>
> He chuckled as he recalled the merchant's assurance that he could have an orange or a grape, however, for his same sweaty nickel.
>
> "The episode," the lawyer said, pointed out for him what has long been the rule in Mississippi: "Negroes get pretty much what whites want them to have."
>
> …Many Mississippi Negroes say Meredith's entry into "Ole Miss," in the face of Gov. Ross Barnett's sworn resistance to Federal court orders, was an accomplishment of the impossible. It was the crack in the thick wall of segregation that may someday broaden, they say, so Negroes themselves may choose—and get—what they want.

I returned from Oxford with enough information to file my main story for *The Washington Post*'s weekly Outlook section and was pleased when Al Friendly put it on the front of the prestigious section on October 14, beneath the headline "Mississippi Mood: Hope and Fear." It read:

Hope and fear are the moods of Negroes in Mississippi these anxious days.

You can spot these feelings in the hesitant words of a disenfranchised Negro handyman in Oxford who hobbles heavily to a chair, hikes up his overalls, and talks.

Or in the bold words of a harassed Negro leader [Medgar Evers] who, despite constant danger, declares that James H. Meredith's entry into the University of Mississippi "is a clear breakthrough" for Negroes and will be a springboard for other advances.

"The hope is that Meredith signals the coming of the light for all of them. The fear is that the inevitable changes will bring further death, destruction, and repercussions."

A highlight of covering the Civil Rights Movement in Mississippi was my visit to Jackson to interview Medgar Wiley Evers, that state's first NAACP field secretary, who had held that dangerous job since 1954. Born in Decatur, Mississippi, in 1925 of parents who taught him to demand respect even in Mississippi, he served in a racially segregated army field battalion in both England and France during World War II. Returning home, he joined with four other black veterans in July 1946 and attempted to vote. They found the courthouse entrance blocked by a group of about twenty armed white men.

After graduating from Alcorn College, he worked for physician T. R. M. Howard's life insurance company in Mound Bayou, Mississippi, where he became aware of the sad plight of black tenant farmers who lived in the plains. He sought to help them and became part of a new generation of black leadership that chafed at the rigid legal segregation. In 1954, Evers applied to the University of Mississippi law school. Denied admission, he turned to the NAACP, whose leaders advised him to become field secretary.

My colleague Wallace Terry would cover the movement in Jackson, Mississippi, in 1963 when Medgar Evers pushed for integration of schools, playgrounds and parks. He advocated for the hiring of Blacks as police officers and as employees in downtown businesses.

Wally went to work for *Time* magazine later in 1963 and became deputy bureau chief for *Time* in Saigon in 1967. His breakthrough book *Bloods: An Oral History of the Vietnam War by Black Veterans* was published in 1984.

In Jackson, Withers and I went to Medgar Evers's office on the second floor of a two-story office building in the black business section. Given the pitched battle, with its terror and violence, that had just raged over James Meredith's admission to Ole Miss, I was astonished at this NAACP field secretary's bold prediction about the future.

"We don't intend to let this thing fizzle with Meredith," Evers told me as Withers snapped dozens of photographs of him. Evers assured me steps would now be taken to get Negroes to apply to other state schools, such as Mississippi State University, Mississippi State College for Women, Delta State University, and the University of Southern Mississippi. During our interview, Evers's phone rang. The caller reported that white youths had strafed eight Negro homes with shotguns. Evers immediately called the Justice Department in Washington and asked for federal protection for the families.

Through association with the NAACP leadership and as the organization's highest official in the state, Evers had access to federal agents in Washington who frequented the state, especially in the sixteen months preceding Meredith's entry into Ole Miss.

There was no need to bother with local officials, he declared. Just eight months after my interview with him in his Jackson office, Evers was killed, shot down by an assassin, outside his home on June 12, 1963; he was thirty-seven years old.

How this tragedy hurt my heart. Having met him, I was devastated. His bravery had been astonishing to me. Even as the troops were in Oxford less than a year before, he was strategizing about the next steps he would take to build on what James Meredith had accomplished.

Three days after Evers was killed, hundreds of African Americans marched in a funeral procession in downtown Jackson, in a tribute to a freedom fighter. It took great courage for the people of Jackson to march because the dangers were real, as evidenced by Evers's fate. The march was a recognition of who Evers was and what his sacrifice meant. He was indefatigable. His death reinforced the marchers' resolve to bring about change.

Meredith was deeply saddened by Evers's murder. He considered Evers "one of my best and most beloved friends" and said in a statement, "I had been considered the most likely victim." Meredith stalwartly endured taunts, insults, jeers and indignities during his lonely time at Ole Miss. When the estimated thirty-one thousand troops President Kennedy had deployed left Oxford, three hundred infantrymen and U.S. marshals continued to guard Meredith almost until the time of his graduation. Meredith graduated from Ole Miss in August 1963 with a Bachelor of Arts degree in political science. In June 1966, Meredith began a lone march through the South, which he called a March against Fear. One day into the march, a sniper shot and injured him.

Dr. King, Stokely Carmichael, leader of the Student Nonviolent Coordinating Committee, and others arrived to continue the march on his behalf while he was hospitalized. Meredith recovered and rejoined the march he had originated, and on June 26, the marchers successfully reached Jackson, Mississippi.

I never returned to the South to cover the Civil Rights Movement, but forty-four years later in Jackson, I caught up with Meredith, now white-bearded, but still slender and focused in his mid-seventies. Over breakfast, I told him about a black student I had just met when I visited the Oxford campus. I asked the young man if he knew who Meredith was; he answered, "No, I've never heard of him." When I told him about Meredith's heroic battle to gain entrance for himself and future black students to attend the university, the young man respectfully turned the bill of his baseball cap around to the front and said, "I appreciate what he did."

After listening to my story, Meredith responded, "I'm not sure he needs to know who I am," he said, displaying his always thoughtful independent-mindedness. He said he wasn't certain about how profoundly the past affected the future in the minds of young people. I was pleased, however, that a bronze statue of Meredith was unveiled on the campus a few years later to commemorate his contribution, so future students of all races will always remember the shoulders upon which they stand.

By mid-October I was safely back in Washington from the bloody Battle of Oxford and doing some follow-up stories. I found myself reflecting on my earlier epic encounter in the civil rights struggle, covering the integration of Central High School in Little Rock in 1957. That tumultuous place turned out to be the training ground that helped me to report successfully from Oxford.

That foray into Little Rock had occurred five years earlier in September 1957, when I was twenty years old, a recent graduate of Lincoln University of Missouri and a rookie reporter at *The Tri-State Defender*, a weekly newspaper in Memphis, Tennessee. My boss, L. Alex Wilson, editor of the newspaper, was a veteran of reporting from the South and highly respected by the small band of black reporters from other outlets with whom he shared this highly dangerous beat. That band included Clotye Murdock of *Ebony*, Francis H. Mitchell and Mark Crawford of *JET*, Simeon Booker and Larry Still of *JET*'s Washington bureau, James Hicks of *The New York Amsterdam News* and Moses Newson of *The Afro-American*.

Mr. Wilson, as I always called him, was forty-nine years old, a tall, dark-skinned man who wore dignity like a soft leather glove. He had become something of a hero to me in the few months I had worked under him at the newspaper and witnessed his prowess as editor, reporter, and writer. Lean, lanky, and standing 6'4", he was gruff, no-nonsense, and brilliant as a boss. He taught me how to approach a story, put it into context with literary and historical references, and never overlook the ironies. While I covered local, mostly crime stories in Memphis, Mr. Wilson ran the entire paper and wrote many stories, including articles about the school integration in Arkansas.

Desegregation in Little Rock had been carefully planned and expected to go smoothly for the handpicked nine, cream-of-the-crop black children, ages fourteen to sixteen. Instead, it became a showdown over states' rights, between Arkansas officials and the federal government, fomenting a calamitous event in civil rights history.

After the U.S. Supreme Court issued the historic decision in *Brown v. Board of Education of Topeka, Kansas*, on May 17, 1954, declaring segregated schools unconstitutional, the NAACP attempted to register black students at white schools in the South. In Little Rock, the school board agreed almost immediately to comply with the ruling and unanimously approved the school superintendent's proposal for gradual integration. The integration of a small number of hand-picked black students into one high school was set to begin in September 1957.

The NAACP selected nine who met the criteria of having excellent grades and attendance, registering them to enroll in Little Rock Central High, which had been reserved for whites. The students were Minnijean Brown, Melba Pattillo (Beal), Elizabeth Eckford, Ernest Green, Gloria Ray (Karlmark), Carlotta Walls (LaNier), Thelma Mothershed, Terrence Roberts and Jefferson Thomas.

As the time approached for them to attend, some segregationist organizations threatened protests and Governor Orval Faubus deployed the Arkansas National Guard on September 4, 1957, to support the protesters in blocking the students' entrance to the school. Images of soldiers barricading the school and blocking the crisply attired brown teenagers made international news. The news coverage sparked outrage among supporters of integration and encouraged violent segregationists. NAACP lawyers, including Thurgood Marshall, won a federal district court injunction to prevent the governor from blocking the black students from entering.

Mr. Wilson had tracked many of Arkansas governor Orval Faubus's delaying tactics from our office in Memphis. Then he headed to Little Rock to cover the news, telling me to stay at the office. "It's too dangerous over there for a girl," he told me. It proved dangerous for him, too. Wilson was part of a group of African American reporters that a mob of about fifty white men attacked.

On the day of integration, one of the Nine, Elizabeth Eckford, arrived by bus alone because she had no telephone and had not gotten a message to gather at the home of Daisy Bates, the president of the Arkansas State NAACP, and leader of the integration struggle.

With threats of a swelling crowd echoing in her ears, the fifteen-year-old walked up to the guardsmen, who told her she couldn't enter the school. When the mob surrounded her, and she looked again to the guardsmen, they rebuffed her a second time.

Trembling as the crowd shouted at her, she walked back to the bus stop and waited on a bench, tears streaming behind her sunglasses. A few minutes later, when the other eight students arrived accompanied by two black and two white ministers, they walked through the growing mob of segregationists who shouted obscenities and threats. When the national guard troops sent the black children away, the mob was delighted.

A three-week standoff followed, and Mr. Wilson wrote about the NAACP lawyers' court battle to get the students into school, the governor's machinations, and the whites who convened around the school every morning. The throng taunted many of the print and television journalists who came to the school and was particularly hostile to black journalists. The guardsmen ushered some of them, including Moses Newson, out of the area surrounding the school. Accustomed to the degradation and humiliation that came with telling their readers what was happening in the South, these black reporters went away and rearmed themselves to return another day.

Finally, U.S. District Judge Ronald N. Davies ordered the governor to dismiss the national guard surrounding the school and told him he could not prevent the black children from enrolling. Thwarted in his attempt to circumvent the law, an angry Governor Faubus advised the black students not to try to come to school, or they might get hurt. Then he left town and went on vacation.

On Monday, September 23, Mr. Wilson was among a small group of black journalists who convened at the Bateses' home, along with the nine students. Moses Newson, James Hicks, and photographer Earl Davy rode together in Mr. Wilson's car. Others piled into a second car. When the newsmen in Mr. Wilson's car arrived at Central and climbed out of the car heading toward the school, the mob attacked them.

As I watched the attack on the small television set in our Beale Street office during the evening news, it was a surreal experience. I couldn't believe the flickering black-and-white images that flashed across the screen. People all over the nation could see my dignified boss as the men pummeled, shoved, slapped, and taunted him with cries of "nigger" and "lynch him" as he walked toward the school.

As the nine black teenagers entered Central through a side door amidst a crowd of jeering whites, the swelling, irate crowd turned its wrath on the black journalists. At first, only a few whites taunted them, but their fury and their numbers grew. They started kicking, shoving, and spitting on the black newsmen. Newson, Hicks, and Davy managed to run back to the car and escape, but Mr. Wilson refused to run.

A pack of around fifty white men maneuvered him onto a side street and attacked him from behind with their fists and with bricks. Then one of them suddenly leaped onto his back, steadied himself on one leg, and kicked him, planting his foot with a thud below the base of Mr. Wilson's spine. Then another white attacker kicked my boss so hard from behind that he stumbled toward the sidewalk.

Mr. Wilson picked up his tan hat, stood up straight, smoothed the wrinkles from the brim, and continued walking. He still refused to run even as one man in the crowd shouted, "Run, damn you, run." Amidst the screaming and pushing, yet another man climbed onto his back and yanked his neck backward, immobilizing him in a stranglehold that made his mouth fly open and his arms flail limply. Then the man rammed him to the ground where another one with a brick leaped from the crowd and kicked him in the middle of his chest. Mr. Wilson kept walking, even as another brick hit him directly on the back of the head, until he finally reached his car and drove away.

Watching the chaos and brutality he endured while I sat in the safety of our Memphis office spurred me to action. I was horrified by the scene, furious with its lynching mentality, and by the way the police abetted his attackers by failing to pursue the pack of men who chased him and the other black journalists.

The scenes captured by the television news reporters prompted the familiar fury about injustice that rose from the pit of my stomach. Then I became deeply frightened. How badly had Mr. Wilson been hurt? Would he be able to work? Who would write the story? I knew I had to get myself to Little Rock.

I called Ernest Withers, who had been in Little Rock earlier but had returned to Memphis to develop his film. "Let's go to Little Rock this evening," I urged. He readily agreed but warned me it might be dangerous.

Withers, who had worked as a U.S. Army photographer in World War II and been one of the first black police officers in Memphis, had photographed more of the Civil Rights Movement than anyone else had. He had shot photos at the Emmett Till trial, among other events. Because he was so familiar with the region, he could get us safely to Little Rock and help me navigate the scene.

After we had driven more than a hundred miles we approached Little Rock. We drove directly to the home of L. C. and Daisy Bates, passing police cars that dotted street after street. We found the couple's two-story rambler with its large plate-glass window, surrounded by police cars. Although we had arrived safely, as soon as we entered the large living room, we heard that gangs of white people in town were randomly pulling black people out of their cars and beating them, while others were attacking Blacks in their homes.

The Bateses ran an influential black newspaper, *The Arkansas State Press*. Daisy was also president of the Arkansas State NAACP and was the mentor to the black students who became known as THE Little Rock Nine. The Bates home served as a safe house for the students and for the African American press.

We found Mr. Wilson stretched out on a couch. He had refused to go to a hospital. "Why'd you bring that girl over here?" Mr. Wilson barked weakly at Withers, referring to me.

The photographer looked squarely at me, then at his boss and told him, "It was her idea, not mine."

Wilson then told us why he'd been determined not to run even though the other reporters fled quickly to their car, avoiding the savage beating he had received. Not only had he once fled when chased by the Ku Klux Klan and been angry at himself for doing so, he said, he was also inspired by the valor of Elizabeth Eckford, who three weeks earlier had faced a mob all alone. "If I were to be beaten, I wanted to take it walking if I could, not running. They would have had to kill me before I would run," he said.

I wasn't surprised to hear these words from Mr. Wilson, this former marine, ex–high school principal, and now newspaperman. In the few months I had worked for him, I had seen that life had made him a fighter. Nevertheless, following his injuries, Wilson began to suffer from anxiety. He was only fifty-one when he died four years later of complications from the beating he had received in Little Rock. And, as was the norm for white mob violence against integration, despite the identifiable white faces on TV cameras, no one has ever been arrested or charged for the beatings that resulted in Mr. Wilson's death. When I met his wife many years later, she said he had refused to ever discuss Little Rock.

The Bateses' home was the central gathering spot for black

reporters covering the story. The couple's basement with its wooden bar, normally used for parties, became the reporters' favorite place to hang out. Those present included Ted Poston of *The New York Post* and Carl Rowan of *The Minneapolis Tribune*, who were among the few black journalists in white-owned media in those days. It seemed that the entire black press was represented at that house, and I met journalists who had covered the Till murder and the *Brown v. Board* decision. I soaked up the atmosphere and wisdom as they sat around the bar talking in the basement rec room.

As the discussion went on, I also wondered what kind of male fraternity was I, as a woman, about to join. Down in the Bateses' basement, I learned more about these newsmen as I listened, fascinated and horrified. As they talked about what had happened that day and about other civil rights struggles, they drank scotch and bourbon at the Bateses' bar. These were veterans of the Southern battlefield—Hicks, Newson, Booker, Davy, Withers, and others.

The reporters knew the stories they found and brought to their readers were part of the single most effective tool in bringing change to the South. "Negro reporters still went places white reporters wouldn't go, in search of stories white reporters didn't even know about," acknowledged Gene Roberts and Hank Klibanoff in *The Race Beat: The Press, The Civil Rights Struggle, and the Awakening of a Nation*. The black reporters may have appreciated the Northern white journalists who were finally turning their lenses, especially television cameras, on events and following the story to the innermost sanctums of power to which Blacks were not privy. The black journalists also knew they had been doing great work themselves.

The photographs of Wilson's beating made the front page of *Pravda* in Russia. The television footage went into the living rooms of millions of Americans, helping to shock the nation into action.

The men recalled instances when black press coverage had broken new ground. After fourteen-year-old Emmett Till was kidnapped and murdered for alleged whistling at a white woman in Mississippi in 1954, *JET* Magazine carried the first photo of the boy in his casket when his body arrived back in Chicago. His face was so bloated and disfigured it stirred outrage among Blacks across America. So powerful was that image and the national response to it that some scholars consider it a galvanizing moment in the Civil Rights Movement.

I was proud to become one of many journalists, black and white, who journeyed to Little Rock to report and write about a key event in the Civil Rights Movement that was changing America and the world.

Most of us reporters spent the night at the Bateses' because the only black hotel was full, and we certainly weren't welcome at the white establishments. We slept lightly on sofas, chairs, anywhere we could perch in makeshift fashion in the Bateses' home. A police cruiser guarding the home discovered a caravan of about a hundred cars, only two blocks away. Piled into the cars were white people with guns, clubs, and enough dynamite to blow up the entire neighborhood, including the Bateses' home where we were fitfully sleeping. The policemen radioed for help. Mrs. Bates was quoted as saying later, "I didn't know if the police would or could stop them. They were coming to lynch us."

The next day, I covered the arrival of the troops that President Dwight D. Eisenhower had sent in. When Governor Faubus ignored warnings from President Eisenhower not to interfere with enforcement of a U.S. Supreme Court ruling, the mayor of Little Rock, Woodrow Wilson Mann, asked the president to send federal troops to enforce integration and protect the nine students. On September 24, the president ordered the 101st Airborne Division of the United States Army to Little Rock, and he federalized the ten-thousand-member Arkansas National Guard, removing it from Faubus's command.

When I went to the massive redbrick school for the first time I saw the thousands of soldiers and guardsmen. It made me wonder what kind of country this was that the president had to call in troops to enforce the law. The thing I remember most was the hatred in the faces of the jeering whites as they tried to protect their segregated way of life and exclude Blacks. The troops would stay inside the schools for months to protect the black students—ordinary young people with loving, supportive parents who had the courage to face murderous white mobs to bring about change in America.

The lessons I learned from these brave black journalists covering Little Rock and the other hot spots of the Civil Rights Movement stood me in good stead when I went to Mississippi in 1962. These journalists, mostly from the Negro press, taught me that it would take courage, as well as curiosity and a desire, to help write history as it was unfolding, if I wanted to be a journalist who made a difference in the world. My desire to make a difference was deeply rooted in my family background, the legacy of growing up in the segregated South as the daughter of two former teachers, who later became a preacher and a maid, who instilled in me the will not only to persevere but also to be of service to others.

In 2005, Withers and I were subjects of a documentary, *Freedom's Call*, directed by Syracuse University professor Richard Breyer and produced by George Kilpatrick and Robert Short Jr. When we got together for the filming, I had not seen Withers for more than forty years; his hair was white, but he was as wily as ever. The filmmakers took us on a trip back to the sites where we had covered events together. Starting in Memphis, we went to Little Rock and then on to Oxford, Jackson, and other towns in Mississippi.

During our week together filming, I thought Withers acted a bit strangely at times, such as when he insisted that black people in Memphis "obeyed the law" during the civil rights struggle, as opposed to engaging in nonviolent protests. I chalked up such absurd statements to his being a forgetful, cantankerous old man. He was eighty-two at the time. When the famed photographer died in 2008 at age eighty-five, the people of Memphis gave him a hero's funeral.

I was stunned when in 2010 *The Commercial Appeal* revealed that he had been a paid FBI informant supplying information he gleaned from his insider status. I was devastated, deeply disappointed, furious even. How could he have revealed information to the hideous FBI director J. Edgar Hoover that further jeopardized Dr. King and the other freedom fighters who faced dangers daily while helping Blacks obtain their rights as American citizens?

Many months later, I heard Andrew Young, former United Nations ambassador and one of Dr. King's principal lieutenants, suggest that the damage that Withers had done was probably limited. With time, I came to accept that Withers was a deeply flawed man. Nevertheless, he did create a legacy of iconic photographs that will forever bear witness to the black struggle for freedom.

In 1962, back at *The Washington Post* after Mississippi, I went back to covering the D.C. Juvenile Court beat and stories about poverty and pending welfare cuts. I was relieved to get back to a regular routine, especially because I soon learned that I was pregnant and was excited about that.

My beat offered its own challenges and rewards. One series I wrote about Junior Village, the city's home for toddlers without homes, attracted the attention of Jacqueline Kennedy. Later, I covered her holiday visit to see the children, in an article that appeared on December 14, 1962:

FIRST LADY PLAYS SANTA TO 'VILLAGE'

Distributes Gifts to Youngsters and Home for Aging

The First Lady distributed Christmas gifts at Junior Village for dependent children and D.C. Village for the aged, and spent twice as much time doing it as she had planned.

In a crowded dining room at Junior Village, she strolled about shaking hands and greeting the youngsters.

"Didn't you bring us anything?" piped up one.

Mrs. Kennedy went first to a 65-year-old cottage where 96 toddlers, aged 18 months to three years, live in space for 45.

"Hi, Mommy," greeted a little girl with a white towel tied around her neck.

Others crowded around as she gave out candy from a basket adorned with a huge red bow.

Although Mrs. Kennedy did not comment on conditions at the overcrowded institution (population 709; capacity 320), President Kennedy did at his press conference Wednesday.

He called it "unfortunate" that the District "had inadequate expenditures for the needs of the people... particularly the younger people."

Five years out of a Louisville housing project myself, I was saddened by these stories. So many Blacks were living in such horrible poverty. I cared about them and felt situations would improve if the city had home rule and if the nation would address the larger problems of black poverty. My heart broke as I reported on such lack and destitution, but I did see some change. By then, some restaurants had begun opening to Blacks, for instance. Positive things were happening for the few middle-class Blacks who could walk through the doors.

In the most unlikely of incidents, I was having a rare lunch with my former Columbia classmate Nina Auchincloss Steers, stepsister of Jacqueline Kennedy, on Friday, November 22, 1963. The waiter had not yet brought our orders when the news began spreading like a fire in dry sagebrush that President Kennedy had been shot in Dallas. A few minutes later, we heard he had died, and we leapt from our seats and gathered our belongings to leave. Startled, unbelieving, then shocked, I ran back to *The Washington Post* to see how I could help cover the story. I lost touch with Nina in the chaotic moments after we left the restaurant.

Back at *The Washington Post*, I was assigned to work the phones, calling the newspaper's stringers in *The Washington Post*'s circulation area in Maryland and Virginia for reactions from officials and citizens. Writing and covering this "story of the century" was the domain of the White House press and other national reporters, and I worked in a supportive role reporting "man on the street" interviews with mourning Americans on Sunday, November 24, and Monday, November 25.

Police estimated that by Monday morning up to 250,000 mourners had passed through the Capitol rotunda to file past Kennedy's casket and pay their respects. My most vivid memory occurred that Monday, the day of the funeral, after the casket was carried from the Capitol to the White House grounds and on to St. Matthew's Roman Catholic Cathedral. Family members and dignitaries left their cars to walk behind the casket, down 16th Street over to the intersection of Connecticut Avenue, Rhode Island Avenue, and M Street to St. Matthew's.

I took up my station along the route at 16th and K Streets on this cold and clear day and watched the president's family in their solemn procession, followed by heads of state from more than ninety countries. The leadership of the free world was passing by.

I was proud to see a few African heads of state from newly independent countries, dressed in full regalia. Yet, I was most struck by the towering figure of the French president and former general Charles de Gaulle in full military dress. Clearly, my world was expanding. The sight of de Gaulle marching briskly past me to the cathedral reaffirmed the perception I had as a teenager that journalism would open new worlds for me.

Growing Up a Preacher's Kid, 1936–1961

Adee Conklin Butler Sr., my father, shown in his late forties, was a minister in the African Methodist Episcopal Church and served at Youngs Chapel A.M.E. Church in Louisville during my growing-up years. *(Courtesy of the Dorothy Butler Gilliam personal collection)*

Jessie Mae Norment Butler, my mother, had been a teacher but later could not work in her field and worked as a maid. She gave birth to ten children. *(Courtesy of the Dorothy Butler Gilliam personal collection)*

I posed in 1946 with the Sunday school students and teachers at Youngs Chapel A.M.E. Church in Louisville. I'm seventh from the top left, holding the stair railing. *(Courtesy of the Dorothy Butler Gilliam personal collection)*

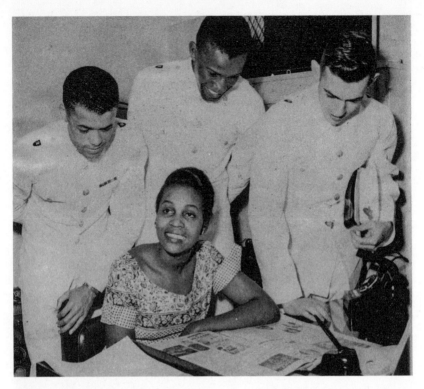

About 1954 at age seventeen or eighteen while working part-time at *The Louisville Defender* and studying at Ursuline College, I talked with cadets from West Point. *(Courtesy of the Dorothy Butler Gilliam personal collection)*

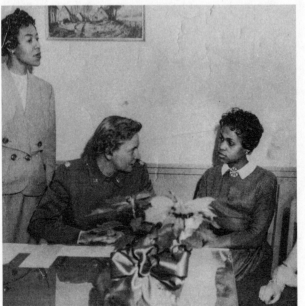

Circa 1956 at Lincoln University in Jefferson City, Missouri, from which I graduated in 1957. Here, the dean of women (left) looks on as an army recruiter talks to me. *(Used with permission of Lincoln University)*

A librarian named Louvan Gearing mentored me at a pivotal time in my life: after the death of my father, when we lived almost as sharecroppers in Anchorage, Kentucky. She was the librarian at Lincoln Institute, the colored high school in Lincoln Ridge, Kentucky. Louvan attended a ceremony with me in 1998 when I received a University of Missouri Honor Medal in Journalism. *(Courtesy of the Dorothy Butler Gilliam personal collection)*

The Butler family in Louisville, Kentucky, in 1957, the summer after my graduation from Lincoln University. From left, standing, Lynwood, Juanita, Evelyn, and Adee Jr., and from left, seated, Dorothy, Blair, Jessie Mae Butler, and Margaret Springer Butler. *(Courtesy of the Dorothy Butler Gilliam personal collection)*

Clifton Daniel and Kay Lawrence presented me with the Anne O'Hare McCormick scholarship from the New York Newspaper Women's Club for 1960–61 while I was a student at Columbia Journalism School. *(Courtesy of the Dorothy Butler Gilliam personal collection)*

I arrived at the Embakasi Airport in Nairobi, Kenya, in June 1961 for the Operation Crossroads Africa Program and posed for a photo with a fellow Crossroader and a member of the welcoming committee. *(Courtesy of the Dorothy Butler Gilliam personal collection)*

Six years old, I was holding my father's huge hand as I walked up the steps into Youngs Chapel A.M.E. Church in Louisville, Kentucky. He made me feel secure even as he let go of my hand as we entered the church and I went to join the other children in my class in the small brick edifice. It was long and narrow, but the new building Daddy would lead this congregation to build was already taking shape in his mind. That frigid night, the Sunday school was having its Christmas program.

Love blossomed among us kids because many of us lived within walking distance of 16th and St. Catherine Streets, where the church and parsonage stood. We were friends and happy to be together, but jittery about saying our poems before the grownups. I saw Brother Ransaw, the Sunday school superintendent, talking to Miss Wilhite and the other teachers who were scurrying over last-minute details.

Our church had rows and three aisles, one down the middle, and it soon filled up with families and children. My friends and the older children were agog over the beautiful Christmas tree, but a special thrill ran through me when I saw it. I knew after the program church officials would bring the fully decorated tree to the parsonage and place it in our small living room. My brothers and sisters and I would have at least one gift and a box with fruit, nuts, and candy for each of us—all under those twinkling lights.

Finally, it was time to recite our poems and, one by one, a church member called our names, and we walked up to the stage near the pulpit. Even my sister, who had a stutter, was encouraged to speak in church and learned to communicate with pride and a strength that came from the loving support shown by our church leaders and the entire congregation. Protocol that made the pulpit primarily off-limits to anyone but the ordained preachers, elders, and bishops was set aside when we kids said our speeches at Easter and Christmas because children were special, precious. While the other children said their poems, I mentally rehearsed the one I would recite. Daddy—tall, strong-jawed, thick-set—pursed his lips in a smile. He wore on his large body a dark suit, vest, and white shirt Mother had ironed in the parsonage next door. Soon, it was my turn to mount the stage. I stood for a minute and looked out at the faces of Negro men and women of all ages, shades, and hues, from the darkest brown to could-pass-for-white. I didn't look at the other children so I wouldn't giggle. I began—softly but loudly enough for people to hear me in the back:

'Twas the night before Christmas, when all through the house
Not a creature was stirring, not even a mouse.

The poem lent itself to action, and I got louder and spoke faster:

"Now, Dasher! now, Dancer! now, Prancer and Vixen!
On, Comet! On, Cupid! on, Donner and Blitzen!
To the top of the porch! to the top of the wall!
Now dash away! Dash away! Dash away all!"

The applause was deafening when I finished. I was breathless, but I had remembered the whole poem! I learned to speak from a stage in church. I enjoyed being a "star performer."

It was natural for my brothers, sisters, and me to go to Sunday school, church service, and the Allen Christian Fellowship (A.C.F.), a youth group gathering that aimed to promote "intelligent and practical Christian living among young people," at six p.m. on Sunday. By then, my father had to drag me to A.C.F.

because I had had enough church for one day, and my mind was more focused on my friends than on spiritual principles.

In Sunday school, our teachers were showing us God's power and how the Almighty worked miracles through human beings. I learned about David, who with five smooth stones slew the giant Goliath and helped save the nation of Israel. I studied Daniel, who was put in the lion's den by his enemies but emerged unscathed the next morning. I heard the story of Queen Esther, who risked her life to save her people. And, of course, I was introduced to Jesus Christ, whose birthday we celebrated at Christmas and who had died to set us in right standing with God. "Jesus loves me this I know," we sang in the Buds of Promise children's choir, "for the Bible tells me so." It was very comforting to know God loved me and that I was "precious in His sight."

Daddy taught that faith was "the substance of things hoped for, the evidence of things not seen" (Hebrews 11:1) and that faith came by hearing God's word. I didn't understand what it meant. When I asked, he explained it in practical terms: it meant "there's no such word as 'can't.'"

During church services, I loved to hear Sister Inez Kalfus, a tall, light-skinned woman, sing "It's a High Way to Heaven." I didn't know where heaven was, but believed it was somewhere beautiful, and I wanted to go there when I got really old and died. Daddy used to say to us: "If you're wrong, admit it, say you are wrong, and get on with life. But if you are right, fight to the death for your beliefs."

As I grew up, my best friend was Margaret Springer, who loved when Daddy would serve Holy Communion to us children on the first Sunday of each month. He would squat down, not bend over, crouching before each child, and hand us the bread and wine. Margaret said it made her feel so close to him. "He was massive in his robe," she recalled years later, "but so kind, gentle, and loving."

I liked seeing the church stewardesses in their white uniforms preparing communion. Mother was a stewardess in addition to her special duties as the pastor's wife. Annually, the stewardesses took a photograph outside the church with Daddy standing behind them. I later learned it was for an annual report on the church's progress Daddy and the church secretary prepared for the person above him—the presiding elder—who would then report to the bishop. I didn't know at the time, but I was learning about the structure of the A.M.E Church, which had a well-organized doctrine and discipline that provided the security I felt as a child.

My father, Adee Conklin Butler Sr., was a big man, about 6′1″ and more than two hundred pounds, who struggled with his health throughout his adulthood. Once when he became ill, as my sister Evelyn remembered, he said, "God, if you bring me through this, I will serve you." In other words, he would stop fighting and running from the inward call to the ministry that he had felt for some time.

However, when he told my mother, Jessie Mae, née Norment, he wanted to go into the ministry, she was horrified because she knew the financial instability that life would bring. He would be giving up a job as a teacher, which was one of the most stable and well-paying jobs a black man could have at the time.

Evelyn said Mother told him, "I didn't marry a preacher. I married a teacher." She was so angry that she left my father and fled to her parents' house, where she stayed for about two weeks. She returned home after her father urged her to accept her husband's decision to enter the ministry.

Though raised as a Baptist, according to my sister, my father decided to become a minister in the African Methodist Episcopal (A.M.E.) Church. My father's sister-in-law, Aunt Gussie Butler, told me a neighbor had advised him that the A.M.E. Church was a denomination in which a young, smart, and ambitious minister could flourish, while doing good for others. In addition to worrying about financial sacrifice, Mother, who had grown up in an A.M.E. family, might also have been concerned about Daddy's choice because the church moved its pastors around at the discretion of the denomination's bishops. The pastors held assignments on a year-to-year basis and were subject to transfer annually, though they might not actually have to move to a new church.

I don't recall that my father ever went to seminary (though he might have audited occasional classes at nearby Payne Theological Seminary while attending Wilberforce College). He didn't decide to go into the ministry until after he had started teaching. He was certainly influenced by books he read. I have some of the books that were his. One was called *A Tribute to the Negro Preacher,* by Charles Spivey. It details the role of the African American clergy in helping the formerly enslaved make the transition to selfhood necessary to function as citizens during the post-Emancipation, Reconstruction, and separate-but-equal, legal-segregation periods.

The A.M.E. Church appealed to my father because of its power, the great black men who had led it, and the opportunity it offered, not only to serve God but also to be a part of a denomination that had grown out of an anti-segregation protest within the Methodist Episcopal Church in Philadelphia in 1787.

Its founder, Richard Allen, was a civil rights leader and vocal advocate for African Americans, denouncing slavery, opposing the removal of free Blacks from the United States to Liberia, and positioning the church to be active in the Underground Railroad. The church spread rapidly and later became involved in the education of the formerly enslaved by establishing colleges and universities. The A.M.E. Church continued its activism into the twentieth century, playing a role in the resettlement of Blacks during the Great Migration when many abandoned the rigidly, brutally segregated South for economic opportunities. The A.M.E. Church was a place where my father could be a part of changing the social and economic status of black people and make a difference in their lives. He saw his role as helping to build upon the legacy of the denomination, as well as to serve the spiritual needs of people.

My parents met while working as teachers in a rural school in Woodstock, Tennessee, in Shelby County, about fifteen miles north of Memphis. They were born at the dawn of the twentieth century: my mother on May 30, 1900, in Lucy, Tennessee, also in Shelby County, a little farther north, where she grew up on a farm with her parents, Robert and Eliza Norment. They lost the farm during the Depression.

My mother went away to attend Lane College in Jackson, Tennessee, a Christian Methodist Episcopal normal school that trained teachers. It is the kind of institution that today would probably be considered a junior college or community college. She completed the two-year course and returned home after graduating.

My father was born September 10, 1898, in Woodstock. His parents were John Henry Butler and Mary Lena Sharp Butler. Mary was the daughter of Joe Sharp, born about 1830, and Ann Sharp, born in 1838, who lived during slavery times in Tipton, Tennessee, according to the 1870 U.S. Census.

In 1900, the census lists John and Mary Butler, my paternal grandparents, as living in the Sharp household, two years after their marriage, along with their child Adee (misspelled "Ade" by the census) Butler, my father. Eventually, John and Mary Butler had four sons (my dad, Adee, John H., Clarence Odell, and Herman) and three daughters (Iris, Mary, and Ida).

The boys had to help on the farm and customarily attended school only until the sixth or the eighth grade. Somehow, my father talked his father into letting him go off to high school at Rust College in Holly Springs, Mississippi, about thirty-five miles from Memphis. Founded in 1866 by the Freedman's Aid Society of the Methodist Episcopal Church, the college offered second-ary education until 1953 and still operates as a historically black liberal-arts college.

Granddad's decision to allow my father to go away angered his brothers, who were left to work on the farm without him. None of the other children pursued higher education, but Adee Conklin Sr. pressed on. He attended the Hampton Normal and Agricul-tural Institute in Hampton, Virginia (later Hampton University) on a football scholarship and studied agriculture. According to the school newsletter, *The Hampton Student*, my dad and a roster of other players were awarded the Hampton letter, "H." He loved football. Transferring after two years, Dad enrolled in Wilberforce College. Located about twenty miles from Dayton, Ohio, it is the oldest college for Negroes in the U.S. and the flagship university for the African Methodist Episcopal Church. One of Wilberforce's claims to fame was that a twenty-eight-year-old professor named W. E. B. Du Bois came to teach classics at the university in 1894, three decades before my father matriculated there.

After Daddy became a minister, my parents moved from Woodstock, Tennessee, to Memphis, where he became pastor of St. John in North Memphis, a small church, and then advanced to Ward Chapel A.M.E. Church, then at 1372 Woodward Street.

With more than a quarter of a million people by 1930, Mem-phis was a big city, compared to Lucy, Tennessee. Memphis was in the heart of cotton country and served as the largest market for cotton in the world. It had also once had the largest slave market in the country. During the Civil War, thousands of Blacks fled enslavement and flocked to Memphis after the Union Army cap-tured the city in 1862 and held it throughout the war.

In the 1860s, Beale Avenue became a mecca for black travel-ing musicians, and by the early 1900s, many clubs, restaurants, and shops lined the street, including many owned by African

Americans. When W. C. Handy published "Beale Street Blues" in 1909, the name was changed from "Avenue" to "Street." The song established Memphis as the hub for this emerging music genre dubbed "the blues." Handy's lyrics paint a picture of what the neighborhood was like around the turn of the century:

I've seen the lights of gay Broadway,
Old Market Street down by the Frisco Bay,
I've strolled the Prado, I've gambled on the Bourse
The seven wonders of the world I've seen
And many are the places I have been.
Take my advice, folks and see Beale Street first.

You'll see pretty Browns in beautiful gowns,
You'll see tailor mades and hand me downs
You'll meet honest men and pick-pockets skilled
You'll find that bus'ness never closes till somebody gets killed.

You'll see Hog-Nose rest'rants and Chitlin' Cafes
You'll see Jugs that tell of bygone days
And places, once places, now just a sham,
You'll see Golden Balls enough to pave the New Jerusalem.

If Beale Street could talk, if Beale Street could talk,
Married men would have to take their beds and walk
Except one or two, who never drink booze
And the blind man on the corner who sings the Beale Street Blues.

Beale Street was still hopping in the early 1930s when my mother and father settled into a house at 226 Ivory Street, only about three miles away from the bustling strip. But it might as well have been thousands of miles away. The life of a minister did not allow for such entertainments, and the pay wouldn't cover it. Mother had settled into being a pastor's wife and rarely complained about the extra work that role meant for her or about the lifestyle she might have given up. Before Daddy was a minister, they had played cards and gone to house parties with other couples. For the sake of propriety, she felt she couldn't do those things anymore.

My parents did not drink alcohol, but Mother blurted out once that she just wished, at the very least, she could have a beer! My father went out, got one, and brought it back to her. It sat in the cabinet untouched for years. I remember that after I first joined the church on my own, if I walked near a beer joint, I felt an urge to cross the street. I didn't even want to get close to it. Temperance was that strong in my mind.

My mother's life was far more constrained by the fact that in Memphis she was unable to continue teaching because she didn't have a degree from a four-year college, as was required there. In the country, her diploma from a two-year course at Lane had been good enough. But Memphis was a bigger district, and standards were changing. In Memphis, she took on what was the only available work for black women—domestic work cleaning, laundering, and cooking for white families. At least it gave her the flexibility she needed for her growing family.

I was born in 1936 in Memphis, and named Dorothy Pearl Butler (after a next-door neighbor who loved children and never had any). Mother gave birth at home, and records vary as to the date. My parents always told me I was born on November 24, and I claim that as my birthday. However, in later years, as I saw copies of my birth certificate and other records, I found that the date was variously recorded as November 22, 23, or 24. This was common in an era when midwives delivered babies in homes and might not have been able to record the birth immediately.

I was the eighth of ten children, only five of whom survived to adulthood. Besides me, the survivors were an older sister, Evelyn, born May 1, 1926; an older brother, Adee, born January 23, 1935; a younger sister, Juanita, who had Down syndrome, born August 31, 1938; and a younger brother, Lynwood, born October 19, 1941. Twin brothers who would have been older than Evelyn were still-born. My birth certificate indicates I had a stillborn twin. A sister, Mary Elizabeth, died February 10, 1937, when she was four years old, of bronchial pneumonia and influenza, according to her death certificate. I was barely two and half months old at the time. My sister Theo died of tuberculosis around the age of seventeen after we moved from Memphis to Louisville, in 1941. In all likelihood, she had contracted the disease living in the slum conditions of our neighborhood, the Queen Bee Bottom area of Memphis, where most residents had to use outdoor toilets and pump their water from wells. She was often ill throughout her life. My mother knew pain from many sources; not the least was the loss of so many of her children.

When Adee was born, Daddy finally had a boy who survived and he named him Adee Conklin Butler Jr., but my older brother's nickname was simply Son.

When I was about eighteen months old, my family had the good fortune to move to the Memphis housing projects, the Dixie Homes. That was a step up back then because the homes were new. Built in 1935, Dixie Homes was on Poplar Avenue, between Ayers Street and Decatur. (It was demolished in 2006 to make way for a new housing development.) In the late 1930s, the housing authorities were looking for "good" colored folks to move into what was one of the first housing projects in the country. Housing officials screened families carefully, and many of those accepted had lived in the Queen Bee Bottom. Conditions there had made Blacks especially vulnerable to a yellow fever epidemic, so our family was happy to have new housing and healthier living conditions. Some white citizens were not thrilled to see Blacks getting such "fine" housing, but the city also built projects for poorer whites and per-suaded the more well-to-do that if their maids and laborers had decent places to live, sanitary toilets, and water to bathe in, they would not bring diseases into their homes.

I learned a lot of this history when I was invited back to make a speech for the rededication after Dixie Homes was torn down due to years of decline and replaced by Legends Park. I was flattered that people in Memphis apparently considered me one of the success stories from Dixie Homes. It was the only home in Memphis that I really remembered. I was so young when we moved there that I had no recollection of our earlier home in Queen Bee Bottom.

Most of Daddy's brothers and sisters moved up North to Gary, Indiana; Chicago; or Detroit. Even without much formal educa-tion, all of them could maintain gainful employment that sup-ported their families and allowed them to buy modest homes, as many black men were able to do when manufacturing jobs were plentiful and a laborer's salary could go far. Blacks across the South moved north hoping to exchange entrenched segregation and limited opportunities for decent wages in a freer environment.

On December 7, 1941, the day the Japanese attacked Pearl Har-bor, and about two weeks after my fifth birthday, we rode the col-ored car of a train from Memphis to move to Louisville, Kentucky. As thousands of Southern black families moved north joining the Great Migration, we merely moved "Up South." Louisville was another big, Southern town.

Bishop Richard R. Wright, the presiding prelate of the A.M.E. 13th district, which encompassed Tennessee and Kentucky, had asked Daddy to go there to direct the building of a new, larger church edifice for Youngs Chapel A.M.E. at 1039 South 16th Street and lead the congregation.

Daddy had gone a couple of months before us and had converted the parsonage, a single-story, narrow house at 1037 South 16th Street, next door to the existing church, into a two-story, with two rooms and a bath for us upstairs. Downstairs were a formal parlor (living room), my parents' bedroom, a dining room, the kitchen, and a bathroom. We were the only family in the neighborhood with two bathrooms. Our house also had a front porch, where the family sat in the summer, and a small backyard.

Louisville would soon become a hub of industrial activity to support the war effort. World War II ushered in a new era of prosperity and energy for the African American community after the long, lean years of the Depression. A catastrophic flood in January 1937 had followed that economic disaster. The floodwaters destroyed more than half the city's homes and displaced a quarter of a million people. Blacks, who were concentrated in the flood plains, were particularly hard hit.

As the war continued during my childhood, there were times when we could not acquire certain foods, owing to wartime rationing. I can't forget the margarine that we had to use instead of butter. It was colorless, like lard, and came with a dye pack to add the color to it.

I am sure my parents were very worried about the war. As an avid reader of newspapers, my father was well informed. He subscribed to the dominant daily paper in the region, *The Louisville Courier-Journal*, and the black paper, *The Louisville Defender*. His example impressed upon me that newspapers were an important source of information. He read critically. He sometimes used stories from the papers in his sermons, as other ministers often did. My awareness of the newspaper, through having it in our home, was one of the things that gave me the courage to apply for a secretarial job there later.

My father admired President Franklin D. Roosevelt, and I can remember headlines announcing that FDR had died on April 12, 1945, of a massive cerebral hemorrhage. Those news headlines brought great sadness to the neighborhood and great concern, especially with the war still going on. I was nine years old when the war ended.

After the war, to earn my spending money, I began to sell *The Louisville Defender* in the neighborhood, which helped me get to know people. I would deliver the paper after school to the apartment building across the street and to church members on the surrounding streets. It was a way to socialize. People were kind and often invited me in. I wasn't thinking then that I would work for that paper and eventually become a reporter, but the experience did make newspapers very familiar to me.

We lived in the segregated, working-class neighborhood known as the California section, south of downtown Louisville. We did not live around white people. The doctors, lawyers, and business owners were black, except for Mr. Tom, who ran the store two or three blocks from our home, and the life insurance man who came around to collect premiums. My father was a significant person. I didn't know it then, but he was among the Blacks who had a voice and prestige in the black community. He was a reverend, one for whom another black man might take off his hat. Black preachers were highly regarded because they could summon everyone together—the laborer, teacher, lawyer, and domestic worker. My father encouraged, led, and guided his flock—and, by extension, his family was among the elite, despite our lack of wealth.

We children attended the neighborhood school for the colored: Phillis Wheatley Elementary School, named after the African

American poet, on St. Catherine Street. I started at age six and skipped the fifth grade. That put me in the same class as Adee—much to his chagrin. After sixth grade, Adee and I attended the colored Madison Junior High School, a three-story, large redbrick building, at 1719 West Madison. The school had a gym and a swimming pool. I was eleven when I started in the seventh grade there and I attended through the ninth grade. All of the black students from the West End went there.

Segregated schools operated under the guise of "separate but equal," and funding was far from equal. In many Southern rural areas, the school year for white children was eight months but six for black children, so that they could be available for crop growing and other field work on the farms. Many rural black schools had a shorter day, while white children attended a full day. Schooling for most Blacks ended at sixth grade while whites matriculated to twelfth grade. But none of this was my experience in Louisville, even though I attended segregated schools. We were happy in our schools and felt we got a good education. In the areas of Kentucky where I grew up, we went to school for the full day and had the opportunity to complete twelve years. We didn't know then that the white schools were far superior, with new books instead of used ones and better equipment in general. We knew that education was very important, and our parents raised us to do the best we could with what gifts we had.

My mother embodied the can-do spirit and worked very hard as a domestic, doing what people called day work—serving as a maid for white families, typically one or two days a week for each. To me, she always looked tired, but she never said "Can't." I resented the fact that, despite her education, she had to do this type of work. I disliked it when some of the women she worked for would call and ask for "Jessie"—using her first name. If I answered the phone, I would respond, "Do you mean Mrs. Butler?" Most southern whites called all black people, no matter their age or station in life, by their first names—or worse, by arbitrary nicknames, or Uncle for every adult black man and Aunt for every black woman. My mother was a pastor's wife, who commanded respect in our community; there, everyone called her Mrs. Butler. I felt she deserved that. But Mother would shush me away from the phone and answer sweetly, "This is Jessie." She refused to let anything destroy her dignity. Working as a maid was, I'm sure, very hard for her at first, but she became used to it. Early in life, I was angry at the system of segregation that forced her into work that demeaned her when I knew that she had been educated and had worked as a teacher.

No matter what cares the outside world put on us, our home life was pleasant and simple. Like other children in that generation, my siblings and I did not ask for or expect a lot of material things. As children we were considered precious, but we were also to be seen and not heard. We were to respect older people. We definitely said "Yes, ma'am" and "No, ma'am." At Christmas, we were happy to get one gift; we all got a box of special fruit or candy or nuts. Looking back at the crushing segregated system of that time, I do not recall growing up in fear. My parents, church, and community shielded me from the emotional, psychological, and physical horrors that are today so well documented—though still unreckoned. My only fear growing up was of cats!

My parents loved and admired each other. They provided a supportive and affirming atmosphere, but they didn't take foolishness from us children. We had breakfast as a family before school every morning. My father was usually next door at the church or near home in the neighborhood for much of the day unless he was away doing church business. As a pastor, he didn't have to be out during working hours like most of the men in the neighborhood, and his office was in the church basement next door. My mother usually went to work once we left for school and was home before we were or just a little later. After school, we did our homework, and we all had dinner together every day.

In the afternoons and evenings, we listened to the radio, as most families did in those days, long before everyone had a television. I especially liked to listen to the soap operas on the radio, particularly when I got older. I would listen to the "stories" while I did the dishes. When Adee and I started junior high at Madison, our days were longer because we had to walk farther to school—thirty to forty minutes each way. It seemed as if we had no time to ourselves during the week. In the summer, our routine would be much less rigid, and I could go to Camp Sky-Hi, a facility out in the country sponsored by a local nonprofit group. Being out of school and able to play in the country brought me such a sense of freedom.

In the segregated South, public education and religious education in the black church commingled. We went to school five days a week, but our church members included schoolteachers who were also Sunday school teachers. They had a deep commitment to equip and prepare us black children to face a racist society. We felt our teachers were genuinely concerned about us. They would explain racist attitudes to us again and again until we internalized that it was the attitudes that were wrong, not us. They wanted us to succeed despite oppression. If we were good students who did bad things occasionally, our teachers were lenient, saying, "I'm not going to tell your parents. We're going to sit down and talk about it." They prepared us both academically and socially, knowing we would move beyond school and church. Church, school, and community all taught us to take pride in ourselves, taught us who we were. They aimed to equip us with the social smarts and the intellectual skills we needed. They told us we had to be twice as good to go half as far as white children. Church gave us spiritual fortitude, told us we were people of pride and integrity. The school, church, and community combined to "raise" us. When we excelled, we knew it was for the generations before and after us. No matter what the season, our lives revolved around the church. My closest friends were in church, especially Margaret Springer, who lived several blocks away on Oak Street, and who later married Adee and became my sister-in-law.

The elders in the church loved children and felt every child belonged to them. They taught us to love those people who spitefully used us and not to exact revenge. My sister-in-law Margaret recalls that when we were walking on the way to Madison, white kids would throw rocks at us and we wanted to retaliate. But our Sunday school teachers had taught us not to. She said, "It was such a struggle all the time, [but] our teachers went the extra mile." Our parents and our teachers told us to do better than the best. The elders held out to us the promise of hope.

Church teachings are the reason my experiences on the front lines of integration never made me a hater. As much as I disliked racism and white supremacy and felt their pain, insult, and isolation, what made it possible for me to go into white institutions and be humiliated and rejected yet somehow not hate white people was this early faith-filled life. I learned to pray, to have conscious contact with God. Faith gave me the strength and the power to do the things that I can, rather than reel and flail and deal with things in anger. Anger and fear have been big in my life, but my faith showed me how to manage my anger, manage my fear, and channel them in a quiet, positive way even when seeing Southern racists attack and witnessing unrestrained white hatred in Mississippi.

We children also had surrogate relatives—our parents' friends—who were invested in us. Special to me were Sister Pearson, an evangelist, and Mrs. Jessie Mae Patton, who had the most beautiful flowers in her garden. She sent me dollar bills folded in an envelope when I was at Lincoln University. My family hosted dinners with guests after church every Sunday. Mother loved to cook, and the more people complimented her, the more food she would prepare.

On Sunday afternoons, I am embarrassed to say, I used to steal money from my daddy's pocket to buy candy. Unlike in Memphis, the public buses in Louisville were not segregated, and I would ride around on Sunday afternoons with some of the young neighborhood kids just to sightsee, catching glimpses of the more well-to-do neighborhoods of Louisville. We would eat candy and ride to the end of the line and back, pointing at the pretty houses.

My father spent a decade building the new church structure and serving the congregation. He poured his life into his calling and would often take money out of his own modest salary to pay the endless stream of workers building the church. Mother always seemed to have a pot of food on hand to share with them, no matter how empty her purse. At one point, the church wall fell. We were devastated. Daddy rallied the congregation to continue, the construction progressed, and the huge building with the large, beautiful, stained-glass windows was built. But Daddy's health suffered. In 1950, with the new Youngs Chapel well on its way to completion, he gave up his role as a full-time pastor because of his declining health. At age fifty, he became the presiding elder of an A.M.E. church district, overseeing several churches. He traveled to different churches but did not have to preach every Sunday and did not have the responsibilities of caring for a congregation.

We could no longer live in the parsonage because a new preacher's family would come to live there. Evelyn, already an adult, had attended Louisville Municipal College and graduated from Kentucky Industrial College in Paducah. She stayed in Louisville to help our family financially, working five days a week as a domestic who "lived on the place"—that is, she stayed overnight with the white families. On the weekends, she stayed with a black family, Dr. and Mrs. Love, in a California section neighborhood of nicer homes. My father found the other six of us a three-room cabin out in the country, in Anchorage, Kentucky, a small town about ten miles northeast of Louisville where wealthy residents from the city summered on their estates.

We lived on a farm owned by a white attorney's family, the Kammerers. My brother Adee, only fourteen when we moved there, took care of the farm, and my mother kept house for the owner's family, working five days a week. Essentially, we were sharecroppers, farming and living on someone else's land. We had to use an outhouse and pump water from a well. Our daily routine was much more rigorous in the country. We helped Mother bring in water from a well for us to wash each morning.

It was a shock to go to this from being a preacher's family in Louisville, where we had status and could entertain after church every Sunday. We didn't even have a dining room in Anchorage, just a kitchen table, and we didn't host dinners the way we had in Louisville. Ordinary tasks were made more difficult by the lack of running water and by having to use an outhouse. It was shameful, but we didn't complain because we had strong spirits, and we got through it with our faith in God and our belief that something better would come. Our part was to make the best of it until we could find our way out of it, so we dealt with it as well as we could.

We children had to get up earlier than we had in Louisville to walk a half mile to a bus stop for school. Adee and I attended Lincoln Institute in Lincoln Ridge, Kentucky. The Lincoln Institute was an all-black boarding high school in Shelby County that had operated since 1912, but we were day students. The school existed so that school districts across Kentucky that had only a handful of Blacks would not have to let them attend school with white children or create schools just for them, under the separatist laws. The boarding school provided education for the colored without necessitating integration of the local schools.

Lincoln Institute was an attractive place. It had a long drive- way from the highway that led up to the school. The campus was dominated by Berea Hall, the main administration and class- room building. The school also had dormitories and a dining hall. Had our family remained in Louisville, I would have attended Central High School, for Negro students. I was better off at the institute because it was a smaller school and I got more personal attention.

Although Adee, Juanita, Lynwood, and I walked some distance to the same bus stop for the ride to school, Adee and I rode to Lincoln, and Juanita and Lynwood took a different bus to the one- room colored elementary school. Such schools were still relatively common in rural areas in Kentucky and elsewhere. One teacher would teach all the children, giving each lessons appropriate to their grade level, one through six.

My father was very sick. He slept in a hospital bed in the front room and wasn't able to help with the farm work. I was scared. I was angry with him for being ill. I dealt with these feelings, as I would well into my adulthood, by eating.

Adee got a special driver's license, although he was only four- teen, and would take Daddy to the churches in his district, in an old Cadillac my father acquired. Adee would then drive the family back to Louisville to attend Youngs Chapel and get the things we needed for the farm. I was in the car with Adee and my father at a gas station when Daddy suffered his final heart attack and died on April 8, 1951. He was fifty-one. I was fourteen. I was a daddy's girl, and his death was the first major turning point in my life. For years, I hated to pass by that gas station because the memory of his death there haunted me. I have little memory of his funeral, though I know it was at Youngs Chapel, and it must have attracted A.M.E. dignitaries, as well as others who admired my father.

It was a devastating loss to us all. Mother went through a difficult time after Daddy's passing, but his long illness had prepared her for his absence. She was left alone to raise us. Evelyn was twenty-six, Adee was fifteen, Juanita was eleven, and Lynwood was eight. Mother was gripped by grief after losing Daddy but was never able to stop and fully grieve because she had so many responsibilities caring for us and working for the Kammerers. She cooked for them and then would come home and cook for us.

As young as he was, Adee, as the first-born son, became almost a surrogate father for the rest of us. He became the man of the house. He was already providing a large part of the support for the family by doing all the Kammerers' farm work, and he took on additional responsibilities after Daddy's death. It was a tough time for him. It was also rough on Juanita because she adored our father. Lynwood was so young; he really needed a father figure, and Adee played a big role in guiding Lynwood, who turned out to be a fine man. Lynwood earned a law degree at Washington University in St. Louis, married Earline, and had a son, Lynwood Butler Jr. Adee graduated from Bellarmine College in Louisville and went on to become an outstanding entrepreneur in Louisville's black community. He and Margaret Springer Butler had a son, Blair Davis Butler.

I became overweight—almost two hundred pounds by the time I was fourteen—and miserable. It was a terrible time for me. I knew that Daddy's poor health was somehow related to his excess weight. While many in the black community accepted or even admired big women, extremes (too thin, too fat) were often frowned upon. I didn't feel comfortable at that weight, and I later became aware that I was a compulsive eater, especially of sweets. Because of my weight, I did not have a very high opinion of myself and avoided sports in school. I did not care much for clothes because I didn't think they looked good on me—unlike my friend Margaret, who sewed and always dressed well.

Linking Daddy's death to his weight eventually awakened a desire in me to do something about my own weight. I was aware that the doctor had given him a diet to lose weight after his first heart attack. His losing battle with weight made me aware of the connection between excess pounds and poor health, and it frightened me. I asked my mother to let me go to General Hospital, the segregated hospital where all Blacks went for health care, so they could put me on a diet as an outpatient to lose weight and become healthier. She did it and encouraged me in my weight-loss efforts by cooking the special meals I needed for the diet. Although my mother herself was plump, but not necessarily concerned about her weight, with her help, I lost more than sixty pounds and kept my weight under control. Losing the excess pounds—bringing me down from 196 to 136 pounds—was in many ways like becoming a new person.

I sometimes had crushes on boys, and a few church guys came to my sixteenth birthday party just after I'd lost weight, but to the best of my knowledge, these were unrequited "likes." I never had a boyfriend, anyone I held hands with. One young gentleman in our church would take ladies out. He was my birthday "boyfriend" date when I turned sixteen.

I began to have a more positive outlook on life. I had always done well in school, getting As and, rarely, Bs. One of my high school teachers at Lincoln Institute, Charles Mucker, was especially encouraging. He would single me out to write and deliver speeches to the other students, for example, about proper behavior and the evils of smoking.

The school librarian, Louvan Gearing, was also special to me. The library was small, and the books were not new. Many were from white schools in Louisville and around the area. When those schools got new books, they gave old ones to Lincoln. Schools for Blacks were not provided money to buy brand-new books. I liked classics such as *Little Women* and *Wuthering Heights* and other novels by the Brontë sisters. I also read contemporary works, like *Native Son* by Richard Wright. I would also sneak and read *True Confessions*, a popular romance magazine that sold millions of copies. I bought it for about fifteen cents at a drugstore. In the library, I would put the *True Confessions* inside a big scholarly tome and read the magazine. Miss Gearing caught me one day and admonished me, "Don't you ever do that again." I'm sure I continued to read *True Confessions*, but not in her library. Miss Gearing, a young black woman from Cincinnati, became a favorite role model. I knew she just didn't want me to waste my time. She showed me that she saw something special in me and treated me accordingly—encouraging me but also chastising me when I was wrong, as did Mr. Mucker. Being sneaky was one of my bad habits.

In the summers, I did clerical work in the school office to earn money, occasionally typing letters for the principal, Whitney Young Sr., when his secretary was on vacation. He was a formidable figure, the father of the civil rights leader Whitney Young Jr. At Lincoln, I always made the honor roll, and I emerged from my cocoon after losing weight. I also became highly involved with my church youth group back in Louisville at Youngs Chapel, serving as president and representing the group at regional youth A.M.E. conventions, an experience that helped me develop confidence and leadership skills and meet other young black Christians across Kentucky.

Though Mr. Mucker told me I was a good writer, I aspired to be a children's lawyer, not a journalist. My own helplessness and feelings that I couldn't change my circumstances as a child led to a desire to advocate for children. I knew children were vulnerable, dependent on adults to do right by them. I didn't even know any lawyers, but law interested me, and I always had affection for children.

After Daddy's death, Mother determined that as soon as Adee and I graduated from high school, we would move back to Louisville. Two years later, Adee, nearly eighteen, and I, sixteen, got our diplomas. We moved back to the city into a housing project, the Cotter Homes, in the West End of the city. Construction on the Cotter Homes and Lang Homes had begun in the 1940s, replacing a black neighborhood long known as Little Africa. Decades later, the Cotter Homes would decay and become plagued with drugs and crime, as were many public housing projects across the nation. The city demolished the Cotter Homes in the late 1990s; replaced them with single- and multifamily, mixed-income housing; and renamed the area Park DuValle. In the early 1950s, when we moved in, the Cotter Homes were relatively new, clean, and well tended. To me, they were a godsend. I had grown up in a working-class Negro community with the esteemed status of minister's daughter in a prominent church family and hadn't felt poor until we moved out to the country, when Daddy was very sick. I felt really poor then. When you don't have an indoor bathroom you know you're poor! Moving back to Louisville into a new housing project after those three horrible years in the country with few amenities was like heaven. This was state-of-the-art, modern living with an up-to-date kitchen and a bathroom.

Evelyn lived and worked with well-to-do furniture store owners, the Bensingers, when we lived at Cotter Homes. Evelyn had studied tailoring in school. She wanted to do something with her hands, rather than a job where she might have to talk much, because of her stutter. She made beautiful clothes that brought in money to help support our family, and she made many of my clothes. Eventually she had to move to Chicago to find work as a tailor. There she worked at Kuppenheimer's, where she made men's suits. Taking care of the family was her nature, and she showed an added sense of responsibility after Daddy died. She used to say that growing up, she always had one of us with her. In the early years, Adee would be on one hip, and I would be on the other; then when we got older, Lynwood would be on one hip and Juanita on the other. With Evelyn helping to shoulder childcare, I was free to pursue my academics.

After high school graduation from Lincoln Institute in 1953, I was fortunate to get a scholarship to Ursuline College, a Catholic women's institution established by the Ursuline Sisters of Louisville in 1938. I had never heard of Ursuline. Miss Gearing and others had worked hard to get me that scholarship. Ursuline apparently was making a concerted effort to integrate. I was one of eight girls from different high schools in and around Louisville and nearby Indiana invited to be the first colored students to attend. Gwendolyn Mumford Buggs was another, and our time together as Ursuline "firsts" forged a friendship that lasted more than sixty years.

Ursuline was on a beautiful, shady campus in an exclusive neighborhood on Lexington Road in the East End of Louisville. I took the bus there directly from Cotter Homes. When my mother was a maid for families in Louisville, I would hear her mention the street addresses of the families for whom she worked—the same street names I now saw from the bus as I rode to college.

Our professors were religious sisters in habits and priests in collars. I can remember seeing the traditional long, flowing black-and-white habits swooshing around the campus. It looked as if the wearers were floating.

Our integration into the academic life of the college went peacefully and smoothly. I don't recall any racial incidents like those we would see on television after the U.S. Supreme Court decision the following year forcing the integration of schools nationwide. None of us black students at Ursuline had ever attended school with whites before, and we wanted to do well and represent the race well. We attended classes without event as day students, although I learned that one black girl had attended Ursuline before our group and hadn't had a good experience. But I don't recall any trouble with my classmates. These were not wealthy, well-traveled, and accomplished white women like those I would encounter at Columbia. Most seemed to come from modest backgrounds. Our relationships were not up close and personal, but the students, as well as the faculty, were accepting of us. Perhaps because their Catholic upbringing encouraged tolerance, they did not treat me as if I were invisible. Still, I don't recall having any real friendships with the white girls at Ursuline.

Attending classes with white girls, sitting next to them, was initially almost an otherworldly experience. The first time I went into a restroom there and washed my hands, a white girl stepped up to wash her hands beside me. I had never been in a restroom with white people before. I had only seen white people at a distance or in passing downtown. I had also seen their images on screen the few times I could view a friend's television or watch a movie at the segregated Lyric Theater. In the mirror, I noticed our reflections side by side, the contrast of our skin colors. Neither of us spoke or acknowledged the other. Standing right next to a white person in my classes, a girl my age, in the flesh, felt more like a dream than a reality.

We black students made no attempt at social integration on campus at Ursuline. We did not try to be a part of the events there, because we felt we would not be welcomed or comfortable. I sang in the school choir, which I found enjoyable, but did little else on campus outside of class. The other seven black girls at Ursuline and I made our social life in the city, with other Blacks who were studying at local colleges and universities.

While at Ursuline, a citywide chapter of a national sorority, Alpha Kappa Alpha (AKA), invited me to join. That chapter brought together young women from the various colleges and universities, not from a single campus as most chapters did. Founded at Howard University in 1908, AKA was the first Greek-letter sorority in the country founded by black women. I enjoyed the opportunity to get to know the other AKAs and participate in social and service activities.

I majored in English and pursued a liberal-arts curriculum, including courses in music and art appreciation, but I also took shorthand and typing to enhance my work skills to help pay my way through college and help support my family. One of my favorite courses was on marriage, taught by a priest, who, of course, was not married. What stuck with me was his description of love as "the willingness to abandon yourself to the person you are able to make happy." Years later, life would teach me how problematic this view of love is.

As a freshman at Ursuline, I began working as a part-time secretary at *The Louisville Defender*, the paper I used to sell as a child. A few weeks after I started in the job, the editor, Frank L. Stanley Sr., came over to speak to me. "Dorothy, you know [the society editor] is ill." I wondered why he was telling me, and then he said, "I want you to fill in for her—write a few stories—to help out."

I was shocked, though flattered, that he thought I could do the job. I stammered out an answer: "Sure, Mr. Stanley."

Suddenly, with no journalism experience and only recently reintroduced to housing with indoor plumbing, I was launched into "black society." Louisville had a small, thriving black upper echelon of doctors, lawyers, business owners, educators, and school administrators. They lived in the far West End, near Chickasaw Park, in an area called the Gold Coast. My boss was a "mover and shaker" in that world of nice houses and fancy parties, not unlike that sociologist E. Franklin Frazier described in his 1957 book, *Black Bourgeoisie*, in which he charged that the black middle class was marked by conspicuous consumption, wish fulfillment, and a world of make-believe.

Louisville, of course, was the home of the Kentucky Derby, the occasion for at least a week of parties that drew visitors from all over the world, and black Louisville hosted its share of racing enthusiasts, celebrities, and partygoers. In the more modest neighborhoods, like the one I had lived in as a child, everybody tried to make extra money at Derby time. We would rent out rooms in our houses to out-of-towners for Derby weekend, and some families let visitors park on their lawns—for a price.

A teenager living in the projects, I now had access to the Derby parties of the black elite. I saw Negroes who set their tables with fine china and lead crystal, serving the grandest meals and liquors, entertaining the way I had seen white people do in the movies or read about in books. Those experiences showed me that journalism was a key that could open a door to new worlds, and I wanted to enter them. I began to see that I could have a "bigger" life. Without knowing it, at age seventeen I had begun my career as a journalist.

Mr. Stanley let me keep reporting and writing features and other types of stories throughout my time at Ursuline. I no longer did secretarial duties but focused on reporting, and I learned how all the elements of journalism—writing, reporting, observing, and analyzing—came into play.

My self-image had also improved. I considered myself reasonably attractive at a moderate weight. I didn't have many clothes, but my sister sewed them, and they were well-made. I dressed as nicely as possible. And I liked to wear makeup.

On my way to college one day, I was riding the bus route that ran from the Cotter Homes past the campus when I saw a tall, skinny young man get on at Southern Avenue, not far from where I lived. He came over to me and began talking, and I responded. I learned that he attended the University of Louisville, and I told him I was studying at Ursuline. His name was Sam Gilliam; he was studying art. He had a deep voice and was talkative, but I can't say that I was instantly attracted to him.

Years later, he would tell a journalist it was "love at first sight" on his part.

We soon began dating off and on—a new and enjoyable experience for me. With him, I socialized with many of the other students at various colleges in town. Sam accompanied me to the local debutante ball for selected college girls, sponsored by my sorority, and I went with him to the Thoroughbred Ball at the University of Louisville. We would go to the Chestnut Street settlement house on Thursday nights to dance.

Neither of us was ready to make a commitment, however, and it would be seven years before we became husband and wife. The relationship had to wait because I wanted to study journalism. Ursuline did not have a program, and I decided after two years there that I wanted to transfer to a school where I could earn a journalism degree.

Unable to secure a scholarship to attend the University of Missouri, which had one of the top journalism programs in the country, I earned a work scholarship for Lincoln University in Jefferson City, Missouri, a predominantly African American school. The journalism program there got its start after the University of Missouri journalism program denied entrance to Lucile Harris Bluford, later editor and publisher of *The Kansas City Call* newspaper. (Bluford sued after her eleventh attempt to enroll. The case went all the way to the U.S. Supreme Court, which ruled in her favor, but the University of Missouri soon announced it was shutting down its program, citing staff shortages during World War II.)

Lincoln had a relatively small journalism department, but I felt nurtured there and gained the skills I needed. The dean was Armistead S. Pride, and the curriculum encompassed everything from putting out a newspaper to typesetting—those were the days of hot-lead type.

At Lincoln, I also gained a greater sense of my African American identity. I had arrived at school in the fall of 1955—reserved, conservative, and psychologically shackled from living nearly eighteen years in the Jim Crow South. I became co-editor of the school paper, *The Clarion*. This is when I wrote the editorial advocating a "go slow" approach to implementing integration after the *Brown v. Board of Education* decision, as if Blacks had not waited long enough or suffered enough violence over desegregation. Some white people in the South were saying, "It will never happen, or it will happen over my dead body." School systems were shutting down over the issue, and I was saying that maybe we needed to slow down and let things work themselves out. I am embarrassed I ever thought that way.

A black history class with Dr. Lorenzo Green provided the awakening I needed. That class probably formed in me the perspectives that would shape my career. "Black history did not begin with slavery," he would intone as he introduced us to the wonders of Africa, its ancient marvels and its heroes' feats of accomplishment. Dr. Green had worked as an intern under Dr. Carter G. Woodson, the Harvard-educated historian known as the father of black history, and my professor was a part of the Association for the Study of African American Life and History that Woodson founded. What Dr. Green said sounds like such a simple truth today, but at the time, it hit me as if somebody had turned on a fire hose filled with knowledge, new insights, and understanding and soaked me in them. It knocked me back and made me realize both what was possible and what I didn't know. I didn't know anything about Negro history before slavery. I thought, "If black history didn't start with slavery, where did it start? It started in Africa. What did that mean? How do I learn more about that?"

I wrote a column about Dr. Green's impact on me. He helped me understand who I was as a black person in America and in the world. Despite all the positives I had been taught in my parallel black worlds of church, school, and community, I had grown up internalizing feelings of second-class citizenship. Because racial segregation and racism were such facts of American life, I believed that black people were inferior and white people were superior. I had strong values and principles, but they hadn't been enough to prepare me for the tactics that government, the white church, and the state employed to keep black people second-class citizens.

I had been "mis-educated" as Dr. Woodson put it in his book *The Mis-Education of the Negro*, published in 1933, three years before I was born. In it, he argued that our schools indoctrinated African Americans to be dependent and to seek out inferior places in society. "When you control a man's thinking you do not have to worry about his actions," Woodson wrote. "You do not have to tell him not to stand here or go yonder. He will find his 'proper place' and will stay in it. You do not need to send him to the back door. He will go without being told. In fact, if there is no back door, he will cut one for his special benefit. His education makes it necessary."

Woodson challenged the African Americans of his day to think and do for themselves. He started Negro History Week, to encourage Blacks to learn their own history, and black schools primarily observed it by immersing their students in the history of black American heroes, not the history of Africa and its heroes. Having grown up in all-black schools, I know we had an illusion that we were learning about black people and their certain worth. We saw positive images because we did have some "good" black teachers, but I never learned in school about the history of Africans before they came to America. Dr. Woodson said our teachers had a classical education in a European sense, so the "good" ones taught us what they knew. It was a vicious circle that results from mis-educating individuals who mis-educate others. We were not trained to think critically about the history of Africans in the world, and what little we knew was based on distorted views.

For the first eighteen years of my life as a young black woman in the South, I was exposed to the societal concept that I was "less than." Black people had the lowest jobs and the lowest place on the totem pole. I had never even seen Blacks as clerks in downtown stores, and certainly not as airline pilots or executives in corporations. Lincoln University helped to broaden my vision, as would visiting Africa later.

When I went to Lincoln, it was also my first time ever living outside my family's home and away from Kentucky since our relocation there in 1941. However, I had a ready-made social circle because I already belonged to a national sorority, and I quickly affiliated with the AKA chapter at Lincoln. That immediately connected me with people, which was helpful, especially since I was coming in as a junior.

I lived in a dormitory and had a roommate, Lucille Johnson, an AKA, who became salutatorian of our class. Another friend, Velma Crossline Nance, who was a year behind us and not interested in joining a sorority, would come to our room and talk. She and I have remained friends. Also among my friends at Lincoln was Mary Justice from Texas, also an AKA, who was always talking about her friend Barbara Jordan back home. Many years later, when Jordan became the first African American congresswoman from Texas, I found out Mary had not been exaggerating Jordan's enormous merits.

In my senior year at Lincoln, the Alpha Phi Alpha Fraternity chapter chose me as their "sweetheart." All the fraternities and sororities on campus picked one. We sweethearts rode around on top of cars for the homecoming parade, waving to the crowd. I was pleasantly surprised and honored to be chosen because I had never seen myself as a beauty queen, especially given my past as a two-hundred-pound adolescent. The fraternity sweethearts tended to be the very fair-skinned, not dark like me.

In June 1957, I graduated cum laude, went home to Louisville, still a legally segregated city, and applied for jobs at the daily newspapers owned by the Bingham family. *The Courier Journal*, the morning paper, had a liberal bent and a national reputation for excellence, and *The Louisville Times* was its companion evening paper. I received a discouraging rejection letter. The letter said the papers had already hired interns from Indiana University in Bloomington, one of the colleges in the region with a journalism program. I took them at face value, but the tone of the letters implied "and don't bother applying again." I felt that racism had slapped me in the face again and that white newsrooms weren't ready for people like me.

In August, I got a job as a reporter working for *The Tri-State Defender* and returned to Memphis, my childhood home. Three weeks after I got to Memphis I covered the desegregation conflict in Little Rock.

Among the black journalists I met in Little Rock were editors from *JET* magazine, who offered me a job. Soon, after only three months at *The Tri-State Defender*, I accepted a job as an associate editor for *JET* and moved to Chicago. *JET* was then known as the black Bible. Black people used to say, "If it wasn't in the *JET*, it didn't happen." The small-format, glossy weekly owned by the Johnson Publishing Company was a companion to the monthly *Ebony*. I enjoyed Lerone Bennett of *Ebony*, whose writing influenced me powerfully. *JET* covered everything there was to know about black people—news, entertainment, sports, weddings, and society happenings. John H. Johnson founded *JET* in 1951 as "The Weekly Negro News Magazine," and it circulated nationwide. Working at *JET* fueled the attitude that Dr. Lorenzo Green's black history classes had ignited in me, a complete change from my "go-slow-with-integration" attitude.

I lived in Chicago with my sister Evelyn, who was working there as a tailor. We lived in an apartment building, Lake Meadows, on East 33rd near Lake Shore Drive on the South Side. With our combined salaries, we could afford a one-bedroom, and we shared the bedroom. We also had a living room, kitchen, and dining area, far more luxurious than the kitchenettes or rooms with shared baths rented by so many transplanted black Southerners. At twenty, I was one of the youngest associate editors *JET* had ever hired and the only female associate editor at that time. My job was to write feature stories and rewrite items from other sources about the African American community.

Despite Mr. Wilson's best efforts to teach me during those three months at *The Tri-State Defender*, my writing was probably only up to par for the Lincoln college newspaper or the Negro society pages of *The Louisville Defender*—not exactly fluid and lyrical. My editor at *JET*, Ed Clayton, told me, "You write like you've got concrete in your fingers." The copy chief, Mr. Carter, who affectionately called me Rookie, helped me to deal with the criticism and improve my writing. He was also like a big brother and helped give me perspective on how to deal with the actors, singers, sports figures, and others who came to visit the Johnson Publishing Company. "Keep your distance. Some people may want to use you to get their pictures in the magazine," he said.

During my time at *JET*, from November 1957 to September 1959, I met black celebrities and leaders. Stars like Sammy Davis Jr. came to our office to visit. I interviewed Ray Charles and was unnerved by his constant shaking, presumably from his drug addiction. I went to prisons to interview inmates, and did captions on the "beauty of the week."

My vision of the history and role of the black press expanded. This was at a time when the Civil Rights Movement was beginning to snowball, and the drive for independence from colonialism in Africa was reshaping the landscape for black people on that continent. Undoubtedly, the most unforgettable African I met during this time was Tom Mboya, a handsome, charismatic, twenty-eight-year-old labor leader from Kenya. In December 1958, he was chosen chairman of the All-African Peoples Conference in Ghana, and in 1959, he was in the U.S. for a two-month tour to solicit scholarships for his "Student Airlift" to the U.S. and Canada for young Kenyan students and to push for the cause of independence from colonial rule. We met at the home of my colleague Rose Jourdain, in nearby Evanston, Illinois, and he asked me out. We dated briefly, as he made numerous trips to the United States. In 1959, for example, he gave the commencement address at Howard University and received an honorary doctorate.

Writing for *JET*, a weekly, kindled in me an ambition to be a journalist for a daily newspaper, which meant I would need to find some way to work for a white-owned publication. To have any chance of getting a job on a white daily, I had to earn "white" credentials. Black professionals who had gotten their baccalaureate degrees at black colleges often followed a pattern of enrolling in a Northern white institution to get a graduate degree.

After researching journalism schools, in 1959, two years out of college and with two years' experience at *JET*, I applied to the most famous graduate journalism program in the country—Columbia University's. The school turned down my application on the basis that I didn't have enough liberal-arts credits on my transcript from Lincoln University to meet Columbia's criteria. I didn't question their decision. It was routinely felt that black universities were not equal to white ones. They certainly lacked the financial resources of white universities.

What I didn't know at the time was that the interviewer, a Columbia alumnus in Chicago, also had written a note to the school officials that they should be aware that I was "very dark-skinned." That suggested that I might have gotten in more easily if I had been a light-skinned Negro. Lighter skin was sometimes seen as more acceptable, even among black people. I found out about the interviewer's remark decades later when the school recognized me as one of the Columbia Alumni of the Year, and a professor, my old *Washington Post* colleague Luther Jackson, found it in my records.

I considered how to get the additional hours in liberal arts that I needed to reapply to Columbia. Samuel Yette, a Johnson Publishing colleague who worked for *Ebony*, told me he was leaving to launch a public-relations office at Tuskegee Institute. Yette would go on to be executive secretary of the Peace Corps and the first black Washington correspondent for *Newsweek*. (He was fired from *Newsweek* after the publication of his incendiary book *The Choice: The Issue of Black Survival in America*.) Yette suggested that I come work for him in Alabama as associate director and earn the additional hours at Tuskegee. I took him up on the offer and enrolled in several history courses while writing for the institution's internal publications. Charles Hamilton was one of my professors. He expanded my views of blackness, continuing the influence of my classes with Dr. Green at Lincoln and my readings of Lerone Bennett's writing at *Ebony* magazine. These were mind-changing times!

One of the highlights of my time at Tuskegee was hearing, on more than one occasion, the young reverend Martin Luther King Jr. preach at his church. Dexter Avenue Baptist, in Montgomery, Alabama, was close enough that I could ride to church on Sunday

with Sam and his wife, Sadie. Four years after his success in leading the bus boycott, King had emerged as the central figure in
the mushrooming movement for civil rights. It was electrifying
to be in the audience of the always-packed church. I could hardly
contain myself as King brilliantly articulated the plight of African
Americans and the aims of the movement to secure our rights.
I marveled at the spiritual power he had that got poor people in
Montgomery to organize, walk, and take alternative transportation for a year to protest segregation on the buses. As long as I
was in Alabama, I took every opportunity to hear him. King's
sermons, added to teachings from professors Green and Hamilton
and the writings of Bennett, transformed my thinking. I began to
believe integration might be possible, or at least worth fighting for,
as my daddy had said.

In 1960, I formally reapplied and gained admission to Columbia University to pursue the master's degree in journalism. I was
excited for the opportunity to live in New York City for a year
and attend the J-school known as an incubator of talent, at 116th
Street and Broadway.

While the James Meredith and other civil rights battles raged in
Mississippi and throughout the South, my classmates and I worked
nine to five, several days each week, or however long it took to
complete our stories to put out daily newspapers. My favorite
professor was John Hohenberg, a 1927 graduate of the J-school,
who roamed around the news-classroom reminding us we were
on deadline by shouting, "Go with what you've got!" In addition to faculty professors, many of our teachers were journalists
from prestigious New York dailies, including the film critic Judith
Crist. We also heard lectures by leading reporters, editors, and
newsmakers such as New York governor Averell Harriman, which
helped me become familiar with interviewing highly placed

government officials. One memorable assignment was to write about the retired prime minister Winston Churchill, who was visible seated on his yacht docked in New York City. I didn't go onto his yacht to interview him, but the experience was nonetheless interesting. I did a story capturing the scene, describing Churchill and the yacht, and I interviewed bystanders about what they saw and their impressions of the British leader.

At first, I felt intimidated by some of my classmates' experiences, knowledge, connections, and prestige. Many had traveled to Europe more than once; I had never left the country. My classmates knew so much more about the general culture. As most educated black Americans of my generation were, I was raised bicultural. I had been steeped in Western thought and tradition and read some of the same books in school as my white classmates had. However, I had also learned about the contributions of black Americans. In the segregated Negro schools and colleges I attended, in my community, and in my church, I had regularly been taught pieces of the history of Blacks in this country. Negro History Week was celebrated. I was even beginning to learn about Africans fighting for independence. This knowledge came from Tom Mboya. Moreover, my family exemplified a strong spirit of Negro pride that was passed on to me. My classmates didn't know anything about my culture. It occurred to me years later that Blacks had always had to be bicultural in our education and experiences, but it had never been a two-way street. Blacks had to know about white culture, but whites did not need to know about black culture.

Much of what my white classmates at Columbia "knew" about Blacks was based on people who worked as maids, cooks, drivers, or butlers for their parents or on stereotypes they saw in the movies. The only film roles available to African American actors and actresses at that time were what film historian Donald Bogle would later aptly describe in the title of his award-winning 1973 book,

Toms, Coons, Mulattoes, Mammies, and Bucks. He was referring to the servile "Tom," the simple-minded and cowardly "coon," the tragic female "mulatto," the fat, dark-skinned "mammy," and the supersexual "buck." Later came "the asexual sidekick." I was none of these, so Columbia University was quite an adventure, and a very difficult one at times.

I was pleased to have saved money for graduate school when I worked at Tuskegee, but the J-school also helped me to land a scholarship that paid an extra dividend. The scholarship was awarded by the New York Newspaper Women's Club. I attended the awards dinner in correct attire, including long white gloves, and was delighted when my photograph appeared in *The New York Times*.

One day in late 1960 or early 1961, I received a call from a writer named Alex Haley, who had seen the photograph in *The Times*. He invited me to his home in Greenwich Village and took me to dinner more than once. Haley was about forty then, soft-spoken and kind. He was wonderful, encouraging me to go into daily journalism, and he shared that he had honed his writing skill during his spare time in the Coast Guard before retiring in 1959 with the rank of chief journalist. A freelance writer then, Alex shared with me that he was working on *The Autobiography of Malcolm X* and had begun interviewing him. We sporadically kept in touch when I left New York. I was working at *The Washington Post* when *The Autobiography* was published, and in the Style section of *The Washington Post* when he published *Roots* a decade later.

As civil rights protests made headlines, graduation drew near, and I sat in Hohenberg's office one spring afternoon for a final meeting. "Being a Negro, and a woman, you face a double whammy, but you have so many handicaps you'll probably make it," he said, shaking his head slightly and his voice fading into silence. He knew I would be diving into daily journalism's ocean of white men in newsrooms where the sparse number of white women were assigned to women's pages and the occasional person of color would be clinging to a life raft called novelty.

That spring, I was among those interviewed by *The Washington Post* city editor Ben Gilbert. It was customary for an editor from the paper to come to campus to interview members of the graduating class. Gilbert was very pleasant, and he asked me numerous questions about my experience. Not long after the interview, Gilbert wrote me saying that *The Washington Post* was interested in me, but that the editors didn't think I had enough daily newspaper experience.

He advised me to go to a smaller paper first, get some more experience, and then get in touch with *The Washington Post* again. This was standard advice to young journalists; his letter did not make me feel summarily rejected as the Louisville paper's reply had. I wasn't surprised that he didn't hire me right away, because I really didn't have experience working for a daily newspaper, and *The Washington Post* was not a small-town paper. It wasn't the paper then in size or stature that it would become by the mid-1970s, but it was still a major newspaper in the nation's capital city.

Gilbert had also told me that if I ever happened to be in Washington, I should let him know so he could arrange for me to meet the managing editor, Alfred Friendly. Friendly was largely credited with elevating *The Washington Post* from a not-particularly-distinguished local paper to a newspaper of national and international prominence. When he returned to reporting, he won a Pulitzer Prize for his coverage of the 1967 Arab-Israeli War.

I graduated in the spring of 1961 and received a scholarship to participate in Operation Crossroads Africa that summer. Under the program, North American students would travel to Africa—to Kenya, Nigeria, Ethiopia, and other countries—to participate in work projects alongside African students. A black Presbyterian minister from Harlem, the Rev. James H. Robinson, had founded the program in 1958, and it is still running. President Kennedy called it the progenitor of the Peace Corps, which he launched in March 1961, and Robinson later became a vice president and advisor of the successful U.S. government program that sends volunteers abroad.

Orientation for Operation Crossroads in the summer of 1961 happened to be in Washington, so I contacted Gilbert and told him I would be in town. True to his word, he invited me to meet Friendly, who asked me why I happened to be in D.C. When I told him I was going to Africa, Friendly seemed genuinely interested in what I would be doing there. Editors are always looking for what is different about someone they meet, and the fact that I was going to Africa at a time when very few Americans, black or white, had ever traveled there or even met an African certainly made me different. He asked me to submit some articles about my experience while I was in Africa. Encouraged and excited at the prospect, I agreed to send back some stories.

Before I left for Africa, I had also asked *The Louisville Times* editors if they would be interested in having me write an article from Africa. Surprisingly, they were open to the idea.

I would find much to write about in Africa. What I saw there expanded my vision beyond the caste system of the Jim Crow era, during which I had come of age, and the distorted pictures of Africa most Americans associated with that vast land. While I knew only too well about the racial divide, before I went to Columbia, I was less conscious of class differences. They were more obvious to me at Columbia because everybody I met seemed to have had so many experiences. Some had been traveling to Europe since they were children, and I had never even been to the West Coast. One reason I wanted to go to Africa during the summer after graduation was to deepen my understanding of that great continent and its people, broaden my knowledge of culture, and enlarge my scope of experiences.

The trip more than met my expectations. In Nigeria, I saw black people in leadership positions that those of my race were denied in the United States. When we landed at the airport in Lagos, I was amazed to see Blacks working in all kinds of jobs. In 1957, Ghana had become the first African nation to declare independence from European colonization. Nigeria had gained its independence from the United Kingdom in October 1960. Clearly, the continent was undergoing extraordinary change.

We were in Nigeria about a week and then went to Kenya for two months. The first thing our group was assigned to do was build a road leading from a highway to what was going to be a children's hospital a few miles from Nairobi. Working in the White Highlands, where Blacks were forbidden to own land, we stayed on site in tents and used sleeping bags.

Eighteen people were in our group, including three Blacks. The rest were white. Sometimes when we weren't working, we would try to hitchhike into Nairobi to see the sights. More than once, I was the lone black person in the group going to town. White drivers would stop and let the white students get in but refuse to take me. The British had declared a state of emergency from October 1952 to 1959 in response to increasing African resistance to colonization, so the slight reflected the racial tensions. But it really hurt to be as badly treated in a black nation as I had been in my predominantly white homeland.

While there, I met with my friend Tom Mboya, who by then was a member of the Kenya Legislative Council (and a close friend of President Barack Obama's father, Barack Obama Sr.) One of the reasons I had wanted to go to Africa was to see Tom. I liked him a lot, and I had naively harbored some romantic notion that we might have a future together. It became clear, however, that that was far from his mind. Marriage to an American, had he been so inclined, would have been a political disadvantage.

One of the highpoints of my visit to Kenya was getting to meet Jomo Kenyatta on August 21, 1961, the day he got out of prison after years of confinement because of his role in the struggle for independence. Operation Crossroads allowed me and another woman in the group to go to his compound to help prepare his house, which had been unoccupied for a while, for his return. We cleaned and washed dishes that had long been sitting on the shelves. His impending arrival was a huge event. People lined the roads for miles and miles. We could hear the sounds of excitement echoing through the beautiful air of Kenya. The area around Nairobi is about six thousand feet above sea level, and I remember the air as thin and fresh. It's one of the most beautiful places in the world. The reason the people were so excited was that they anticipated that in another couple of years, Kenyatta would become Kenya's first president. The winds of change were drifting across Africa.

Kenyatta had been the leader of the rebellion against British rule. As head of the Mau Mau rebellion, he was widely portrayed in the Western press as violent, but Mboya defended him all over the world, refuting that characterization. Kenyatta would go on to lead Kenya as prime minister and later president from independence in 1963 to his death in 1978. Meeting him at the historic moment and playing a small part in that day was an honor.

On our way back to the U.S. from Kenya, we met with Emperor Haile Selassie, who governed Ethiopia from 1930 to 1974. We arrived at his palace early for our appointment, and the lions that protect the palace at night were still in view, as were the guns and other weapons of the palace guards.

Before arriving home, where civil rights protests and white mob violence were so prominent they made headlines around the world, I sent articles in to *The Washington Post*, as promised. The editors apparently read and liked them, because when I returned to the States, *The Washington Post* hired me as a general assignment reporter. *The Louisville Times* also published one of my articles when I got back, and the editors of that paper also offered me a job. A new era of openness seemed to have dawned at my hometown paper, but I was on my way to *The Washington Post*.

I find it ironic that if I had not gone to Africa in the summer of 1961, *The Washington Post* probably wouldn't have hired me at that point in my career. The trip had given me a chance to show the editors that I could write, and think broadly. I had no work experience writing under daily deadline pressure, and *The Washington Post* was a real daily newspaper. The editors at *The Washington Post* were taking a gamble on me. I had to prove I was up to the challenge. I had no idea how difficult or fulfilling that would be, or that I would spend nearly my entire career there.

Being Mrs. Sam Gilliam, 1962–1982

I'm posed sitting on a car in 1958 in Chicago while working as an associate editor at *JET* magazine. *(Courtesy of the Dorothy Butler Gilliam personal collection)*

This picture of Sam and me was taken by *The Washington Post* for an article on Sam and his career after I left *The Post* in 1966 to care for our growing family. Behind us is one of Sam's paintings. The photo was taken during the seven-year period when I was not working for the newspaper, thereby avoiding any ethical conflict. I was rehired in 1972. *(Photo © 1964, Matthew Lewis/ Washington Post)*

My family in 1967. I'm on the left, with Stephanie, four, on my lap, and Sam has Melissa, two, and Leah, eight months, on his lap, at our home in the Mount Pleasant community of Washington, D.C. *(Courtesy of the Dorothy Butler Gilliam personal collection)*

Maurice Sorrell of *JET* magazine presented me with an award from the Capital Press Club on June 13, 1964, while I was still one of only a handful of black reporters for *The Washington Post*. My good friend Wallace H. Terry, right, who preceded me at *The Washington Post*, also received an award that day. *(Used with Permission of Capital Press Club)*

With my family at my eightieth birthday celebration. I'm in the center, with, from left, Dr. William Grobman, Dr. Melissa Gilliam, granddaughter Eve Grobman, grandson Ben Grobman, granddaughter Olivia Hanley, Thomas Hanley (rear), Stephanie Gilliam, Melissa Anderson, and Leah Gilliam. *(Kea Dupree Photography)*

When Sam moved to Washington after our wedding in Louisville, I was happy we were finally together. Our families approved of our marriage, and we loved each other. He had been ready to leave Louisville. And he had heard that Washington, D.C., had "a pretty good art scene."

One thing that brought Sam and me together was that he, like me, was a "pusher out." He wanted to get out of Kentucky. I had already gotten out of Kentucky. We each had a vision of what we wanted to do and who we wanted to be. That shared thinking was a part of our attraction for each other, perhaps even when we first met on the bus while I was a student at Ursuline and he at the University of Louisville.

We both went to white schools then, but our social life was with other black people. I was definitely not part of an artistic circle. I had just moved back to Louisville, after three years in sharecropper country. Sam was tall and thin and had a deep voice. He was the first man I dated, although I don't remember exactly when we started dating. I am sure I gave *him* my phone number because *I* didn't call boys or young men. They would call *me*. All the black students who went to white colleges in the area would gather at the Settlement House on Chestnut Street once a week on Thursday night to dance. That was our social life and how we met other black college students in Louisville. Sam was the one who told me about the weekly dances. He would also take me to a place called Joe's where they played jazz; he introduced me to that world. Sam was a big fan of John Coltrane. The AKA sorority would sponsor a debutante ball. We were young Negroes mimicking white society. We wanted to be like the better whites, society people, not poor whites. I was a debutante. Sam was my escort. My older sister made my dress.

Sam was a little bit risqué for me, a preacher's kid. He was not the kind of boy who was at my sixteenth birthday party, out in the country. But interestingly, my mother always liked Sam. If she had not liked him I definitely would not have married him. Years later, he said, "Your mother was a queen." They had a very real connection. Mother thought he was polite. She saw that he was trying to get an education. He was "going somewhere." He wasn't someone who had no ambition. She didn't understand his art—it took me a long time to start understanding his abstract art—but she liked him. I said nothing to her about his occasional social drinking, and if she detected it, she didn't mention it to me as a problem.

When I met Sam, I'd made it back to city life after three years in the country with no indoor toilet. I had a byline at the local Negro paper. I'd gotten my excess weight off. And I was going somewhere! Sam probably sensed my ambition, that I was a pusher out, too, because when we met I was already working for *The Louisville Defender* even though I was still a student at Ursuline. I was already getting bylines. My children tease me about a picture taken of me about that time. They say it has a kind of a movie-star quality. In it, I'm wearing a poodle skirt and sitting on the hood of a convertible. My girls asked me, "Mom, whose car is that?" They laughed when I told them I didn't know whose car that was, that I'd just hopped up on the hood so my friend could snap a picture. Growing up, I was the bookish person in the family. I was a great reader of books, and the only negative thing I remember my mother ever saying about me was "Dorothy has a lot of book sense, but not a lot of common sense." That picture shows a side of me that was just beginning to emerge when Sam met me. I jumped up on that car because I knew it was going to be a great picture of me. That picture showed I was going somewhere. I wasn't sitting on any old car. I sat on the hood of a convertible.

Sam saw my drive emerging. He saw an attractive brown-skinned woman of seventeen who liked makeup, looked her best going to school every day, and had ambition. I didn't have that many clothes, but my sister Evelyn made me a few nice outfits that I could wear over and over. What Sam saw as special in me was my grounding. He didn't see just the preacher's kid but who I had *become* growing up in the church. Negro women have a certain kind of special when they are the preacher's daughter.

When he came over to me on the bus and started talking, the preacher's kid in me was a little bit put off at first. I thought, *He's talking too much; it's smack talk*, but I also sensed something interesting, so I talked with him. We were kindred spirits, what we called "pushers out." We knew inherently that we were expected to excel among our own, and that was what we wanted, too. But 1955 thrust whole new possibilities at us. I began to feel liberated, seeing the bravery of Rosa Parks and the total lack of fear and concern for their exhaustion that the people in Montgomery showed when they walked back and forth to work. You work as a maid, a domestic worker. You walk to work. You work hard all day—and from my own mother I knew how hard they worked. And then you *walk* home. I was glad when they organized shared rides and car services to help some, but their bravery was, to me, a breakthrough moment in my own personal evolution. It made me want to do more. I wanted to *be* more. I was never someone who was not going to be involved. I was already on a track. I was already the one among my siblings who would probably go away to college and then keep going. But the Montgomery bus boycott was a supercharge that said, "All right, Dorothy, you can do more. You *are* more and you can do more." Certainly by the time Sam and I got married, I was truly ambitious and part of that is what attracted him to me. We were both on a path.

Although we had known each other for seven years before our marriage, we had not even lived in the same city since I left Louisville in 1955 to begin my junior year of college at Lincoln University in Missouri. After earning his bachelor's degree from the University of Louisville, Sam entered the army in 1956 and spent two years in Japan. Sam was passionate about art; loved jazz, especially Coltrane and Miles Davis; and had a large jazz-record collection. He was brilliant, a polymath, and could be extremely talkative at times, and very funny. He was also unusually perceptive about people and highly knowledgeable about history and current events. We had written each other letters and dated casually during my brief stays in Louisville while I lived in other cities.

Marriage was expected of young women of my generation and, at age twenty-four, I thought I was ready for the plunge. Marriage was the biggest turning point in the decade of my twenties, even more important than the choice to leave the Negro press and chart a course in white journalism. I was so excited to get married! It was not only because that was what young women of my generation were supposed to do. I was excited about having a man of my own, being with him all the time, sleeping together, and all the things we didn't do before we got married. These were the days before birth control pills. Just as important, my community, church, and family thought the worst thing that could happen to a girl was to spoil her life chances by becoming pregnant unwed. No more lusting! That was part of my excitement about getting married because, while sex is wonderful in a marriage, casual encounters—I thought then and still think now—can be harmful to people's development. That is my perspective; it is obviously very out of style today. For Sam and me, marriage was the beginning of our deep intimacy—the discovery of each other's temperaments and bad and good character traits.

After the wedding, Sam came to my family's house to pick me

up. As we loaded everything we had into his little Volkswagen bug to drive to Washington, he looked upset. "What is upsetting you?" I asked, wondering how he could be distressed since we had just gotten married. I knew he didn't have much money for the trip, probably only fifty dollars, but in 1962 that was enough to get from Louisville to D.C. with an overnight stay at a nice hotel. He had a job already lined up in D.C. I had already secured our apartment. I never found out what had upset him, but it foreshadowed a pattern.

We spent our honeymoon night in Cincinnati, a stop on our drive to Washington. Unbeknown to either of us, I immediately got pregnant.

I entered marriage with romantic notions based on my Catholic professor's definition of love: Love is the willingness to abandon yourself to the person you can make happy. That was my working intellectual description. The book-sense nature that my mother ascribed to me, as opposed to a common-sense nature, led me to believe that since the professor had said it and gotten it out of a book, it must be okay. I believed a wife's business was to get involved in her husband's feelings, regardless of what that did to my own emotional development. My whole being was wrapped up in Sam, so that if he felt bad, I'd feel bad. When Sam looked upset about something, I would plead with him: "Sam, if you're upset, I'm upset. What's the matter?" Like most newlyweds, I had a lot to learn about the realities of living with another complicated human being and the ups and downs of married life. It took me a long time to learn not to feel his issues were mine, that the way he felt didn't necessarily have to do with me. After all, I was twenty-four.

Our first apartment was a sparsely furnished one-bedroom apartment in Adams Morgan. At the end of our workdays, we would sit on the floor on opposite sides of a cloth-covered wooden crate that temporarily served as our table, and we'd enjoy our meal with candles and inexpensive wine.

Sam's ambition was to become an exhibiting artist in Washington, and he was most interested in abstract painting. Setting out to learn the local scene, he met with James Porter, chair of Howard University's Art Department, noted scholar of African American art, and a figurative painter who wrote the first comprehensive history of black art. Despite wide differences in their artistic expression, they eventually became friends.

Sam initially worked on a series of paintings in oil and watercolor featuring his impressions of Rock Creek Park. "Park Invention" was his first solo exhibition. The Adams Morgan Gallery held the show in 1963 during our first year of marriage.

That show led to Sam's meeting Tom Downing, Corcoran School of Art professor and a prominent member of the Washington Color School. The Washington Color School was made up of a group of artists whose work contained neither object nor representation but instead used large areas of color. Painters Morris Louis and Kenneth Noland, its first members, stained unsized, unprimed canvas with acrylic-based pigment to make their colorfield paintings. A trio of other Washington painters followed, with Downing as the fourth major figure in the group. Downing, well-known in New York and Washington art circles for his "spot" paintings, became an important friend and colleague of Sam's. Sam talked to me about how Tom's expansive ideas produced new intellectual challenges for his own painting.

In addition to my work at *The Washington Post*, I was expanding my knowledge of art beyond the Old Masters and the art-appreciation course I had at Ursuline College. Sam, a good teacher, enthusiastically shared insights about his work and that of other contemporary artists. We visited art exhibitions and museums, with him walking through quickly and me lagging behind, study-ing more closely the works that attracted me. Tom Downing's col-orful paintings were strange to me at first, but I learned to see the same beauty and brilliance in them as I did in Sam's developing abstract work. I brought to art a reporter's curiosity and my deep interest in people, new ideas, and fresh inspiration.

Three months into our marriage, Sam observed that I was gaining weight. Given my battles with weight in my teens, it was a sensitive subject, but in this case the doctor confirmed the added girth was the result of my having gotten pregnant, apparently on my wedding night. I was thrilled. I was especially grateful we had not known I was pregnant when I traveled to Mississippi. As my pregnancy advanced, however, my joy in giving birth was mildly tempered by the daily stories I was writing about hungry and poor black children in the nation's capital. One day I remarked to assis-tant *Washington Post* city editor Steve Isaacs, "I'm not sure I should be bringing a black child into such a terrible world." I worried about the state and future of black people.

Our first child, a beautiful daughter named Stephanie Jessica (her middle name was in honor of my mother, Jessie Mae Nor-ment Butler), was born on May 7, 1963, one month prematurely. She weighed 5.6 pounds.

During my four-month maternity leave from the newspaper, we moved from our apartment and rented a small house with two bedrooms in Manor Park, a modest black, middle-class neighbor-hood in Northwest Washington, a few blocks from the Maryland border. Sam painted in the basement at night and on weekends. We now had a nursery for our daughter. The depth of love pour-ing from my heart for my baby added a bright new dimension to my life. I wanted to love and protect this beautiful child, but my inexperience made the responsibility sometimes frightening. Stephanie was colicky and choked occasionally when I was giving her a bottle. "Sam, Sam!" I would yell. "Come here! The baby's choking." He would run upstairs from his studio and calm us both down.

I was in my final weeks of maternity leave when the March on Washington for Jobs and Freedom occurred, on August 28. For once, I would not be an observer but a participant. (This was before newspapers banned participation in marches by reporters.) Sam and I left the baby with friends and went to the march with other artists. While he had engaged in some civil rights activism in Louisville before our marriage, Sam's main interest was in art rather than politics. The day of the march was hot. As a Southerner, I was glad to join the peaceful, interracial throng of 250,000 people. Change was in the air as black Americans and their supporters were rising up and demanding equality, and the momentum of the Civil Rights Movement continued to gain force. The newspapers had been full of predictions of possible violence because of the huge number of protesters expected. President Kennedy was nervous, but the march proceeded peacefully. I clapped when the unparalleled gospel singer Mahalia Jackson's glorious voice shouted out in song. I responded "yes" when Bayard Rustin, the chief strategist and organizer for the march, shouted out the demands for effective civil rights legislation and fair housing. Movie stars like Sidney Poitier and Harry Belafonte flew in to be at the march, but of course the star was Dr. King. I was mesmerized as he spoke of the need for economic parity for black people, his soaring address climaxing with his "I Have a Dream" speech. To my sorrow, *The Washington Post* didn't write about the speech. "We were looking for the bad guys," my colleague Robert Asher explained many years later.

I found it an awesome, unforgettable experience. I was pulsating with joy when we picked up the baby at the end of the day.

★   ★   ★

The changes sweeping America had not yet liberated women in the fall of 1963 when I went back to reporting on *The Washington Post* City Desk. I was still the only black woman on the entire reporting staff of the newspaper. I still coped with the challenges of covering stories in a largely segregated city. I also yearned to spend more time with the baby and asked to work extended hours for four days a week in order to take one day each week for family time. My request made one of the assistant city editors indignant.

"No, you can't work part-time," he told me. "There are men here who might want to work part-time so they can write the great American novel. Why should we give you that special privilege?"

Later, however reluctantly, the City Desk relented and allowed me to work a four-day schedule. The arrangement didn't work for long. Soon, a City Desk assistant editor told me my arrangement was lowering the morale in the newsroom, and it came to an abrupt halt. I went back to working five days a week.

The demands of a reporter's schedule made it tough to work and make childcare arrangements. My official hours were ten a.m. to seven p.m., but in reality, I worked until my story for the next day was completed, sometimes as late as eight or nine, to make the late edition. I often had early-morning interviews. I don't recall seeing any other female reporters on the City Desk pregnant or having babies in the early 1960s. I had no role models for mothering as a journalist. I stumbled along the best I could.

Having come of age in the segregated South in the 1940s and 1950s, I hadn't given much thought to discrimination against women, issues of racial segregation that oppressed both men and women so shaped the contours of my life. I wasn't consciously aware of how much my personal experience was part of a larger issue for women. I knew I was not the only working woman who experienced these problems during the days before the women's movement, flextime, and the Family and Medical Leave Act. It would take the women's movement years to turn things around for young working mothers like me.

As the daughter of an educated mother forced by segregation to work as a maid and of a college-educated father, I had seen notions of white racial superiority debunked by my parents' example, but the South's gender bias was not discussed. My father's progressive attitude about roles for black women was evident in the female evangelists who preached at our church. But he may have been the exception to the rule, for many black denominations discouraged or even banned women preachers. Daddy was clearly the head of the household, but his Christian dedication to love permeated our lives. I had no doubt that I was expected to achieve all I could professionally, even as I was also expected to get married and have children, which I certainly desired.

After Stephanie's birth, Sam looked after her when the sitter left at six p.m. until I returned home by bus around eight p.m. I foolishly panicked one day when I found blue paint on her shirt and arms that he had gotten on her when he'd heard her cry and rushed up to her nursery from his basement studio. I thought the paint might harm her if she got it in her mouth, but mainly my fear was a reflection of my general unease of being a new, working mother.

These forces came to bear on my marriage and childrearing.

I had romantic ideas of marriage and family. Yet, I was also ambitious. Sam represented both of these things: a chance to have a family along with the ambition and drive that came with a new life in the nation's capital.

The signs that my marriage would be far more complex than I realized came early. Sam and I had taken Stephanie home to Louisville to visit our families at Christmas in 1963, when she was seven months old. During the visit, Sam became agitated and then deeply depressed, ending up hospitalized for two weeks. Perhaps it was the stress of parenthood and the responsibility of a family.

I was crippled with fear—fear for him, fear for our lives, fear for our time together, fear for our daughter. We returned to D.C. when he was better, and he was eventually able to go back to work, but I lived with an underlying uncertainty of what would happen next. Although it was a frightening time, it didn't stop me from moving ahead with our marriage and our life. It would be a backdrop to Sam's artistic genius, brilliance, creativity, and success throughout our marriage.

I was happy when we had a second child. Our daughter Melissa Lynne was born on August 21, 1965. She was even more premature than Stephanie, about seven weeks early, and weighed a mere 4.23 pounds. Melissa had to stay in a hospital incubator for several days—even after I went home. Leaving my baby at the hospital for the first night or two by herself made me feel desperate. I was so upset that she had to stay in the hospital—not that I thought anything would happen to her. It was just that I couldn't see her and hold her and touch her. I had never loved anyone like that before. When the time came, I was elated to bring her home!

I returned to the paper after another four-month maternity leave and felt still in the game when the Capital Press Club, a local African American organization, selected me as one of the city's top journalists of 1964 and 1965. When I became pregnant with our third child, I resigned from the newspaper before her birth because finding childcare would be too difficult. I joked that I became pregnant a third time so I'd have an excuse to quit and end the mounting stress. Our third daughter, Leah Kathryn, was born February 12, 1967. She was full-term and weighed just over six pounds.

Growing up, I had never thought about having children. I'm

not one of those women who dreamed of motherhood from an early age. I always saw myself as a career woman. When I got pregnant so early, it awakened in me an ability to love in a different way. This was someone to whom I'd given birth!

I had many choices to make regarding my family. Sam and I, newcomers to Washington, weren't interested in mimicking the typical lifestyle of Washington's traditional black educated elite, though I admired their accomplishments. We were part of the "Crossover" or "Breaking Through" generation, part of the artist/intellectual class embracing a diversity of race, income, and culture. Seismic movements in national consciousness were opening new areas in the capital and across the country. Citizen activism focused a spotlight on the once-hidden or -ignored issues of poverty, racism, and gender.

Washington had become the largest American city with a predominantly black population. I was a brown-skinned woman on the cusp of social change and very comfortable in my skin. I had fallen in love with and married a dark-brown-skinned man, and we had three healthy, beautiful daughters in various shades of chocolate. Skin-color variations did not matter, in my view, and we were determined to succeed against the odds.

Later, my daughter Stephanie would tell me that I had not talked to her about the nuances of "colorism" and how some African Americans judged one another based on the color of their skin. I had made her aware of how people of other races judged black people, she said, but not ways some African Americans judged one another with light-skinned/dark-skinned prejudices. She didn't know anything about it until she was in high school and our family joined Jack and Jill, a historically black national organization that offers social, cultural, and educational activities for mothers and children.

By 1967, Sam was making extraordinary strides, developing prodigiously as an abstract painter. He had a second solo exhibition

in D.C. in 1964 at the Adams Morgan Gallery. In 1965 and annually from 1966 to 1971, he exhibited at the Jefferson Place Gallery,
where he displayed his breakthrough suspended paintings for the
first time in 1968. In 1967, he had earned a rare distinction—a
solo exhibition at the prestigious Phillips Collection. In 1968, he
exhibited at a New York gallery and in 1971 at the Museum of
Modern Art in New York. He showed in group exhibitions at the
Studio Museum in Harlem and the Minneapolis Institute of Art.
His impressive works were reviewed regularly—mostly in glowing terms but at times critically—by writers in *The Washington Post*
and national magazines. But financially we were just getting by.

A significant influence on our family, by way of his financial
and intellectual support of Sam, was Walter Hopps, an important art-world figure who came to Washington in 1966 from Los
Angeles to be a fellow at the Institute for Policy Studies, a liberal
think tank. Walter thought and wrote about public policy toward
the arts and helped open my understanding of the dynamics
behind the art world. He aimed to revitalize the city aesthetically
through art and was determined to strengthen the role of the arts
in the neighborhoods where artists lived, to foster cultural growth
and community development. Hopps helped many black artists. In
addition to supporting Sam as he prepared for his solo exhibition
at the Phillips Collection, one of the most important things Hopps
did was to find funding for Sam to acquire and use a studio workshop downtown.

From 1967 to 1970, I worked from home doing freelance writing, placing occasional articles in *The Washington Post*, *McCall's*,
and *Essence* magazines (which launched in May 1970). I also briefly
taught journalism courses at American and Howard Universities. The absence of my full-time salary was a financial shock to
our family. Sam taught high school full-time at McKinley and
worked most summers teaching at the Corcoran School of Art,

while still finding time to paint—on weekends, at times all night long. During these years, as he prepared for exhibitions, it also was imperative that he invest heavily in canvas, paints, and other materials—thousands of dollars per year. With my sporadic earnings and the costs of raising three children, I worried about how we would make it from month to month. I was thrilled when in 1967 the National Endowment for the Arts awarded Sam a $5,000 grant, which he used to take time off from teaching at McKinley to paint. At my urging, we used part of the money as a down payment on a house and purchased a four-level brownstone on Lamont Street N.W. in Mount Pleasant for about $20,000.

Racial redlining was still so rampant in the gentrifying, racially and ethnically mixed Mount Pleasant neighborhood adjacent to Adams Morgan that we had to have a white lawyer friend front for us.

We made the choice to be in the Adams Morgan/Mount Pleasant area because we wanted to be in a diverse, creative neighborhood. We had been married only five years when we moved there. Our first move had been right after Stephanie was born. We lived in Adams Morgan in a one-bedroom apartment, and I was mugged coming up the back steps of that apartment house. It was the second time I had been mugged. (The first was when I was single, living on Capitol Hill. I had just come in my back door and some guy standing there got me. Very scary. He used a choke hold and took my money. Thankfully, he didn't use a knife or gun or rape me.) I was ready to leave that building after the mugging, and I also wanted to move to a place with more than one bedroom, so we ended up in a lower-middle-class, predominantly black neighborhood on North Dakota Avenue N.W. We stayed there for about four years until Sam received the grant.

The neighborhood public schools were overcrowded, with thirty-five kids in a classroom. Sam and I decided to send the children to private schools, annually going into debt to do so. I joked that my car automatically headed to the bank every August to get a loan to cover tuitions; we repaid the debt by the end of each school year. We did not apply for scholarships, so as to leave them for other black children. I knew private schools had more money and better facilities—things whites had denied us. I wanted to expose our kids to as much as we could. I questioned whether the negatives of sending them to predominantly white schools outweighed the positives. "I don't want them in schools where white people are feeling their hair," I remarked to friends. Ultimately my feeling was that the negatives of being one of the few black students did not outweigh the positives of private education. I tried to be careful about how our girls reacted to school. And they each liked their schools, even though they obviously weren't perfect. My job, I thought, was to serve on the trustee board and get more minority teachers; that is what I did.

We selected Georgetown Day School, which was predominantly Jewish and had the city's most racially and culturally diverse student body. We felt the girls would not be an oddity there. The school was located on MacArthur Boulevard, west of Rock Creek Park, the rigid racial dividing line, in a predominantly white neighborhood. In their early years, we carpooled with the children of writer/journalists Judith and Milton Viorst, who lived ten minutes away from us. I ran for and was elected to the board of Georgetown Day School with a goal of increasing the small number of teachers of color, and I had some success.

The girls' lives straddled black and white worlds. They took dance lessons at black dance studios: Carolyn Tate in Maryland and the Jones-Haywood Dance School on Georgia Avenue. The girls were members of the D.C. Youth Orchestra in upper Northwest, and they made many of their friends at the predominantly white schools they attended.

Looking back, I was parenting children who were growing up in parallel black and white worlds at the dawning of integration. With no models to follow, I wanted to impart to my daughters my high regard and respect for black people, the black community, and the black ability and resilience to thrive against horrific odds. They were educated and socialized in a white world, and would lament when, while they were watching television, I would break in with insightful, precise analysis about race. But I did it anyway.

"We would be sitting there watching MTV," said Leah, "and Mom would say, 'Black people have made such a strong contribution to music from the blues to R and B to rock and roll,' and then ask us, 'When you watch MTV, do you ever see anyone black there? No you don't. This is the way that whites control industries and Blacks aren't recognized for their talent and expertise.' Mom would come out with these criticisms. As a kid I thought, *Oh, must she ruin everything? There's no joy. Why is she talking to us about all this stuff?* She would slice through such moments with really incisive critique—that I can now channel in my head. When Melissa expressed an interest in rock and roll, Mom brought home three records by Jimi Hendrix and two other African American musicians who played rock, so that she would see that rock was not music that only white people played. Mom was consistently Afrocentric and black-forward in her thinking and in her communications with us."

I wanted my children to grow up in an integrated community where they could see many different possibilities for their lives. But I wanted them to always know that they were different from whites and came from a proud black lineage. I searched for dolls of color. I finally found some, although they weren't black, black dolls. But they were definitely brown dolls. I was so happy to be able to give them to my girls. When they were older, I very tentatively put the girls in Jack and Jill, concerned about skin-tone prejudice.

One day they were playing and they tied scarves around their heads as if the scarves were long, flowing hair. "Your own hair is so beautiful! Why would you want to do that?" I asked them. The girls viewed these as little lectures, but I was trying to encourage them to love themselves. It took me a long time to learn to love myself. My need to shape black children in a predominantly white world deepened my understanding of love, relationships, and self-love.

The 1960s heralded new changes. As President Johnson began to expand laws around voting and public accommodation, Washington, D.C., home to Howard University, was an epicenter for black life. We could live in more places in the city, enter new careers, and socialize in a less segregated environment. Just as Merle had helped me navigate New York City and its cultural barriers, Sam and I did that when we moved from our predominantly black neighborhood in Northwest D.C. to be one of the first black families on Lamont Street in Mount Pleasant, another section of Northwest D.C.

At the same time, the country was undergoing a cultural revolution. Washington had a thriving arts and progressive community with a lively social scene. We would occasionally go to artists' homes and visit their farms for the weekend. We would tuck the kids into bed, and the adults would stay up talking late into the night.

While most black families longed to live on the Gold Coast, we did not want our children to have a typical black bourgeoisie upbringing. I wanted them to understand what racial and economic diversity looked and felt like. So we selected Mount Pleasant, a neighborhood with some elegant row houses near Rock Creek Park. Yet it was home to many low-income African Americans and new Latino immigrants. Thus, my children had to run the gauntlet of drunken men and boys on the corner after they came home on the bus to our leafy green, quiet street.

I had to make difficult choices about the cultural influences for my children. Each of them was so bright, and I deeply believed that education was crucial to their future success. We decided that the local public school could not give them the opportunity and intellectual rigor that we sought. Yet it set up a sharp dichotomy for them as they crossed town to their tony private school and returned home to our far more complex neighborhood. While Sam and I were comfortable in our choice, the day-to-day experience of walking to the corner could be frightening for children. At times, they preferred to play at school friends' homes rather than asking friends to make the trek to their own house.

We lived in a multiethnic and socioeconomically diverse, gentrifying neighborhood and sent them to private, upper-middle-class, mostly white schools. All three of our daughters later revealed how much they disliked the neighborhood. "I remember being ashamed to bring people home because of the neighborhood. There were drunks and lecherous guys on the walk home from the bus to the house," said Melissa. "There were no others like us. The black kids in our neighborhood went to public schools." Melissa also recalled that Sam would sometimes send the girls on errands, like cashing a check. "You taught us to just smile and speak and keep walking— always together, so we could walk the streets without getting hurt." Stephanie, our first child, was old enough to remember that we had chosen the neighborhood "to teach us to be accepting and respectful of all people regardless of race, wealth, or class, to keep us well grounded, but we didn't embrace the lesson."

Years later, my daughters revealed how our attitudes and use of money confused them. "There were a lot of complex class and wealth and race issues going on," recalled Leah.

Despite the challenges of growing up in a multicultural neighborhood and attending predominantly white schools, my daughters now agree that learning to navigate those differences between class, race, and wealth was important. I don't regret sending them to private schools because they couldn't have gotten a good education in the neighborhood public school they would have had to attend.

"It was very difficult," Sam recalled, when some people criticized our educational decisions. I felt hearing my viewpoint at home about Africa and black culture would provide balance to the stories of Europe and Western triumphalism. "We were reading books on the African child, the dynamics of Kenya and Senegal," Sam added.

I was among a group of parents who participated in an African culture group for our children that met on Saturday afternoons at Howard University. At home, we exposed them to important and interesting black people.

One disagreement Sam and I had about raising our children concerned the role of religion. Sam had been raised in a Baptist family that attended church regularly. We had married in the A.M.E. church my father built, and we even christened our first daughter there. But Sam insisted he "didn't want the girls brought up in those old dogmatic religions." Agreeing that spending Sunday mornings watching television wasn't a good idea, we compromised on Unitarian Universalism, a liberal religion that focused on a search for truth and meaning. I took the girls to nearby All Souls Unitarian Church. One neighbor said we looked like a mother duck and three ducklings walking down Lamont Street to All Souls at 16th and Harvard Streets on Sunday mornings. Sam never attended.

For the first few years, I felt comfortable with the compromise because All Souls was an activist congregation, taking the need for social justice in America as seriously as I did. James Reeb, a martyr of the Civil Rights Movement, was assistant minister at All Souls prior to his murder at Selma, Alabama, in 1965. A. Powell Davies was the minister when we began attending church. Davies became nationally prominent for his progressive views, advocating for civil rights for African Americans and women and for desegregation. Later, the Rev. David H. Eaton became the church's first African American senior minister. All Souls' religiously and racially diverse membership and progressive vision were evident during our time there in the 1970s and 1980s. (J. Edgar Hoover was so deeply distrustful of the direction in which Eaton was leading All Souls that he planted an undercover FBI agent in the church to monitor the congregation and undermine Eaton's ministry. According to *The New York Times*, in 1981, Eaton was one of four political activists awarded damages, along with a peace group, by a federal district judge in a suit against four former FBI agents. In a case spanning ten years, the judge ruled that the activists' civil rights had been violated by various acts of defamation, infiltration, and intimidation.) I enjoyed Rev. Eaton's messages focusing on social justice, and the church gave the girls an ethical structure and a church community.

During those years, however, I missed hearing the gospel message of Jesus Christ. All Souls provided a general moral compass, but I wasn't experiencing spiritual fulfillment. As the daughter of an African Methodist Episcopal minister, I knew something about God and Jesus's love and power. A few teachings of the Old and New Testament, the gospels, some scriptures, hymns, and anthems remained with me from my youth, yet I felt disconnected from God at All Souls. That feeling would dog me for years and decades later return me to my A.M.E. roots.

Did I succeed totally as a parent? No. But all my children feel their educations gave them a head start in life, and each of them has achieved outstanding career success through hard work of their own. Leah became a tenured professor at Bard College, had a career as a new-media artist and technology leader, and until recently was the vice president of strategy and innovation at a wonderful nonprofit called Girls Who Code. Stephanie earned two master's degrees and is a member of the Art Directors Guild, as a film and TV art director. Her movie credits include *Man of Steel*, *Contagion*, and *Conviction*. She helped produce *Christmas at the White House* and served as art director of the television series *Chicago Fire*. Melissa obtained her medical degree from Harvard Medical School and became the Ellen H. Block Professor and a researcher at the University of Chicago. She co-founded a research center that focuses on improving the sexual and reproductive health of young people of color, and she serves as a vice provost at the University of Chicago.

I am proud of my daughters, and I love being a grandmother to Ben, twenty, Eve, seventeen, and Olivia, fifteen.

Sam moved his studio from the third floor of our home and eventually to a new location, near U Street. Then he began to further renovate our home. We had painted the walls and done minor fixes when we moved in, but Sam envisioned a home with light, space, and openness. His architect friend and neighbor Jim Whitley remodeled the front door and foyer. Renovation occurred in stages. The most dramatic change was when a small living room was transformed by a talented female interior designer to include built-in circular sofas around the entire perimeter, making room for eight to twelve people to sit and talk intimately and comfortably. One day, when I came home, Sam had torn down a wall in the large dining room, exposing the brick. The third floor, which had been his studio, was changed into bedrooms for the girls, and the second floor, where once the entire family's bedrooms had been, was made to contain our bedroom suite and an office for a part-time secretary who would keep up with the business end of his work. He traded paintings for some of the renovation. For example, Whitley became the owner of a beautifully shaped yellow painting. The interior designer who transformed our first floor also selected a painting. I enjoyed the end results of the renovation but not the constant upheaval.

While my life lacked a newspaper reporter's daily intellectual stimulation and public recognition, it was busy with the excitement, stress, and challenge of mothering the girls and being the wife of an artist on an extraordinary rise. The development of Sam's career was a major turning point in my life.

Sam was always searching for and talking about new techniques of painting. I watched him over the years explore new territory with abstract painting, and he made beautiful work. I received an ongoing education about the development of his painting, and I joined him in Washington and as far away as Paris to attend artists' parties, museums, gallery openings, and dinners at the homes of the collectors who purchased his work. At these social events I'd order—much to the chagrin of the bartenders—a scotch and ginger ale. I was such a part of his world that I told an art critic, "Being Mrs. Sam Gilliam is a full-time job." I helped with business affairs, listened to his conversations about painting, and arranged travel until we obtained part-time secretarial help. I got to know the artists who were important to him and their families. When Morris Louis, the legendary leader and co-founder of the Washington Color School, invited Sam to visit Vermont, our entire family traveled with him.

Entertaining poets and other artists was an important part of our life. One of our favorites was poet Léon-Gontran Damas, who was born in French Guiana. He was one of the leaders of the Negritude Movement, a literary and philosophical movement begun in Paris during the early 1930s that attacked colonialism and racism and celebrated African traditions and black culture. One memorable Christmas, he read one of his poems to the children. We also hosted a buffet dinner party for Sterling Brown, the illustrious and celebrated poet.

My daughters recall going to sleep while hearing artists downstairs arguing and making all kinds of noise. But those evenings were full of excitement and of people talking about ideas and caring passionately about their work. Making art was serious. Our girls grew up in a household with two very strong role models doing very different things but going after their careers a thousand percent without letup. It wasn't quiet. It was noisy. There was always a lot going on, and yet I still worked—freelance, part-time, or full-time—and met my deadlines. I was navigating so many things, but the times were lively and exciting, too. It was the sixties. I wore minis, although I never had good legs; my daughters still tease me about my white miniskirt. Around this time I also began smoking cigarettes—a habit I would not kick until I tired of hiding it from my mother when, a decade later, I returned home to help care for her when she was sick. Sam was not practical in many ways. He would buy me a fur coat instead of getting me a wool coat. We would go to Paris and shop at Givenchy instead of a regular boutique. But I've always been drawn to people who have a certain kind of energy, like Merle Goldberg from my days at Columbia. They rile me a little bit, or they push me a little bit. I provided stability in the household. I don't know if Sam always appreciated that, but I think he recognized it.

In 1968, Sam and I made our first trip to Europe, traveling to Paris, Nice, and London. My mother came up from Louisville and looked after the children during these trips. We had no local relatives, but a good friend, daycare owner Gail Whitley, was always willing to keep the children when I needed her. In 1970 and 1971, Sam's growing recognition and exhibition schedule took us to Rome, Greece, Germany, and India, where he exhibited in the Indian Triennale. He was sent to Poland by the State Department, and we visited a Holocaust exhibit, where I recoiled at the horrors.

Sam's enormous creativity, growing reputation, and living-on-the-edge mentality brought many rewards to him and some satisfactions to our family. We sometimes took the children on Caribbean cruises after we annually visited our families in Louisville at Christmas.

The ancient monuments, museums, exhibitions, and new people we met on these trips were stimulating, but the pace and stress had another impact. The highs and lows Sam had suffered since early in our marriage continued, and the doctors and psychiatrists had no effective medications for them. The bright, toothy smile I once had sometimes gave way to a look of bemused solemnity.

This period coincided with the awakening of the Black Arts Movement led by Amiri Baraka. In that era, Sam was criticized by some black activists because he chose to engage in the full sweep of post-Renaissance history and aesthetics. That is what he saw as central to his work. Yet, Jeff Donaldson, one of the movement's leaders, was a good friend of Sam's. Some charged that Sam's work did not portray his black heritage; the criticism was so vocal, and it sometimes hurt Sam deeply. Privately he expressed anger. I would comfort him and strike back as I could when these attacks occurred. I believed deeply in his right as an artist to go where his creativity led him.

Yet I also understood and appreciated the Black Arts Movement, which reached into literature, painting, film, theater, and music. I knew how desperately all our people needed what it embodied—freedom from the necessity of assimilating and inspiration for many more black Americans to explore their creativity. While that wasn't Sam's calling and the criticism stung, he appreciated the sacrifice artists of the Black Arts Movement made.

Sam was already getting a reputation for what he later said was his "artist personality," and I tried to serve as a buffer. He was not always easy for people to deal with. But he could also be charming and kind. I also knew Sam was unfaithful to me. I was a preacher's kid and had been raised to frown on divorce, and beyond that, divorce at that time—especially in a certain "class"—was a no-no.

Our daughters remember challenges and painful episodes growing up in our household, including arguments and outbursts that they found frightening. "Growing up, our household was lively and exciting but didn't always feel safe," Leah said. "There wasn't physical violence or abuse, but it could be emotionally charged. It wasn't directed towards me but it was in the atmosphere."

In the early 1970s I took a part-time job in local television, working for *Panorama*, a popular talk show on WTTG-TV, channel 5, with Maury Povich, who would later emerge as a national television personality with his own syndicated show. *Time* magazine Washington correspondent Bonnie Angelo and I worked as special reporters on the show. She focused on politics at the White House, and I concentrated on the greater Washington, D.C., community.

I enjoyed having a twice-weekly opportunity to bring African American community leaders and local and regional issues to the forefront. It was a step toward acknowledging that D.C. was more than the seat of the federal government, with power centered in the Capitol and White House, but was also home for hundreds of thousands of people, 70 percent of whom were black, with lives, opinions, and talents. I interviewed leaders in education, politics, science, civil rights, sociology, and culture.

In 1972, I went back to *The Washington Post* as an assistant editor in the Style section. Sam supported my desire to return to print journalism. The security of my full-time salary would help our family. Leah was now nearly six years old, Melissa was eight, and Stephanie almost eleven. As Sam was busy painting in his studio, now away from home, I hired a succession of young women I called creative companions to be with our daughters after school, give them dinner, oversee their homework, and stay with them until I came home about eight in the evening. My daughters got along well with these women, and Sam and I ate a simple supper together most nights and talked while the girls finished their homework or prepared for bed. I tried to make sure we ate together as a family on weekends. I became aware in this period of my life of the parallel development of career and marriage/family. Sometimes the two lines of my life would move at a constant pace. Other times career would accelerate, and marriage/family would stall. Then career would stall, and marriage/family would flourish. No time was ever easy; I was always punishing myself for one parallel line of my life or the other, even experiencing anxiety attacks and serious health issues. Eventually therapy, an overeaters twelve-step group, and a deepening spirituality—what I call living in the sixth dimension—helped me make peace with these dual challenges.

Our girls were growing up, experiencing the pros and cons of having a mother who was a journalist and father who was an artist. "I liked that you could edit papers and help with schoolwork, but I didn't like having personal struggles and other things about me showing up in the newspaper," Leah said. Melissa recalled that she sometimes found it exciting to have us as parents: "We could open the newspaper or turn on TV and see you there. It gave our family a special status and helped make us feel connected to many of the local leaders of the day in Washington."

In 1976, there was a highly public and embarrassing altercation aboard an airplane. Sam was later exonerated. That finally led us to one of the few psychiatrists in Washington who had worked with artists, Dr. Simon Auster. He took Sam on as his patient, and prescribed the new drug lithium, while I worked with a female therapist, Myra Wesley King.

For a brief while it appeared that things were going smoothly, and it was a time when we were enjoying some national recognition both for me individually and for us as a couple. In 1977, I was profiled in a two-page article in *Essence* about my work in Style as one of the Washington women on the rise in "Chocolate City," as Washington was called because its population was more than

75 percent black. In November 1979, Sam and I were selected by *Ebony* magazine as one of "America's 10 Most Exciting Couples," along with such luminaries as Sammy Davis Jr. and his wife Altovise, Ashford and Simpson, and Ossie Davis and Ruby Dee. I had hoped we would finally enjoy our lives together more, but despite our valiant struggle together, Sam and I were growing apart.

Despite the accolades and recognition, my self-esteem had plummeted. I was a bundle of nerves. Returning to the coping behavior I'd begun when I lost my father, I ate compulsively to deal with and mask painful emotions. Frequently, I'd stop and eat a large ice cream cone on my way home from *The Washington Post*. My weight fluctuated up and down, yo-yoing as high as 185 and down to 120, when my good weight was 136 to 142 pounds. I had several illnesses during my marriage to Sam, including peritonitis, which resulted in my having a hysterectomy.

My romantic notions about marriage began to fade. I realized that I would have to balance a career, children, and a marriage for which I was ill-prepared. I had a husband who at times would be my greatest support, at others would require tremendous support from me, at times would be a person I could barely recognize, and at times be my greatest detractor.

It is hard to describe the isolation that I felt. I could not discuss the details with my mother. I was so close to her, and yet I had entered a new world that was so distant from her own experience. Mental health was not discussed; problems in marriage were not discussed. I wanted to appear like a success, and it was hard to admit that there was more going on.

While we had close artist friends, there too I felt that I needed to save face. Similarly, I could not undermine Sam's career, which had begun to have a meteoric rise. Yet these behaviors were commonplace. Indeed, so many of our friends from those years faced similar challenges, including suicides and other deaths. In many ways, these experiences were so much more serious than what I was seeing. Often I rationalized it; perhaps this was just what it meant to have an artist's personality. Perhaps it was the source of his creativity.

At work, I was still one of the few women of color. To bring issues of marriage and personal life to work was unthinkable.

Like any family in search of answers, we did seek doctors, but there were simply no answers for us.

It was not until the public episode on an airplane that we finally got to a doctor who homed in on the problem and treatment could begin.

For me, this was a continuation of a pattern: becoming isolated when tragedy struck and covering my hurt and fear by consuming food. In some ways, I too was demonstrating patterns and behaviors to my children that could have consequences for their health. It is ironic that I always thought I was the good one and only later would I realize that I was complicit and at times even to blame for some of our family patterns and dynamics.

Why do people stay in marriages that are damaging to their self-esteem and psyche? For me it was to support my children. I recalled my own feelings of being without a father after his death and did not want that for my children. They were close to their father, and he loved them deeply. He was a part of their success. On weekends, the dinner table was particularly important to our family. We would spend late hours discussing art and artists. We would go to museums, sometimes in New York City. We took family trips to the Caribbean some years after spending Christmas in Louisville.

There was also the excitement and the thrill of his career. Sam and I traveled all over the world, often to wonderful art openings, and I too benefited. I was occasionally frightened by this newly integrated world I was emerging into. Sam was so confident of his genius, his intellect, and the value of his art and contribution. He would say he was the best abstract painter in the world. I not only admired his confidence but appreciated the ways in which he would push me to the next level, telling me to ask for a raise, demand what I deserved.

He also pushed me to be a public figure, so I bought clothing that we sometimes could not afford. In many ways, he helped me withstand what I would later understand was sexism and gender bias at work. I saw the example he set forth, and it helped me understand the politics and machinations that I was experiencing at work. When my courage faltered, often it was Sam who believed in me. He would tell me to fight and would help me plan a strategy, and so often he was right.

When things were not going well, I carefully monitored the toll that his outbursts took on the children. I had been taught that marriage was forever and that you do not abandon someone because of problems that they neither created nor could control. He was being failed by the medical establishment; could I fail him, too?

Yet at last I realized I was miserable and that what I thought of as heroics and bravery were no longer helping my children, me, and perhaps not Sam. I had underestimated his ability to survive and even thrive without me. He has an incredible charisma and intelligence and an important career. In some ways, he had more support than I did. I realized that I could leave and, in fact, that I had to leave.

So in October 1982 I did just that. Leaving a marriage is not easy. I left because it was time, and I felt it would be better for the girls, for me, and for Sam.

The children were tense and unhappy. Sam said he was deeply unhappy with me. And I was unhappy with him. He loved his daughters very deeply, but I decided we needed to separate. I told Sam I had to leave "to get myself together," promising to talk in one year about our future together. Since I knew he needed the emotional security of the family home, and since it was my decision to leave, it fell to me to find another place for the girls and me.

On October 1, 1982, after more than twenty years of marriage, I moved into a two-bedroom apartment near American University with our two younger girls. Stephanie had left to begin her second year at Brown University. Melissa was a senior at Georgetown Day School, and Leah was a sophomore at Sidwell Friends. It was a difficult, heart-wrenching time. I felt incredibly sad that our life together had to dissolve, but at the same time, I was relieved to be in an atmosphere that lacked stress and tension. Sam adored his daughters and supported them and their education.

When I interviewed him years later, he said, always the charmer, "The twenty years with you were the most wonderful twenty years of my life." I'm happy that within a few years Sam was able to resolve his issues, settle down, and find happiness with a companion with whom he has lived for more than thirty years. He is truly an artistic genius.

As my career trajectory reached upward, I began a long period of personal reconstruction. I faced the challenge of making a new life for myself as a single woman. For the first three years, I was largely focused on my daughters, but when the youngest went to college I faced the loneliness of an empty nest. Washington is a city where one's social and business lives often merge and many of the events I covered led to friendships with interesting people. I also still had many old friends. But it would be nearly a decade before I met a man with whom I had a deep and lasting relationship. Eventually my traditional view that marriage and love go together, among other issues, prompted me to cut off the relationship with this commitment-shy man. Another important relationship ended similarly. Part of my journey was to learn to be happy, whatever my circumstances.

Return to *The Washington Post*: The Style Years and Founding the Institute for Journalism Education, 1972–1979

Don Graham (far left), publisher of *The Washington Post*, and Arthur O. Sulzberger Sr. (right), publisher of *The New York Times*, attended a reception for the Institute for Journalism Education (IJE) Diversity Conference with IJE founder Robert C. Maynard (third from left) and me. *(Courtesy Evelyn Hsu, co-executive director Maynard Institute)*

Pictured with Institute for Journalism Education founders Robert C. Maynard, Earl Caldwell, Walter L. Stovall III, Leroy F. Aarons, Frank O. Sotomayor, Nancy Hicks Maynard, A. Stephen Montiel, and John L. Dotson Jr. *(Courtesy Evelyn Hsu, co-executive director, Maynard Institute)*

With co-founders and fellow board members of the Institute for Journalism Education, John L. Dotson, left, and Frank O. Sotomayor, right, at the 1987 conference. *(Used with Permission of Mrs. John L. Dotson)*

Institute for Journalism Education's diversity efforts received financial and personal support from media companies.

Jerry Sass of the Gannett Company talked with me at the 1987 Institute for Journalism Education conference. *(Used with Permission of Jerry Sass)*

John Quinn of the Gannett Company shared the podium with me at the 1987 Institute for Journalism Education conference.

The Metro Seven, who charged *The Washington Post* with racial discrimination: Michael Hodge, Ivan C. Brandon, LaBarbara Bowman, Leon Dash, Penny
Mickelbury, Ronald Taylor, and Richard E. Prince, and their attorney, Clif-
ford Alexander, at a March 23, 1972, news conference. *(Credit: Ellsworth Davis/
Washington Post)*

During the years I was Mrs. Sam Gilliam, the Civil Rights Movement hurtled dramatically into the Black Power era, and a path suddenly appeared for me to help bring knowledge of black culture into the mainstream media and expand its appeal to a broader and more diverse audience. It would be an exhilarating adventure.

On February 29, 1968, shortly after the wave of urban insurrections, the National Advisory Commission on Civil Disorders known as the Kerner Commission blasted the nation's white press, charging it had "too long basked in a white world, looking out of it, if at all, with a white man's eyes and a white perspective." The American press frequently portrayed African Americans "as if Negroes were not a part of the audience," said the report, adding, news organizations "failed to communicate to both their black and white audiences a sense of the problems America faces and the sources of potential solutions." The commission's report urged the hiring of black reporters and editors to counter a press that "repeatedly…reflects the biases…paternalism (and) indifference of white America." Amen to that. The press was under fire for its hiring and promotion policies.

The Washington Post was under heavy internal pressure to recruit, hire, and promote Blacks. By the time of Dr. King's assassination on April 4, 1968, and the urban rebellions that ignited immediately thereafter, *The Washington Post* said it had enough Blacks "to field nine biracial teams of reporters and photographers in radio-equipped cars to cover the riots that erupted, a then–unprecedented deployment of staff…that enabled its news gatherers to move with ease through police roadblocks along still-smoldering riot corridors."

On February 7, 1972, nine black *Washington Post* reporters had given Ben Bradlee a list of twenty questions and asked for answers in four days. For example, they asked, "Why are there no black originating editors on the foreign, national, sports, financial and Style desks.... Why was a white reporter assigned to cover the [Representative Shirley] Chisholm [presidential] campaign after two black reporters suggested coverage and volunteered for the assignment?"

The next month, that group known as the Metro Seven (two had dropped out) filed a discrimination complaint against the newspaper with the U.S. Equal Employment Opportunity Commission (EEOC), calling attention publicly to the paucity of black editors. Lack of hiring and promotion of Blacks was the core of the complaint at a newspaper that published in a city that was then 71.1 percent black. The reporters who stood up were all junior reporters: Michael Hodge, Ivan C. Brandon, LaBarbara Bowman, Leon Dash, Penny Mickelbury, Ronald Taylor, and Richard E. Prince. They put their careers on the line by participating in the complaint charging the newspaper with racial discrimination. I wasn't surprised that at the management level, sensitive people privately recognized that the paper's performance in black hiring was lagging. Donald Graham, the publisher's son, wrote a memorandum to John Prescott, *The Washington Post*'s president, about the situation. Graham, who was beginning to work his way through the different departments on his way to becoming publisher, said, "We have talked a lot and thought a lot, but we haven't worked a lot or spent a lot on black hiring and promotion." Describing meetings with executive editor Bradlee, LaBarbara (Bobbi) Bowman, one of the seven and who was at her first paying job, said, "His hands were shaking, and I thought, 'We have scared Ben Bradlee.'" Sitting amid the bustle of an NABJ convention decades later, Bowman explained, "You cannot cover a community without people who look like that community." Leon Dash, who won a Pulitzer for his series on an African American family struggling with poverty, later was the paper's West Africa bureau chief. Ivan Brandon became an editor for the city staff. One hundred reporters, photographers, and editors were involved, including fourteen Blacks. The paper had also hired its first black editorial writer, Roger Wilkins, nephew of NAACP president Roy Wilkins. Bradlee later acknowledged the newspaper "still had 'a redneck streak' especially on some news desks and sensitive Blacks often had a hard time from some editors." Yolanda Woodlee said, "All of us reporters had a hard time."

A letter of support for the Metro Seven signed by other black staffers showed that the problem went beyond obtaining jobs: "The lack of black participation in the shaping of the news about the society in which they play so vital a role has led to unfortunate distortions of the basic posture of the community on such vital questions as crime in the streets and the busing of school children." Richard Prince recalled that in 1972 the EEOC "issued a finding that we had grounds to go to court. However, we did not have the money to go to court."

I was proud of the Metro Seven and felt certain the complaint had helped me land an editing job. A push for new editors had also been prompted, I later learned, by critics within and outside the newspaper who contended that the entire newspaper was not well edited.

Though I was not yet back on staff, I admired those who took a stand, and I applauded all the challenges to a newspaper industry that was still only paying lip service to hiring and promoting Blacks. The complaint by the Metro Seven never evolved into a lawsuit, but it did cause movement inside *The Washington Post* newsroom. Managers broadened subject beats, increased the number of columnists of color, and stepped up promotion and hiring.

Looking back at the diversity-in-media mission, I know from my own rehiring at *The Washington Post* that a key element of diversity has been the collective work of minority reporters. The progress in hiring Blacks in daily newspapers was not simply due to the largesse of white editors.

The traditional ladder to become editors in daily newspapers was to obtain junior supervisory positions and then be considered for higher management positions. However, that ladder was often discarded, with no path to advancement clearly drawn. There was not even a bottom rung on the ladder for Blacks; white managers considered minorities less capable than whites to be editors.

One early spring day in 1972, while Sam and I were in the middle of our score of married years, Paul Richard, art critic for *The Washington Post*, visited our home in Mount Pleasant to interview Sam over lunch. As I was serving them at the long table in our recently remodeled dining room, opposite one of Sam's huge color-field paintings, we were talking about current shows when the conversation turned to my own career. Paul turned to me and said, "Why don't you come back to work at *The Post*?"

I was surprised, flattered, and intrigued by the question. Working as a freelance writer and part-time television personality (at *Panorama*, a popular talk show on WTTG-TV Channel 5), I had jobs that provided the flexibility I needed when our daughters were young. However, Leah, our youngest, was now five years old and about to be in school all day. And with all three girls in private schools, our family could certainly use more income.

The idea of returning to print journalism was also compelling, after my stint in television journalism. While I enjoyed nice clothes, I was beginning to find the attention to wardrobe, makeup, and hairstyling that television demanded was a distraction from the elements of journalism I most enjoyed. It had been important to me to show local African American personalities, feature stories that wouldn't otherwise have been aired, and provide a lens for items that didn't fit into the news shows. Black stories in those days didn't often receive air time otherwise. My interviews added to the white audience's knowledge of African Americans, informed black Washingtonians, fostered their self-esteem, and taught me more about the city. I was interviewing personalities such as Calvin Rolark Jr., a native Memphian who moved to Washington in the 1950s and started a weekly community newspaper, *The Washington Informer*, and anti-segregation crusader and home-rule activist Julius Hobson Sr. But I was a print journalist at heart. I preferred the daily hurly-burly of newspaper journalism—long interviews, digging deeply into information from all sides in search of the truth, and writing on deadline.

After Paul Richard left our home that day, Sam and I discussed his suggestion, and shortly afterward, I told Paul I was interested. He conveyed my interest to the executive editor, Ben Bradlee, who invited me to lunch. Selecting an outfit to wear for lunch, I chose one I had purchased when Sam was exhibiting his art in Paris, tan pants and a jacket from Yves Saint Laurent.

I met with Bradlee and Managing Editor Howard Simons, a former science writer, at a restaurant a block from the paper. I felt a few eyes following me as I walked into the restaurant and proceeded to Bradlee's table near the front window. I remembered my humiliating early days at the paper when I usually had had lunch at Sholl's Colonial Cafeteria. Now, the public-accommodations portion of the Civil Rights Act had made segregation in restaurants illegal, and I felt somewhat liberated, although I knew black customers still had to rebel when the staff tried to seat them near the kitchen. Bradlee wasn't a total stranger to me. I had seen him at art gallery and museum openings with his wife, Antoinette (Tony)

Pinchot Bradlee, a striking blond artist, so I knew who he was, though we had not formally met.

He radiated confidence, mental toughness, and something of the same blue-blood aura I had seen in my graduate school colleague Nina Auchincloss Steers. I felt no hint he was lording white superiority over me. He spoke in a vigorous, impatient style common to men of his background, and he had a salty tongue. We talked about the art scene, which I knew well because Sam had by now been featured in numerous solo exhibitions in Washington, New York, and Europe. Bradlee asked about our foreign travels, which recently had included Rome, India, Greece, Poland, Yugoslavia, and Venice, all generated by Sam's growing fame. I shared that I often felt freer in Europe than in America. Bradlee and Simons didn't inquire further, probably because black writers like James Baldwin had expressed that same sentiment that I did, as had black soldiers who returned to Europe after World War II. We felt relief in Europe at the absence of the debilitating racial prejudice we hated so much in America. My conversation with Bradlee about the art world somewhat consciously excluded Simons, I felt, but the managing editor was a sharp listener and observer, who was no doubt sizing me up.

Bradlee talked about Style, the section he had launched in 1969 when he assigned the innovative David Laventhol to rework the For and About Women section, becoming the first newspaper in the country to take this major step. The section launched on January 6, 1969, and covered people, the arts, books, and leisure. Entertainment, fashion, food, and interior design were also part of the fare, as was television, social, and cultural trends and even travel. Focusing on the human dimension, it even included wars and politics. Its aim was a more diverse and inclusive audience—male and female, black and white, suburbanite and city dweller, decision maker and homemaker.

I knew the vast and complex black cultural world, which was unknown to white readers, was largely missing from the section, and I longed to help unveil what some called a secret world and make the marvelous culture of black America better known and understood by all races. Bradlee finally asked if I would be interested in becoming one of the new assistant editors. I don't recall my exact words, but the sense of them was a strong "Yes!"

Inexperienced as an editor, I faced an uphill battle, but I was a reasonably good candidate for this supervisory role—with a master's degree from Columbia; weekly and daily reporting experience, including civil rights coverage; and a link to the art world through Sam. I would later see confirmation that my experiences, reading, and insights translated into interesting stories that had not been on the radar of Bradlee and other white editors. I eagerly offered ideas for articles and sometimes brought in copies of *Ebony*, *JET*, or *The Afro* as resources to support my ideas.

When I began working in Style, the women's movement was opening doors for women, but I still didn't know whether the newsroom I would be reentering would be more accommodating to me as a wife and mother than it had been before. White women journalists, who often bore the stigma of being considered less capable than white men, had been tolerating gender discrimination in the media, as most were segregated as reporters for the women's pages. The first significant breakthrough had come in 1933 when Eleanor Roosevelt "nervously" announced plans to hold weekly White House press conferences only for "The Newspaper Girls," said historian Maureen Beasley. Mrs. Roosevelt continued the press conferences during the twelve years she was First Lady. "Covering a president's wife who was believed to wield power herself appeared to enhance (women's) own importance," Beasley said. World War II provided another breakthrough when women all over the nation replaced men in defense plants, took jobs as drivers, flew as pilots of cargo planes, volunteered for women's units within the military, and became reporters. When the war ended, retrenchment followed, and most white women were again relegated to the confines of the home. This was not true for most black women, who out of necessity had always worked outside the home and continued to work in previously closed occupations, in factories, in low-level government jobs in Washington, and in other roles when possible.

I had long admired several women journalists of the black press. The courageous Ida B. Wells, editor of *The Memphis Free Speech* around the turn of the nineteenth century, who became the nation's leading anti-lynching crusader, especially awed me with her courage. At Lincoln University, I learned of Lucile Bluford, who tried eleven times to enter the University of Missouri. When the state supreme court finally ruled in her favor, the School of Journalism closed its graduate program rather than admit her. She later graduated from the University of Kansas and became editor and publisher of the black weekly *Kansas City Call*. I had met the very personable Ethel I. Payne, Washington bureau chief of *The Chicago Defender*, in 1962 and admired her and Alice Dunnigan of the Associated Negro Press for badgering U.S. presidents with questions about civil rights that white reporters wouldn't ask. Working at *JET* magazine from 1957 to 1959, I got to know the impressive *Ebony* editor-in-chief Era Bell Thompson, one of the few women in the nation to hold such a leadership position. *Ebony* reporter Clotye Murdock became my role model when I covered the integration of Ole Miss in 1962. Covering the trial for the gruesome murder of Emmett Till in 1955, she never flinched in the face of insults from the police chief who nodded at black reporters sitting at a Jim Crow table and said, "Maw'nin', nigras."

Later, I was introduced to a strong but small cadre of white women journalists, including Bonnie Angelo of *Time* magazine, who worked at *Panorama* with me and was deeply knowledgeable about national affairs. While I didn't know her personally, I had high regard for Nancy Dickerson, the first woman network correspondent at CBS News.

As a black person, I had been fighting racial discrimination in the media for more than a decade, when in the late sixties and early seventies white women began fighting back in earnest against gender discrimination. Under pressure from the Women's National Press Club, the formerly all-male National Press Club admitted women as members in 1971. For years, women who attended National Press Club functions had been permitted only to sit in the balcony and were not allowed to ask speakers questions. Finally, women could now sit anywhere and ask questions. The women's club, which recently had admitted men and changed its name to the Washington Press Club, was headed by another woman I admired, the capable Elsie Carper, my occasional lunch buddy in the early days at *The Washington Post*.

Against this backdrop, in 1972, I hoped to negotiate a four-day week at least for the first year or so. I had been laughed out of the newsroom in 1962 for that request. Then flextime for parenting had been a pipe dream. Would I succeed this time? Yes, I was finally able to negotiate a four-day weekly schedule, gaining an extra day for my home and family. There was real gender progress at last. As our children grew older, I would eventually transition to a regular five-day schedule.

As I walked around the newsroom, I saw more white women sitting among the masses of males and no longer segregated in the For and About Women section. Many were in Style, but others worked in the Metropolitan section, and a few worked for other sections, such as National and Business. Women at *The Washington Post* protested the limited roles they played. On May 29, 1972, the Washington-Baltimore Newspaper Guild and 117 women filed an EEOC complaint charging the paper with discrimination in employment practices. Bradlee pledged to "increase substantially, as fast as possible, consistent with quality and opportunity, the role of women as newsroom employees, particularly in top and middle-management positions."

Management appointed a newsroom equal-employment-opportunity committee composed of white and black employees to report to editors periodically. The essence of the committee's first report, in late 1972, was to urge management to break out of "its normal pattern of recruitment... now badly lopsided in favor of white males." By 1974, the federal EEOC had charged the paper with discrimination against women, particularly in promotion opportunities. By January 1976, almost 20 percent of all *Washington Post* news employees were women.

When I returned as an editor in the Style section in 1972, in what became another major turning point in my life, *The Washington Post* had moved into a new $25 million building, fronting on 15th Street N.W. and joined to the old L Street building in which I had worked earlier. The new newsroom now was large, stark, and bright, located on the fifth floor, and Style had its own territory in an adjoining section. The paper had more than doubled the space for its 2,600 editorial, business, printers, and other employees, and additional mechanical equipment. The building included a small factory consisting of a print shop and pressroom where workers put the paper together and printed it.

I was pleased that the expanse of white faces I had left was now sparsely flecked with African American ones—male and female. Little more than ten years before, when I had been the first and only black woman reporter, in 1961, City Editor Ben Gilbert and other white editors had seen me as one of three "bright young black 'would be' journalists with college degrees with the same background *The Post* sought in its white job candidates." Writing years after that time, Gilbert penned that insulting line in an article entitled "Toward a Color-Blind Newspaper: Race Relations and *The Washington Post*" for the journal *Washington History*. He credited our performance with "diminishing some of the newsroom tension around race," adding, "these reporters, Luther Jackson, Jr., Wallace H. Terry, and Dorothy Gilliam, did what came naturally for survival; they assisted each other. They exchanged experiences, educated each other on the mysteries of the newsroom and warned about 'rednecks' in the office." I was offended that he called us "would be" journalists. Luther, Wally, and I were experienced journalists and did good work under adverse circumstances that white reporters didn't have to face. We had the scars of Mississippi and Vietnam, for starters. I came to forgive Gilbert, who was basically a supporter, because I had had a lot of exposure to bad white people as I was growing up in the South, and when I entered white institutions I had learned that not all white people were the same.

At *The Washington Post*, despite many, many problems, there were progressive—albeit imperfect—people like Ben Gilbert. He and his wife, Maureen, invited me to my first social event in D.C. and, when my three girls were growing up, invited us to swim in their pool. I would take the girls to their house in northwest Washington from our house in Mount Pleasant and Maureen entertained us with delight. Of course, the girls enjoyed it and later remarked: "We owned that pool!" And I enjoyed it. We would stay all day and just eat and relax, the girls running all over the place. Maureen would bring food out again and again. No, even when they hurt me, as did Ben's insulting line, I learned that not all white people are alike. So many people at *The Washington Post* didn't like Ben Gilbert. He got sick at one point and Maureen confided in me that she'd called Bradlee and told him Ben was sick and had had a blood transfusion. "Blue I hope," was the response from Bradlee. Maureen never got over that remark. Everyone knew they didn't like each other. Ben was seen as too close to the black community, because he heard and understood our concerns.

On the surface, at least, *The Washington Post* under Bradlee seemed to be responding to the pressures from Blacks and women both inside the newspaper and in the society.

Several days after I returned, I met the African American journalist who would one day have a major impact on my professional life. I was walking toward the ladies' room in the main newsroom when I saw him, a dark-skinned black man of medium height, gliding toward me, heading for the editorial section. He was wearing mules, very avant-garde, backless shoes, and looking very relaxed, even cool. Cool was not how I'd felt in the newsroom when I was one of only three black reporters. He told me his name was Bob Maynard and he was an editorial writer. I recalled the byline "Robert C. Maynard." He had covered the 1968 urban insurrections, and I knew his reporting had received special attention from Gilbert, when he was the city editor. An African American from Brooklyn, Maynard was one of those pioneers everyone wanted to know and emulate. He had dropped out of high school and then joined the staff of *The Gazette and Daily* in York, Pennsylvania, in 1961, before coming to *The Washington Post* in 1966. I was not on staff during his initial years there, but I've been told that from the beginning, his voice resonated throughout the newsroom, and his writing on national stories stood out like songs. Maynard was pleased that I was going to be the first black female editor in Style. We bonded immediately and talked often thereafter.

At one point Maynard became the paper's ombudsman, publicly sorting out what the readers liked and disliked about the coverage and monitoring the paper's content. In a long, groundbreaking career, he found time to help Blacks succeed at *The Washington Post*, giving advice, reading their copy, even writing recommendations.

A few years later, Maynard found his larger cause, helping to train minorities of all ethnic groups from around the country to enter daily newspapers. When that effort got underway, he asked me to join his inner circle, which I did gladly.

Following the assassination of Martin Luther King Jr. on April 4, 1968, and the release of the Kerner Commission Report, Fred Friendly, a former president of CBS and a Ford Foundation executive, was one of the first white power brokers to build a roadmap for bringing more minorities into the news business. At my alma mater Columbia Journalism School, he started a summer training program and received an initial grant from the Ford Foundation. He not only used the Columbia faculty but also enlisted the experienced and solid journalists Maynard and Earl Caldwell, a reporter for *The New York Times*, who used their networks to recruit young reporters from college papers, entry-level internships, or other careers. The two veteran journalists convinced the recruits that they could get the experience they needed for television or newspapers in the Columbia program. Well-known journalists, such as Charlayne Hunter-Gault, gave lectures, sent the reporters on assignments, and edited their work. At the end of the summer program—what many called a boot camp—the reporters were guaranteed a job in a broadcast or newspaper newsroom.

The first session had been in the summer of 1969. In its short history at Columbia from 1969 to 1974, the program produced a Who's Who of journalists in print and broadcast, placed in the best newsrooms. Geraldo Rivera, Maureen Bunyan, J. C. Hayward, Milton Coleman, and Michele E. Clark were early students, and Clark later became the first black woman network television correspondent.

When Bob Maynard approached me, however, I never dreamed that through him I would become one of the leaders in a decades-long struggle to help diversify the nation's mainstream news media companies.

I later came to know some of the other Blacks who had come to the paper during my absence. Blacks were in the photography department—the gruff but personable Ellsworth Davis and soft-spoken, sensitive Matthew Lewis, a brilliant photographer. Lewis went on to win the 1975 Pulitzer Prize for Feature Photography.

I also got to know the supertalented William Raspberry in his new role as a columnist. He had been a teletype operator in 1962 when I was a reporter, but by early 1965, he had begun to alternate with several white reporters in writing a Potomac Watch column. In early 1966, Bill took over the column as his own—much to my joy as a reader and to the benefit of the metropolitan area.

What I saw was invigorating and had the potential for creating new approaches to coverage, new ways to write about people who had formerly been outsiders. I was excited about my new role in Style as one of five assistant editors, an originating editor, to create story ideas, work with existing reporters and scout for new ones. Reporters spent time in the field, traveled, interviewed, and dug deep, sifting fact from fiction, truth from lie in stories. Editors worked in the office, generating ideas, editing reporters' copy, and helping them produce their best work, trying to bring a sense of order to events. I aimed to focus on black culture and to report occasionally and write features when I could find the time.

The paper I had left in 1966 dominated the market in advertising and gained a reputation for being good and liberal among knowledgeable white observers like David Halberstam, who wrote in *The Powers That Be*, that *The Washington Post* "always seemed on the verge of becoming a great newspaper but it was not yet a great paper. Its editorial page was distinguished, but there was a certain softness to its reporting, as if good will and good intentions could substitute for hard work and toughness of mind.... There was an essential decency to the paper's political outlook: *The Post* clearly wanted the city and the nation and the world to be a better place."

During the years I was away, however, the newspaper had undergone tremendous change, and the biggest change was the impact of Bradlee, who had become managing editor in August 1965 and then been selected as executive editor in 1968. Publisher Katharine Graham, who had taken the helm of the paper in 1963, succeeding her husband, Philip, told one interviewer she had hired Bradlee "for his ability as a talent finder, because I essentially think that is what any business is all about."

Bradlee, formerly the Washington bureau chief for *Newsweek*, also brought a magazine flair and style; his primary goal was to make an impact—to get people reading and talking about the paper. While the emphasis was heavy on substance in news coverage when I had left, Bradlee wanted to influence the city of Washington and the nation. I found a different journalistic environment than I had left, and it was Bradlee, with his creative tension, that was the driving force. I was pleased because a positive impact on the predominantly black city had been missing.

The newspaper's biggest national story to date under Bradlee had been the Pentagon Papers, a struggle that brought into stark relief *The Washington Post's* ongoing rivalry with the venerable *New York Times*. That institution had, Halberstam wrote, "the money and the power and the prestige to stand up to the government, to hire the lawyers, to stand equal to the Solicitor of the United States, to fight if necessary not just City Hall but 1600 Pennsylvania Avenue." *The Washington Post* had been gaining on *The Times*, but had still been lingering behind it in its coverage of Vietnam.

The Pentagon Papers story broke on June 13, 1971, when *The Times* made public a secret bureaucratic history of the Vietnam War compiled by Secretary of State Robert McNamara. The Pentagon Papers had been provided to *The Times* by anti-war activist Daniel Ellsberg. *The Times* printed over six pages of the top-secret documents daily over several days before the Nixon administration obtained a court order halting their publication. *The Washington Post*, furious at being scooped by *The Times*, then obtained some of the papers for itself, preparing to run them, but there were arguments against doing so, at the top levels of the business side. The publisher, Mrs. Graham, sided with Bradlee, who was itching for a piece of the action. As Katharine Graham's memoir recalled, "Publishing the papers went a long way toward advancing the interests of *The Post*. As Ben Bradlee later said, 'That was a key moment in the life of this paper.' One of our unspoken goals was to get the world to refer to *The Post* and *The New York Times* in the same breath, which they previously hadn't done. After the Pentagon Papers, they did."

The fight brought the conflict between freedom of the press and national security to the forefront. The legal maneuvering involving both newspapers led to the Supreme Court, where the two cases were enjoined and argued. The Court ruled for the newspapers. The newsroom morale shot up at *The Washington Post*.

Bradlee rehired me just as *The Washington Post*'s stature as a newspaper was about to be magnified worldwide by its reporting about the Watergate break-in on June 17, 1972. The story began as an unusual crime on the police blotters: a break-in by five men at the Democratic National Committee headquarters in the Watergate Hotel and an arrest at two thirty a.m. One of the men arrested, James McCord, worked for the Committee for the Re-Election of the President (CREEP). Another, Bernard Barker, had money that had been raised for the Richard Nixon campaign deposited in his bank account.

The story became the most groundbreaking story in U.S. journalism history, accomplished by dogged digging by Bob Woodward, a navy vet and Yale graduate, and Carl Bernstein, a native of Washington who hadn't completed his University of Maryland education. He was a good "shoe-leather" reporter (one who didn't shy away from stories that required going out and knocking on doors to talk to people), but some editors considered him a bit of a loose cannon. I personally admired both of them and their work but Carl was my favorite. Staffers called the pair Woodstein. With them and *The Washington Post* in constant pursuit, the story developed over the course of two years.

The Watergate saga spilled over into the Style section as reporters and editors who wanted to be part of the mix wrote profiles of some of the key players. The latest Watergate developments were a constant subject at our daily meetings. I wasn't part of the editing or reporting of the story, but I was curious about how it was developing. I was also pleased that Roger Wilkins, the editorial writer, was bringing his sharp intellect, racial sensitivity, and eagle eye to its developments. *The New York Times*, CBS, *The Los Angeles Times*, *Time* magazine, and others joined in original reporting, revealing stories about the cover-up by the Nixon administration and publishing stories on the special prosecutor, until everything slowly came to a head, leading to the resignation of President Nixon in August 1974.

The magnificent moment when *The Washington Post* won the 1973 Pulitzer Prize for Public Service confirmed that Bradlee's and Katharine Graham's *Washington Post* had become a great newspaper. Along with reporting by Woodward and Bernstein, Roger Wilkins's editorials on the Watergate scandal, and cartoons by Herbert Block (whom we called Herblock, as was his byline) helped *The Washington Post* win the coveted award. I was thrilled.

It was an exciting time to be at the paper, as the Style section played an important role in enhancing *The Washington Post's* stature. As one of the editors of the section, I wanted to paint a larger world of black culture nationally. The people I wanted to feature in *The Washington Post* were the heirs to a long history of creativity. Black culture's genesis lay partly in the segregated system that had forced us Blacks to live in a world of our own. Blacks built churches, businesses, colleges, and universities despite hostility and oppression. Spirituals, the blues, and jazz emerged—the last as the quintessential American art form—and the Harlem Renaissance of the 1920s and 1930s was important for black expression and self-realization. I knew this vast and complex black cultural world—largely unknown to white readers—was missing from the Style section.

I had to learn the lay of the land and the existing rules before trying to expand them. By 1972, the section had gelled under a strong editor, Thomas R. Kendrick, who knew exactly what Style stood for in its pursuit of personal journalism: "(The) focus is squarely on the human dimension," he wrote, "a dimension that somehow got cut wafer-thin in the who-what-when-where-why formula that seemed nearly computer programmed by the early '60s....Style writers are striving to gather facts without excising their human context...make contact with the private individual behind the public image."

The section's profiles, personal memoirs, and insights on the powerful and the obscure were stirring talk of "the new journalism" in newspapers around the country, and Style became the prototype that newspapers mimicked for its daring, highly intelligent, culture-oriented content. These new and personal approaches were long overdue, and the ideas had been percolating in me since I was at Columbia in 1961.

Influences included *The New Yorker* and *New York* magazines, which became models for what *Vanity Fair* and others would be years later. I had also seen this approach in writers for the black press, including *JET* and *Ebony*. "Don't overlook the ironies in your stories," L. Alex Wilson had told me in 1957 when I worked for him at *The Tri-State Defender*. Washington had become the largest American city with a predominantly black population. Citizen activism focused a spotlight on once-hidden and once-ignored issues of poverty, racism, and gender discrimination.

In cities where large numbers of African Americans have historically lived, the black residents have always had two lives. One was presented to the white world where they worked or interacted in public places. The secondary one was much more complicated. Racial segregation enforced living patterns in neighborhoods, and for much of the twentieth century, Blacks of different economic levels resided with each other. Segregated schools, from nursery to high school, forced interaction between the black classes.

When it came to leisure time, higher education, and professional attainment, the black classes divided themselves. College-educated Blacks had fraternal organizations, and graduates kept up their associations through social clubs. And to further divide, a color line of dark and light-skinned Blacks existed. The lives of working-class and middle-class African Americans in the twentieth century were severely shaped by these patterns and choices.

Having light or dark skin didn't protect African American people from the degrading racist practices of the day. All the Pullman porters were called George because white people couldn't bother to remember their names. By contrast, many black Americans who were porters were credited with helping the expansion of the black middle class. Black history abounds with stories of people who achieved despite being treated inhumanely, such as Thurgood Marshall, a former Pullman porter, who became a lawyer, successfully argued the 1954 Supreme Court case that desegregated the public schools, and eventually served on the Court himself.

What developed was a vibrant one-of-a-kind society built by black willpower, intellect, determination, and necessity. Despite huge challenges, Blacks built institutions such as Spelman College, Tuskegee Institute, and Fisk, Morehouse, and Howard Universities, as well as my alma mater Lincoln University. They provided a blueprint for black progress, even within the confines of segregation.

Churches were houses of worship but also focal points of black activism. The A.M.E. denomination, of which my father was a part, boasted Metropolitan in Washington, D.C., known as the "National Cathedral of African Methodism," which I would join in 1997.

Black leadership emerged. Neighborhoods spawned cultural institutions, such as the Anacostia Community Museum. John Kinard, who started it in 1967, was one of the smartest men in D.C. and one Sam deeply admired. He and the community organizers who founded the museum wanted to inspire local constituencies to examine their own history and engage in public dialogue about contemporary issues. I loved that it was located in a black neighborhood, east of the Anacostia, where few white people lived or visited. Our family enjoyed checking out its exhibitions, as did other black Washingtonians.

White suburbanites wanted access to the downtown business district and had the power to get federal funds and laws to create the Metrorail. Exasperated African Americans waited much longer for the system to provide that transportation in their neighborhoods. At Style, I wanted the editors to know about the growing impatience of the black population so reporters could write about it.

I was glad to see public colleges open, giving more residents access to higher education. The fifty states had such institutions providing higher education, but only D.C. Teachers College had existed in that category in Washington. I was thrilled when federal legislation introducing guaranteed student loans authorized two new public colleges—Washington Technical Institute and Federal City College—in 1968. There were some fifteen thousand applicants.

Just as the 1960s saw the emergence of the Civil Rights Movement for African Americans and, soon after, the women's movement, the 1970s saw the emergence of the gay community, in Washington and around the nation. In 1969, the Stonewall riots, in which patrons at a gay bar in New York City defied police harassment and fought back, caused widespread ripples for freedom from stigmatism for the gay community.

All of this had a liberating impact on Washington and brought a new vibrancy to the city that I welcomed and wanted to write about. As I rejoined *The Washington Post* in the Style section, I knew developments in urban black communities around the country were reflected in Washington. A freed black community had existed in Washington even in the early 1800s, a half century before the Civil War and Emancipation Proclamation. In Washington, as in many other cities, black citizens of all economic classes had created a world of fraternal organizations, philanthropic groups, social clubs, even their own yacht clubs. Women who cleaned houses for the upper-class white women left that job on Friday and dressed in satin and lace for a Saturday-night dance at the Colonnade. Doctors who made house calls and rounds at Freedman's Hospital during the week donned their formal tails and patent-leather shoes for dinner and dancing with the Bachelor Benedicts Club. And while some of the clubs had a serious purpose of raising scholarships and doing other good works, they also engaged in activities that were solely to release the tensions of living in a segregated society.

I was not much of a joiner, so these organizations and activities did not hold much allure for me. But as a journalist, I saw that as segregation was breaking down, Washington Blacks still cherished them. Cotillions, a rite of passage for young men and women, still were important among well-to-do Blacks. Organizations like Jack and Jill, the Continentals, the Links, and the Girlfriends provided social leadership. I wanted the Style pages to reflect this part of black culture.

A social revolution was occurring in America as Blacks were demanding the full equality that the Founding Fathers had promised every American but had been denied us for more than two centuries. I had already been a small part of that revolution, breaking down race and gender barriers at *The Washington Post*. Now the decade of the Civil Rights Movement (1955 to 1965) had faded. It was the era of Black Power. Stokely Carmichael shouted, "Black Power" during James Meredith's "March against Fear" in 1965, and Bobby Seale founded the Black Panther Party for Self-Defense in 1966. Black political leadership emerged across the country in the wake of the Voting Rights Act, as African Americans began to win key offices in the early 1970s. Shirley Chisholm, whose campaign slogan was "unbossed and unbought," ran for president of the U.S., bringing great pride to us black women with her audaciousness. It was an exciting time of hope and promise, a time reminiscent of Reconstruction a century earlier. Although that hope would be cruelly dashed for the poorest African Americans, a small but growing middle class would make solid steps forward, thanks in large part to the Affirmative Action legislation of the late 1960s and protests like the one that helped open a door for me to return to *The Washington Post* as an editor.

More and more, Washington had become the stage for public and behind-the-scenes protests by celebrities against the Vietnam War. Eartha Kitt, the actress and singer, was resoundingly applauded by many black folks when she told Lady Bird Johnson at a White House luncheon, "You send the best of this country off to be shot and maimed. They rebel in the street. They will take pot and they will get high. They don't want to go to school because they're going to be snatched off from their mothers to be shot in Vietnam." I was glad to be in a position at Style to cover her remarks.

One of the most profound local changes I witnessed was political, as the city finally ended more than a century of deeply racist control by Congress, where Ku Klux Klan members like Senator Theodore Bilbo of Mississippi and former KKK leaders like Senator Robert Byrd had served as chairmen of the committee that oversaw District affairs. (Byrd eventually renounced his KKK membership.) I had encountered Byrd in 1962 when I wrote about Junior Village, where hundreds of black youngsters were living in harsh and overcrowded conditions. Because the series attracted First Lady Jacqueline Kennedy's attention, she visited the depressing institution, accompanied by Byrd. I was visibly pregnant covering the visit and was surprised when the senator courteously took my arm to help me over a ditch. Like many white Southerners, even Klansmen, Byrd displayed gentility outwardly to everybody. But I understood that even though he helped me over a ditch he was not accepting me as an equal. Southern whites often had a veneer of courtesy and were not unkind to Blacks in daily interaction, as long as the whites retained a position of authority. They wanted us to stay in our place but, like Byrd, would help us in small ways so they could have a good conscience, while maintaining their power and superiority.

As a news reporter in the 1960s, I had worked to bring to the readers unbiased and objective coverage of D.C. home-rule events, and I was excited that more black Washingtonians were now activists. A new city was emerging, a "chocolate city," that reflected in part citizen activism from such leaders as Julius Hobson Sr., head of the local Congress of Racial Equality, one of the soundest thinkers on the issue of home rule, and M. Carl Holman, the first black president of the National Urban Coalition. However, the citizens of Washington still couldn't elect their own mayor or city council. Representative John L. McMillan, Democrat of South Carolina, was chairman of the House District Committee and blocked any suggestion of home rule. Finally, in the crucial 1972 congressional primary campaign, the stars aligned for change. The city's black leaders, including Walter Fauntroy and Sterling Tucker, set their sights on ending McMillan's reign.

Recognizing that black voters in South Carolina could, if organized, vote him out of office, they traveled to South Carolina to tell their story, and black voters defeated McMillan. Representative Charles Diggs of Michigan, a black Democrat, who had sat on the committee for several years and was in line to become its leader after McMillan, moved up and helped the city attain partial home rule. Walter Washington became the first elected mayor of the capital city, and Marion Barry entered politics and was elected chairman of the school board. I was optimistic, as were most Washingtonians and Blacks in other cities, about the ascendancy of Blacks into positions of power.

As part of our eye on politics, the Style reporters chronicled many developments with the Congressional Black Caucus. The black members of Congress energized the black social scene because they were very involved in the local community. The intersection of the local leaders and the executives of national organizations headquartered in Washington fascinated me. D.C.'s cultural community reflected the trends and issues of the times. Style ran a piece on former Beat poet and playwright Amiri Baraka, a founder of the Black Arts Movement, which used the arts and philosophy to redress the cultural and psychological effects of black oppression. Style also covered another seminal figure in the movement, Maulana Karenga, who started the festival Kwanzaa.

The idea that "black is beautiful" began to take hold in the black middle class, which had for decades rejected any manifestation of African heritage. I embraced this new idea and readers told me they did, too. In Style, we paid attention to the developing black nightlife scene. Early on, reporter Hollie I. West did an article on clubs and restaurants middle-class black Washingto-nians frequented at night. Prime among the destinations was Billy Simpson's restaurant on Georgia Avenue, where I dined frequently with sources or friends. The menu was comfort food, but it had been a gathering place for the movers and shakers to discuss and plan such activities as the 1963 March on Washington, election campaigns for Barry, and efforts to gain full voting rights for the city. So important was the restaurant to history that the location was placed on the National Register of Historic Places in 2009.

Style writers chronicled how the black cultural movement across the nation affected Washington. The 1970s brought a giant leap in the number of cultural spaces in the city, which would change Washington from the cultural backwater it had been when I first arrived there. The John F. Kennedy Center for the Perform-ing Arts opened in 1971, and two years later, 1973, Robert Hooks directed *The Blacks* by French playwright Jean Genet, breaking race and gender barriers on the center's stage. And we reported it in Style.

Style had many excellent critics to cover this explosion of the-aters and museums, including art critic Paul Richard, architectural critic Wolf von Eckardt, TV reviewers Sander Vanocur and Tom Shales, dance critic Alan M. Kriegsman, and others. One of the stars of Style was Sally Quinn, a profile writer with a unique way of portraying powerful personalities. She would become involved with Bradlee, and they later married, which seemed to give her certain privileges. I was startled when she wrote of Rudolf Nureyev: "He has a fabulous behind. Women follow him around and stare at his fanny as blatantly as some men would stare at a woman's bosom."

Two other women joined the section as assistant editors about the same time I did: Sandy Rovner, who was sharp, kind and had a special interest in local personalities and politics, and bubbly

Donnie Radcliffe, who chronicled First Ladies and high society. We were all originating editors with clusters of reporters and subjects for which we were responsible. Lon Tuck, who was Style's managing editor, a sensitive, rotund man, was Kendrick's right-hand man and alter ego. We assistant editors met daily with Kendrick and Tuck to discuss our stories-in-progress and upcoming ideas. Editors discussed their own and their reporters' ideas and shared them in the daily meetings. I mainly reported to Tuck and Kendrick and only occasionally to Bradlee.

As a reader, before I returned, I had particularly enjoyed the thought-provoking writing of Hollie I. West. He and Angela Terrell were the section's only two black writers. I particularly looked forward to working with West. He had joined the paper as a Metro reporter in April 1967 and displayed such wide capabilities with his interest in music and feature writing that he was selected to join the new section when it started in 1969. Hollie wrote the newspaper's first article on Sterling Brown, the famous poet, author, and professor of literature at Howard University who helped establish Afro-American literary criticism and taught many of the nation's black scholars and writers. Brown was connected to the larger Black Arts Movement of the 1960s and 1970s, but some of his seminal works had been written decades earlier. As an elder, he was one of the District's strong voices. West also wrote a long article on Duke Ellington in 1969 when President Richard Nixon chose the great musician/composer/bandleader to receive the Medal of Freedom at the White House, on the occasion of Ellington's seventieth birthday.

When West told one editor he wanted to interview the author Iceberg Slim, the editor responded quizzically, "Do you think a story like that belongs on the pages of *The Washington Post?*" West said, "This is about the social fabric of American culture." Iceberg Slim wrote popular novels about pimping and street life that sold millions of copies. When West's article ran, investigative reporter Morton Mintz told West he had found it "fascinating."

While some white editors and writers knew such stories were important, not many leaped to cover them, so some editors appreciated that the black reporters and now a black editor were handling them. Many white reporters were hesitant to write about Blacks in all dimensions, treading carefully for fear they might be called racist. That eventually faded. In the 1970s, editors were very open to stories because Blacks were in vogue. "I had carte blanche," said West.

Because *The Washington Post* had national distribution through the Los Angeles Times–Washington Post News Service, we were able to introduce black culture to new audiences across America. International audiences also saw our stories via *The International Herald Tribune*, which was then owned jointly by *The Washington Post* and *The New York Times*. The jazz musician Dexter Gordon, who lived in Europe, told West he kept informed about what was happening in America by reading his articles in *The International Herald Tribune*.

My work in Style was a two-way street with ideas coming from reporters to me and from me to my fellow editors and reporters. My insights came from my experience growing up in the segregated South, attending a black college for two years, and working in the black press for several years, experiences the white editors and reporters had not had. Over the years, I was able to suggest good stories because of my reading, interests, and experiences. Stories on important black figures took on an extra dimension because I was familiar with black specialists in politics, music, entertainment, and education to interview and quote in my stories.

If we were going to continue to come up with such compelling stories, however, I needed to find additional writers. As an editor, I could suggest stories but unless I had a team that could report and write strong narratives, I could not be effective. I could coach writers and help them tell the stories that needed to be told. Good reporters would also bring great ideas and their own sources to the table. Together, we could make sure interesting black people and dynamic issues of the black community became part of the mix in the Style section. I was attracted to the writing of Joel Dreyfuss, a twenty-seven-year-old reporter at *The New York Post*, and called him to Kendrick's and Bradlee's attention in 1973. Bradlee was skeptical. "I hear he's a pain in the ass," he told me in his usual off-color language. He agreed to bring Dreyfuss down from New York after I insisted he would be an asset to the section. When he arrived, Kendrick wanted to hire him. He knew his writers were "uniquely diverse, non-interchangeable (a motley assemblage of individuals with roaring talent for certain tasks, howling weaknesses for others)," according to "Writing in Style." Dreyfuss would fit right in, Kendrick felt. Bradlee wasn't convinced.

Years later, Dreyfuss wrote about his interview with Bradlee: "He snarled, threw around F words and popped a trick question, 'We've been accused of racism,' he said, [referring to the Metro Seven complaint filed by the paper's black reporters a year earlier.] I was Haitian-born and black. 'How do you feel about working for a racist paper?' 'If I was going to worry about who was racist, I wouldn't be in this business,'" Dreyfuss answered. "Bradlee roared with laughter." He approved our recommendation to hire Dreyfuss.

I especially related to Joel Dreyfuss's piece for *The Washington Post* on Ted Poston published on January 19, 1974, and entitled "The Loneliness of Being First." He wrote:

> Ted Poston died last week at the age of 67. The first black reporter on the New York Post and for long periods of time the only black reporter on any major white-owned newspaper in the country.

Being the "first black" at something is one experience many members of my generation have been spared and I was not particularly impressed by the disheveled old man who limped over to my desk in the cramped city room of the New York Post to shake my hand the first day I worked there.

I wasn't impressed because some of the young hotshot editors shrugged him off when questioned, and I was ignorant about what he had done and particularly ignorant about what it meant to be "the first."

By the time I got there [to *The New York Post*], Ted wasn't as fast or as productive as he used to be and there were younger people—less talented than Ted in his prime—in the rewrite bank who handled the major stories. But as time went by I got to know Theodore Roosevelt Augustus Major Poston, and when he wasn't suffering from poor circulation or battling a deadline, we would sit at the only window in the newsroom. We would watch the ships glide down the East River, under the Brooklyn Bridge into New York harbor and he would weave those marvelous stories about his experiences in the South.

He talked about a time when any black who went into the Deep South asking questions took his life into his own hands and survived by the speed of his feet and the quickness of his wit. In Ted's case, he had the added weapon of humor. Like the time the mayor of a small town introduced Ted to the sheriff as a reporter from "one of them Noo Yawk papers."

"Do you work for a white paper or a colored paper?" the sheriff wanted to know. Ted kind of ruminated for a minute and said:

"Well, Sheriff, down here you all have a law that says if a man has one drop of black blood, he's black. I'm the drop of black blood at the New York Post so I guess it's a colored paper." And Ted would throw his head back and laugh that big infectious laugh that reminded one he had a tremendous joy of life and had lived it to the hilt.

In that tribute, Dreyfuss did what I hoped my band of reporters would do: bring to the attention of a broad audience, the talent and contributions of a pioneering figure.

In 1975, my colleague Donnie Radcliffe and I "stole" Jacqueline Trescott from *The Washington Star*, where her sensitive and unique chronicling of black culture had already shone brightly in the city. A story she wrote about the historic Metropolitan A.M.E. Church, which was right around the corner from the *Washington Post* headquarters, had attracted *The Washington Post* editors' attention, as had her profiles of Maya Angelou and Nina Simone. Trescott would become one of the Style section's stars, staying on the job for thirty-seven years.

"I was very Afro-centric in dress [and] preferences for what I did in my spare time," she said later. "Because of being immersed in minority culture at *The Star*, I concentrated on the same sort of things by writing about it, talking about it. My monitoring showed that when you look at what most editors wanted covered, you had to fight for inclusion because minority stories weren't always the first things that came to their minds."

One of Trescott's first articles was about Freedman's Hospital, a formidable institution in black Washington, that was transitioning into Howard University Hospital. The article was a behind-the-scenes look at the doctors, most of whom were male, and documented the hospital's importance in the black community in part because so many local African Americans had been born there.

It was an invigorating period. If reporters could make the case for the importance of their stories, they had the freedom to develop them. One of Trescott's favorite subjects was my acquaintance from J-school days, Alex Haley, author of the book *Roots: The Saga of an American Family*, which became a blockbuster television series and dominated the TV coverage from the mid- to late 1970s. She wrote about his writing the novel that traced his heritage to Gambia, and she chronicled the excitement about its publication and the television series and reported on the TV series itself. "Everyone in *The Post* newsroom was so tired of my Alex Haley stories," she cheerfully recalled years later in an interview. "Howard [Simons, the managing editor] said, 'I do not want to see another story about Alex until the TV program comes on, and we'll see if anyone is watching." Trescott pushed him: "After it becomes a monumental hit, can I go anywhere and see how Alex is doing?" He agreed. When Haley became famous overnight, she called him and asked where he was. Disappointed that he was nearby in New York, she joked, "Can't you go to California?"

From New York, Trescott wrote: "Suddenly Alexander Palmer Haley is a folk hero.

"An estimated 82 million viewers, third-largest audience in television history, according to ABC, watched the Tuesday installment of 'Roots,' the eight-part movie based on Haley's best-selling family chronicle and now he is besieged by well-wishers."

One of the pleasures of being in Style was presenting the voice of people like Alex to our readers. Trescott's piece echoed that voice. "In rare quiet spells, when all the autograph seekers are gone, Alex Haley says he feels like 'a total man.' He hopes he's helping many others to feel like 'total' human beings." Haley told her, "We have in this country obscured slavery. To some it's just a word. But no one has really dealt with it. Slavery set in motion two centuries of methodical stunting, a repression of a whole people to have equality. It's time for that to end and 'Roots' has moved us all. When I talk and when I cry the tears are for the whole thing—the gamble paid off. It has paid off beyond the money." Trescott eventually had the opportunity to interview Haley in California, and Haley later wrote her a note thanking her for her excellent interviewing and writing.

Trescott also wrote compelling profiles unveiling unique human dimensions of singers Roberta Flack, Patti Labelle, Nancy Wilson, Donna Summer, the Shirelles, Natalie Cole, Gloria Gaynor, and Lena Horne. In addition, actors Al Freeman, Dorian Harewood, and Robert Guillaume and the great photographer Gordon Parks also received the Trescott treatment, as did the novelist Toni Morrison and Ntozake Shange, playwright and author of *for colored girls who have considered suicide / when the rainbow is enuf.*

Trescott wrote "The Torment of Fame: Donny Hathaway's Struggle with Success" when the singer tragically plunged to his death from a New York hotel. In an article entitled "The Hemings Affair; The Black Novelist and the 'Sally Hemings' Affair," Trescott wrote about the historical novel based on the affair between Thomas Jefferson and the enslaved woman who was his mistress for decades, written by daring author Barbara Chase-Riboud.

As the District and many other cities attempted to rebuild and refocus following the devastating riots of the 1960s, I wanted to help unveil that "secret city" which so strongly influenced America even when it was denied and denigrated. It was a fabulous time for talented black writers to be working in the Style section. Together with the other writers and editors, and the approval of Kendrick, Bradlee and Simons, we were creating a paradigm shift in profiling interesting Blacks—in politics, academia, arts, literature, and entertainment, as well as everyday people—covering them critically and revealing who they were beyond the ordinary celebrity features. We believed people of African descent had to be proactive subjects within history, rather than simply passive objects of the highly touted triumphal nature of Western culture.

Karen DeWitt came to the section in 1977, after several years freelancing for *Essence, Black Enterprise, The Washingtonian, Glamour,* and *Potomac* (*The Washington Post* magazine at the time). She had previously worked at *The National Journal.*

Shelby Coffey III, who became the editor at Style, had been the editor of *Potomac* when Karen wrote for it. "When he became Style editor, I did a short piece for his Valentine's Day special," she recalled. "Afterwards, he took me to lunch, asked me if I had any other ideas. I did, about 25, and he said, 'Save them, come work for Style.'" In Style, she interviewed personalities such as Zbigniew Brzezinski, President Jimmy Carter's national security advisor, and others. She recalled that working in Style "was paradise." She left after only ten months, not because she was unhappy but because *The New York Times* Washington bureau offered her $10,000 more annually than the $20,000 *The Washington Post* was paying her.

In the 1970s, Howard University was at the epicenter of cultural activity as many emerging writers, like Maya Angelou and Nikki Giovanni, made sure they came to speak at Howard, as well as at the D.C. libraries. Howard University Press started in 1972 with Charles Harris, a former editor at Random House, as publisher. Eleanor Traylor, head of the English Department at Howard University, revived the tradition of the literary salon, acting as the grande dame hostess to such major literary figures as James Baldwin, Toni Morrison, and Maya Angelou, as well as the singer Nina Simone. The salons were fun, and I found them informative. As a journalist it was critical to have this relaxed, casual time with these luminaries. Traylor was brilliant and eclectic. Her walls were packed with the work of black artists, and she lived her life much as Angelou did, with performance, writing, teaching, and high-spirited involvement in black art. At Howard, she inaugurated the annual Sterling Brown lecture and helped raise funds to institute an endowed chair for the noted poet.

The breadth of this history of Washington's black culture came strongly into focus during my early years as a Style editor as I tried to help capture the thoughts, strategies, and accomplishments of the energized and changing black community. Style, I thought, must be a daily chronicler of the whole city.

While the editing was satisfying, I still wanted to exercise my own writing skills, and I occasionally "stole" a story from the reporters. For example, I wrote about the actress Cicely Tyson. I was fascinated by her vegetarian diet and daily jogging routine. I also wrote about Sammy Davis Jr., the singer and dancer who had been part of America's cultural landscape for fifty years. When I questioned him sharply on why he had so passionately hugged the disgraced President Nixon at the White House, Davis was moved to tears, presumably because he was still upset by the criticism he had received from black Americans.

The pieces I assigned, edited, or wrote were not merely cheerleading for the race. Through teamwork with journalists like Trescott, West, and Dreyfuss, we covered black celebrities with a critical eye. One example was my approach to the television series *Roots*. In a January 1977 article entitled "The Television Series: Out of Balance with History," I wrote this review:

There is much that is significant about "Roots," the 12-hour saga unfolding this week before a television audience that includes nearly half of America's population.

But de word from dat Kunta is not all good.

True, it has taken a long time for the problem of slavery to be raised to a conscious level as graphically as ABC has with its dramatization of Alex Haley's book about his bloodlines—an indication perhaps that the country now is emotionally mature enough to handle its continuing loss of innocence.

It's significant, too, that this series comes at a time when historians are seriously re-examining the slave experience. The popular and scholarly studies provide a kind of double-barreled spotlight with potential for enormous—if unknown—impact.

Like whites, blacks are learning from the result of author Haley's 12-year search; like him, they too were crippled by the absence of knowing. For ignorance about its roots and heritage lead to a misreading of the culture that has evolved here and its relationship to African traditions.

Like Fanta, the young woman with whom Kunta Kinte shares the crossing, many blacks had "put all that African stuff behind" them. The shame of the period produced a conscious forgetfulness.

The bad word about ABC's "Roots" is that the show's negative underpinnings at times show through, and elements that are important to a truer understanding of black experience in America have been omitted:

Item: An early and unsettling pattern of submission is set from the moment Kunta Kinte runs breathlessly back to manhood training, reports that he has just seen white men less than two days' travel away, and is told by the elders only, in effect, to watch his step. Why didn't they fight back? Why didn't they meet and plot resistance? What was the cultural difference that made them noble, but not very take charge or brave?

Item: From "primitive" Africa to the "Old South" is the voyage ABC promises the viewer. How "primitive" is a close-knit family, organized community structure, reverence for human life, as opposed to the oppression of the "Old South"? ABC romanticized the American experience, but stereotyped the African.

Item: What was the role of the blacks who took part in the process of enslaving their brothers? The serial doesn't offer a clue to their motivation.

Item: The crossing of the slave ship, the Lord Ligonier, was not a typical one, and some passage scenes in "Roots" are mild when compared to the harsh, stark reality. Seasoning camps en route and breeding camps in the New World were also vital parts of the links that chained men's minds and bodies.

One of my favorite and personally most significant articles appeared on April 16, 1973, and led to the publication of my first book. I traveled to New York to write about a "cultural salute" to Paul Robeson on his seventy-fifth birthday. This article was part of a trend that developed in Style of catching up with famous cultural figures who had never been profiled in the newspaper. A capacity crowd filled Carnegie Hall to honor the great black singer, actor, and activist. The audience of all ages, races, and political persuasions had come to see highlights of his career that spanned sports, law school, theater, Hollywood, concert halls, and political forums. The evening included reminiscences of Robeson from actors like Zero Mostel and Sidney Poitier, songs from Harry Belafonte and Pete Seeger, and a tribute from Coretta Scott King. Later, *The Washington Post* assigned me to write Robeson's advance obituary, as is the newspaper custom for famous people. It would be filed away and used upon his death. My research convinced me that I wanted to write his biography. I had to know more about the man who rose from being a poor preacher's son to a millionaire theatrical, screen, and concert star. He was such a large figure, as a man who had been hunted by the U.S. government and virtually eradicated from most history books. He was scorned and humiliated for years because of his political beliefs.

A literary agent who had seen my article approached me about writing a book about Robeson for New Republic Books. Fascinated by the accomplishments of this Renaissance man who had come of age when America did not consider black Americans full citizens, I took up the challenge. I had to fit the writing and research into my already-busy life. I spent my "spare" time on the book and benefited greatly from the assistance of an editor from New Republic, Leon King, who came to Washington and spent days in my home helping me. I went all over the country to interview people who knew Robeson. I traveled constantly to New York to work in the Robeson archives, which were being set up near Carnegie Hall, and tried unsuccessfully to interview the singer, who was then ailing and living with his sister in Philadelphia.

Robeson died on January 23, 1976, and later that year, my book *Paul Robeson: All-American* was published and was well received. It was a thrilling, daunting experience to write a book about such a great American, who loved justice and freedom and hated injustice and oppression. I appreciated Representative Andrew Young's back-cover endorsement. It said that in my "quiet and sensitive work," I took "care in bringing back this gentle giant who lifted our national soul to unequal heights and tested our love of liberty."

Not all our work at Style was about high-profile superachievers. One of the toughest stories was reported by Trescott and Michael Kernan after the massacre in Jonestown. Many of the people who committed suicide there in 1978 were minority residents of poor neighborhoods in San Francisco. I argued that the families of these black residents would feel comfortable talking to a black reporter, and the team produced a series of moving obituaries.

Our work was generally appreciated, and black reporters won awards. Bradlee even submitted our black cultural stories for a Pulitzer Prize, a sign he had seen the gamble pay off and become an essential part of the paper's coverage. We put together a collection of black cultural stories and made a package for the Pulitzer committee. We didn't win, but it was an ego boost that the brass thought our work was up to that level of competition. I felt the irony, however, when the editors made the selections for "Best of *The Post*," in 1975, and they included no articles by our black writers.

My greatest reward was the respect of my reporters. Our mutual aim was to bring about a broader view of Blacks and write stories that showed them as full human beings. These words from West, years later, meant the world to me: "You were fierce in your determination to portray Blacks in a positive manner. I enjoyed working with you because you were serious and regarded stories about Blacks as important. They mattered and figured in the whole scheme of what was going on in African American (and American) culture."

In 1974, during these invigorating years at Style, Columbia University's graduate school of journalism could no longer support the program Fred Friendly and the Ford Foundation had founded to bring more minorities into the news business. Earl Caldwell spearheaded an emergency fund-raising drive. Arthur O. Sulzberger Sr., chairman of the *Times* board, gave his support and handed Caldwell a list of other CEOs and publishers in the upper echelon of the media to contact for additional funding. He suggested Caldwell pay them visits and flatly state *The Times*' support. It worked. Gerald Sass and John Quinn of the Gannett Company were among those executives who stepped forward.

The donors gave enough money to save the program, which then moved to the University of California, Berkeley. Bob Maynard and his wife, Nancy Hicks Maynard, the first African American female reporter at *The New York Times*, had appealed to the dean of the University of California, Berkeley, to use the facility while the regular classes were on summer break.

In 1974, at the end of that summer's session at Columbia, not even 1 percent of the staff at the country's 1,500 daily newspapers were members of racial minorities—only four hundred minority journalists were working in the United States, according to Frank O. Sotomayor, a diligent recorder of minority progress in the media and a *Los Angeles Times* writer for many years. Those low numbers angered and energized us at *The Washington Post* and other papers and gave us a mission. We expanded quite quickly into a national voice for diversity in the media, primarily under the leadership of Bob Maynard.

Sometimes, the combination of talent, ideals, need, and risk-taking come together in a cometlike moment. That happened in 1976 when nine black journalists vowed to bury the often-heard excuse, "We can't find anyone qualified." Robert C. Maynard, Earl Caldwell, Walter L. Stovall III, Leroy F. Aarons, Frank O. Sotomayor, Nancy Hicks Maynard, A. Stephen Montiel, John L. Dotson Jr., and I founded what became the Institute for Journalism Education (IJE). All experienced journalists, we had been witnesses to and participants in the long journey to bring more reporters of color into all parts of the daily news business. I felt very, very blessed that I had been able to move from poverty to the middle class. Thankful to God for those blessings, I wanted to open the way for others.

Though I loved my years at *The Washington Post*, I recognized its flaws. It was a difficult place to work because of its size, its heroic reputation after the Watergate disclosures, creative tension, and the inherent nature of news gathering—things moved quickly. Not everyone had the personality to react quickly. Below the surface, those typewriters (and later computers) were in the hands of many unhappy people. Black reporters were held to a double standard—needing to be "twice as good to go half as far." They often felt the media expected them to become white reporters with a black face, and they didn't want to do that. Blacks wanted to work among white reporters as *themselves*. They wanted to get to the heart of reporting stories they could connect with. For many, personal anger, no matter how hidden, became an issue. For too many years, I had felt this anger, and now I had found a way to channel my frustration and engage with like-minded journalists to remedy the shortage of people of color in our newsrooms.

When IJE incorporated in 1977, our platform was to equip journalists with the best skills; change the image of minority people in newspapers and newsrooms; influence how stories portrayed minorities; and provide an example of balanced reporting on minority issues through training and news gathering. I knew we were on a passionate crusade. I also knew this was going to be an uphill struggle.

The Kerner Commission Report, released in 1968, had pointed to the media as a visible culprit for ignoring conditions in black communities and underreporting or misreporting stories about them. The negative images white America had of African Americans were the fault of a biased white media, the report said, and to correct that, newspapers and television needed more black reporters and editors. My journey from Kentucky to Washington had given me plenty of proof that harsh de facto segregation was entrenched in many corners of my world. Evidence was everywhere that the media was a major part of that pattern of exclusion. As I joined in the creation of IJE, I was excited to be a part of changing that record.

Naturally, the seasoned journalists on the IJE team knew reporters, editors, and photographers had raised these issues and fought these battles before. The names of the small fraternity working in mainstream daily media were well known within our circle— their stories almost legendary. These journalists had known the satisfaction of walking through the door and then the loneliness of being the only one of their race or ethnicity. They had bruises from advocating that hiring more minority journalists would lead to more complex, stronger, fairer, and more balanced coverage of our communities. They were tired of not being heard. They heaved the collective sigh when an editor needed a reporter to go to a poor black neighborhood, looked up, and pointed straight at them. They had heard so many excuses for not hiring more people who looked like them that they knew they had to look for outside help. Advocacy became part of many journalists' extra portfolio.

In the 1960s, which bled into the 1970s, news about black communities was a priority for many media outlets because of the Civil Rights Movement, the continued resistance to integrate in the South, the urban rebellions, the Black Power Movement, and the ascendency of black politicians. After the integration of the University of Mississippi in September 1962 and the University of Alabama in June 1963, the historic March on Washington in August 1963, and the bombing of the 16th Street Baptist Church in Birmingham in September 1963, many national papers created black beats. We as a people, and we as black reporters, had begun to have essential roles.

The white-owned media recruited black reporters like me who had worked for the black press. The black press reflected the broad interest of African Americans when the white press ignored them. It offered news, editorials, features, and entertainment that Blacks trusted, even as it found it difficult to get the advertising that the general media depended on. The black press is and has always been an advocacy press. For me, the black press was an invaluable training and proving ground. I always subscribed to *The Afro-American* as well as *The Washington Post* in D.C. But even with the movement of journalists from the black press to the white media, we knew the number of reporters and editors had to expand. Fortunately, a prototype for training badly needed journalists of color existed, the Columbia program.

Bob was the IJE convener-in-chief. He knew how to build a team, reaching out to a seasoned group who not only had the experience to pass their skills on to another generation of reporters but also upheld the principles of diversity and good journalism. He enlisted his friend Earl Caldwell, formerly a reporter for *The New York Times*, whose refusal to give his notes on the Black Panthers to a federal grand jury led to an important journalism legal case. A lower court upheld Caldwell's right, but the case went to the Supreme Court, which in 1972 went against him. However, the case led to a clarification of reporters' rights and, in some states, a critical shield law, which advanced the cause of journalism writ large.

Another member of the team was Walter L. Stovall III, a white journalist who had worked as a reporter and editor at the Associated Press.

Leroy F. Aarons, a Jewish reporter who joined, had worked as an editor and national correspondent for *The Washington Post*. He had served as the paper's bureau chief in New York City and Los Angeles. When Bob and Nancy later bought *The Oakland Tribune*, Aarons followed as features editor and then became executive editor and senior vice president of news. Long active in many journalism organizations, Aarons, a gay man, was founder of the National Lesbian and Gay Journalists Association.

Another indispensable hand was Frank O. Sotomayor, a Latino reporter and editor, who worked for *The Los Angeles Times* for more than thirty years. He was part of the team that won the 1984 Pulitzer for Public Service for the paper's series "Latinos in Southern California." Sotomayor was a founder of the California Chicano News Media Association. Eventually, Sotomayor turned to teaching at the University of Southern California to continue our principles of training and leadership.

A. Stephen Montiel, a Latino reporter, was a veteran of the Associated Press and had also worked for *Pacific Stars and Stripes*, *The Arizona Daily Star*, and *The Los Angeles Times*. John L. Dotson Jr., an African American, was the publisher of *The Akron Beacon Journal* and was the director of the coverage on race relations that led to that paper's Pulitzer. He later became a member of the board of *The Washington Post*.

In 1976, IJE opened its training program at the University of California, Berkeley, with seed money from the Gannett Foundation. Bob and Nancy, who had married in 1975, were a unique couple, never hesitating to drive across the states and go into newsrooms, even in the remote parts of the country, and point out the lack of diversity. Warren Lerude, editor of the *Reno Gazette Journal*, recently said Bob and Nancy were impressive with their insight and ability to connect on a personal level with individual editors. Always nattily dressed, Bob was cordial, the ultimate salesman, but not one to mince words. He would look directly at the editors and say, "No Blacks in your city got married, have weddings, have babies, have funerals, or achieve honors in school. The only news," Bob would say, "was crime news." Underlying this was an optimism that Bob never relinquished, and that confidence gave him the freedom to speak about the issues in an inviting tone and convincing manner. Addressing the issue in that direct way got the attention of the editors and managers. Nancy said she relished going to corporate meetings and making the case for journalism training, though fund-raising was not her background.

My involvement came about because one day, Bob came to my desk in the Style section and asked me to participate in the training. I had not been part of the Columbia program, but the concept of equipping minority people in eleven weeks to take on a reporter's job—Bob's boot camp—appealed to me. I arranged for a leave from my editing duties. My mother watched the three girls for a while, and later Sam brought the children out for their first trip to California.

I plunged into teaching at the first session of the Summer Program for Minority Journalists, passing on the basics of reporting and writing, underscoring the tenets of what Bob Maynard called "Ms. Portrayal," scrubbing any misrepresentation of the black world from the reporting. I told the young reporters how to be strong in the face of editors who wouldn't believe they had the necessary tools or talent, or the newsmakers who would try to ignore them. We believed our reporters were bringing a perspective to their reporting that had been absent for two hundred years. We knew that at times their backgrounds and talent would be questioned. We prepared them with lectures and tough questions from experienced reporters like Austin Long-Scott, Eileen Shanahan, Stan Chen, Gayle Pollard, Sylvia Moreno, Karen Howze, Bill Wong, and Betty Anne Williams, as well as Aarons, Montiel, and Stovall. We underscored the importance of accuracy for every story and, particularly, for the reputations of minority reporters. Nancy Hicks Maynard used to repeat the quip I'd first heard at Columbia Journalism School: "If your mother says she loves you, check it out."

Eventually we expanded to include an editing program and a management-training program. The news industry was recognizing that qualified journalists of color were everywhere and slowly allowed them to enter the nation's newsrooms. Senior journalists often gave up their summer vacations to help shape our rigorous student newsroom.

I discovered that advocating for and training new black journalists via IJE provided an outlet to my long-held frustrations in journalism. While white journalists no longer refused to acknowl-edge me when they saw me on the street, as they had done rou-tinely a decade earlier, I often felt my voice was unheard or misunderstood in meetings where we pitched story ideas. I was no longer invisible, but I was sometimes muted. Efforts to diversify the media gave me hope and balanced my internal frustrations.

I became fanatic about improving diversity in the media. I pushed my own paper, to the point that the editors knew what I wanted when I asked for a meeting. Under Donald Graham, *The Washington Post* had a keen business sense, and its strong support of the IJE effort was an investment in personnel development, to shore up its reporting and business staffs. At the same time, I had to monitor what was occurring in my own newsroom. When asked about diversity, the editors would always say, "We are doing better than most newspapers, but not well enough." I saw a few Blacks getting promotions from reporting to editing. White women were moving up in larger numbers and more quickly and easily than black reporters. White male editors apparently felt they had more similarities to and bonds with white women than with Blacks. At one point, 20 percent of the editors were white women, a number that had increased with pressure and lawsuits.

Yet the mobility in the newsroom wasn't easy for Blacks or women—the lot of both was a bad one. Several news organiza-tions, both print and broadcast, faced class-action suits by female employees during this period. Soon after the Metro Seven filed their complaint, the Washington-Baltimore Newspaper Guild and the 117 women filed theirs. In 1974, the EEOC, a federal agency, had released findings that shocked some employees, particularly the women: The EEOC said the paper denied female reporters equal consideration with male reporters for assignments on the Metropolitan staff and the female reporters got less pay than men in the newsroom. At *The Washington Post*, one woman had moved through various ranks, Elsie Carper. She had joined *The Washington Post* during World War II and worked as a reporter on the National Desk, then moved to newsroom personnel and served as president of the Women's National Press Club. The club was strictly for the female journalists when she led the group in 1963. Judy Mann was another prominent woman as the first female columnist in Metro, bringing a strong feminist point of view to *The Washington Post* pages. Mann was also a leader when women brought complaints against *The Washington Post*.

Within our minority journalism circles, we had always had respect for women's leadership. I watched with particular interest the lawsuit the women of *The New York Times* brought against their newspaper in 1972. One of its leaders was Betsy Wade, my former professor at Columbia, the first woman copy editor at *The Times*. One question white male editors asked women was similar to questions black journalists faced: "Why would successful people like you have complaints about how women or Blacks, in general, were treated?" (*The Times* denied systematic discrimination but agreed in November 1978 to an out-of-court settlement, with goals for hiring and promoting women, as well as compensation for the plaintiffs.)

As these issues were swirling around the industry, our challenge at IJE was to establish the year 2000 as a goal for reaching proportionality in the newsroom. In effect, we wanted the percentages of journalists of color to equal their representation in the population of the nation. In 1978, the American Society of News Editors (ASNE) reported that 4 percent of newsroom journalists were minorities. This was a decade after the Kerner Commission Report. I remember shaking my head in annoyance. When the board of ASNE adopted the year-2000 proportionality goal, I thought this was too generous a schedule—after all, it was 1978! But Bob counseled that it really was a formidable challenge and that we needed ASNE, the largest organization of editors and executives, as an ally in this fight. Bob was instrumental in getting ASNE to adopt the goal as its own, and I was awestruck. As always, Bob was patient, explaining what a big deal this goal was, no matter who was getting the credit, and reminding us that if it worked, it would be a resounding breakthrough. In addition, Bob cited the promise of an annual census on newsroom employment, to be compiled by Jay Harris, a Gannett reporter who later became publisher of the *San Jose Mercury News*. It would carry weight the industry would recognize. Over the years, that census became a valuable yardstick.

Many of the IJE graduates rose to key positions within the media business, often taking core tenets such as diversity in hiring and balanced minority coverage to their jobs. For example, Kevin Merida rose to the highest ranks in the print business, becoming assistant managing editor of *The Washington Post* in 2008 and managing editor in 2013. He founded an online news operation, The Undefeated, concentrating on the intersection of sports and culture, from a minority perspective. It became part of the ESPN group.

Members of our IJE family won Pulitzer Prizes, including graduates Joe Oglesby, board member Sotomayor, and faculty member Frank Del Olmo.

When we started IJE, we understood an accelerated activism was taking place in newsrooms. We trained reporters to look at all sides of the issues, develop multicultural expertise and present a multidimensional story. Just as important, we realized, was the synergy among black and Latino groups in the streets and the reporters who were hired sometimes specifically to cover their actions. The first wave of minority reporters soon started raising questions about journalistic equity. Austin Long-Scott, the first full-time black reporter for the Associated Press, in his resignation letter to General Manager Wes Gallagher, asked him why journalism wasn't keeping up with other fields. "Why are there more black doctors than black reporters?" asked Long-Scott, carefully laying out the statistical chasm. Long-Scott provided a blueprint for protest: Put your point of view in writing, laced with data.

"What we learned is that if we were just expressing outrage and anger, they would say we were angry," said Joel Dreyfuss in an interview.

Across America's newsrooms, journalists of color were making inroads. Les Payne, a U.S. Army veteran steeped in leadership skills and newspaper practices learned as editor of the army newspaper during the Vietnam War, took notice of the black reporters writing about black soldiers. One—Jesse Lewis—wrote a story in *The Washington Post* about Confederate flags flying on army trucks. "LBJ called Gen. William Westmoreland about 2, 3 o'clock in the morning. Those flags were removed. That showed me the power of the press. That turned my mind toward journalism," recalled Payne, who was part of a reporting team that won a Pulitzer for the thirty-three–part series "The Heroin Trail." Payne was involved in seven of the twelve Pulitzers *Newsday* won.

Good work was the proof of the merit of inclusion, and mentoring became an essential part of the job for some black journalists, activists trying to influence the industry. Paul Delaney, the first black editor at *The New York Times*, said his goal was "trying to beat the single black syndrome."

While minority reporters were building their careers, the output of stories about their communities exploded. Many noted the positive difference in the news coverage. At *The Washington Post*, the company efforts to adopt some of our goals were paying off. I felt vindicated when David Broder, the paper's Pulitzer Prize–winning political reporter, remarked to me, "Diversity has made *The Post* a better newspaper."

We black journalists wanted fair reporting, an unbiased narrative, the inclusion of ethnic sources, and multidimensional portrayals. We believed to achieve this we needed balanced news staffs with many perspectives. In its first years, the IJE summer program training was already changing minority representation in newsrooms, large and small.

While IJE filled a crucial role in training journalists from all minority groups, African American journalists formed an organization in 1975, the National Association of Black Journalists (NABJ). Many black journalists were covering an assembly of the Black Elected Officials Conference and decided to use that occasion for a meeting of their own. The group of journalists met in Washington, D.C., and drew up the guidelines. Forty-four of those attending signed a document calling for the formation of the organization. Among them were Maureen Bunyan, a television anchor; Joe Davidson, a national reporter in Philadelphia; Acel Moore, a columnist in Philadelphia; Max Robinson, a television anchor in Washington; Mal Johnson, an executive at Cox Broadcasting in Washington; and Pluria Marshall, chairman of the National Media Coalition, based in Washington. Chuck Stone, then a columnist for *The Philadelphia Daily News*, chaired the meeting. My first encounter with Chuck had been in the 1960s when, as editor of the Washington *Afro-American*, he called *The Washington Post* a paper for white Washingtonians.

NABJ was to function both as a network for working journalists and as a platform for broad media issues and challenges black journalists faced. It would raise issues from hiring and promotions to images, and then pressure the mainstream media to act on them. NABJ would reward stories and journalists who produced work that reflected the multidimensional lives of African Americans. Through an annual national convention, NABJ would join media executives and sponsor recruiting and job searches.

Looking to the future, the organization would provide scholarships and short-course training on college campuses and would
sponsor workshops for high school and college students.

Years before the U.S. Census confirmed that Latinos and African
Americans would eventually make up the majority population,
the large and small news markets experienced a shift of ethnic
groups in their news base. Editors and reporters couldn't be blind
to these changes. IJE had institutionalized an interactive workshop
to enrich and expand their thinking and coverage and underscore
that news stories about minorities were often too simplistic and
didn't include the complex issues—racial discrimination, housing
segregation, poverty, family structures, job and promotion restric-
tions, and inferior education—that formed our societies. We had
seen many improvements in the 1960s and 1970s through IJE,
even before NABJ.

Things were changing. Black professionals in the news business
had a national organization in NABJ. The black community had
captured the attention of newsmakers. People of color were being
trained in media skills by IJE. When talk about the need for diversity failed, lawyers were called and talks about imbalances became
formal complaints. The Associated Press, *The New York Times*,
The Washington Post, and *The New York Daily News*, among others, found themselves the subject of complaints and unflattering
news about the bias in their own newsrooms. After much insis-
tence, the portrayal of black communities was slowly becoming a
bit less unfair and unbalanced. The Congressional Black Caucus
had become a major leader in monitoring issues of employment
and media images. And, in the early 1980s, the Communications
Braintrust of the Congressional Black Caucus continued its investigation into media practices.

Still, the end of an era was on the horizon for me. For many years, the power of Bradlee had prevailed over the bean counters on the top floor, but now there was pressure to cut costs and make more profit. Working in the fifth-floor newsroom, I wasn't aware of the top-level machinations up on the eighth floor. Daily newspapers like *The Washington Post* erected a "firewall" between the business side and the newsroom so advertisers wouldn't be able to tell us what to write.

A new editor was hired at Style, a bright man named Shelby Coffey III. He was twenty-nine years old, the former editor of *Potomac*, *The Washington Post*'s Sunday magazine, and he believed strongly in the narrative form. I was given an expanded cluster of reporters with whom to work, including some of the white critics. I had rarely edited white reporters, because I had focused on black culture. This was the first time, as an editor, that I had a predominantly white team. Most of them were experienced critics for dance, art, music, and architecture, and editing them was not difficult. I did not have to assign them stories or interact with them closely. Having a mostly white team did not feel like a big deal because by that time there were other black editors at *The Washington Post*.

But the work did not seem as fulfilling to me. By the end of the 1970s, it appeared that the black heyday of Style might be over soon. We grew increasingly aware of talk inside the paper that the Style section was "too black." When I heard an editor say he had looked at Style and thought it was *The Afro*, I knew that was not a good omen for me.

I was traveling to Europe more with Sam and had been assigned to write stories while there. From Paris, in November 1978, I interviewed Ruhollah Khomeini, better known later as Ayatollah Khomeini, who then was leader of the opposition movement that had laid siege to the rule of the shah of Iran and who was threatening to signal his followers to take up arms against the shah's regime. In January 1979, I wrote an article that traced the route of Perrier water from the tiny town of Vergeze, France, to folks willing to pay $1 a bottle for its snob appeal. I later wrote about the delicious French cuisine I sampled in Lyon, France. Though the stories were interesting, I felt they were articles any reporter could do, and I grew discontented with my role. Style had given me intimate dealings with the literati of black America, but by mid-1979, the new editor of Style seemed less interested in my story ideas.

The managing editor of *The Washington Post*, Howard Simons, who had once told West some of his work was "distinguished," by 1981, had told him his work was "too serious" and offered him a job in sports. "I had no choice but to quit," West told me years later. I witnessed the cadre of black reporters I had helped assemble become all but wiped out, one by one. I looked around the room, and the team I had built had disappeared, except for Jackie Trescott. Those who remained seemed to be in a constant competition to get space and prominent placement for their stories. Black reporters joked that the bottom right-hand story, considered the least prominent spot on the Style front page, was reserved for the minority coverage. The most important stories would get three or four columns on the top half of the page, above the fold, and on the right side.

I detected a newer conservatism within *The Washington Post* that probably was in response to the growing conservatism in the country. Newspapers respond to reader feedback and surveys; what they were hearing from readers was the mood of a nation that was about to elect Ronald Reagan. The country had been through the tumultuous Civil Rights Movement, weathering significant changes. After such changes, we hit a wall. We see it today with the election of Donald Trump after Barack Obama. After the Civil Rights Movement and resulting progress in the 1970s, the mood of the country was "We've gone far enough." While media has a powerful influence on the national mood, it also reflects it. The progressive action at *The Washington Post*, prompted by formal complaints by Blacks and women, as well as by societal changes, was coming to an end. Style was exhibiting some of the same halting of forward movement the larger society was exhibiting.

Hollie I. West said that I was "adamant about telling the black story, not telling it in a fawning way, but telling it in a holistic way." I was always conscious of the white-supremacist structure that was and still is permissible in newsrooms and against which black journalists have had to push—and still must. I felt compelled to use my career to get black stories into print.

Style had at first been a world of new opportunity for me, a chance to affect the society in a larger way than I had done as a reporter back in the 1960s. Then an editor was assigning me stories, telling me what to do. As an assistant editor at Style, I assigned the reporters stories. I always welcomed the reporters' input on what they wanted to write, and I assigned to their strengths, but my thrust was always toward bringing our story to the larger society. Style had broadened my world, but I was committed to telling black stories.

I hear that more young black journalists today have the view that I had when I first began at *The Washington Post*, when I was adamant that I did not want to be stereotyped as qualified to cover only black stories. Just as I felt at that time, they say "I'm a journalist who happens to be black and I don't want to be assigned 'black' stories." Today I find that attitude very sad, if they are saying they find something distasteful, even harming their career trajectory, about covering the black community. As I did, they need to examine why they feel that way. When I came back to *The Washington Post*, as more black people were hired, this attitude became more prevalent; there were greater divisions among us Blacks. It is important to have coverage by journalists who care about and understand the black community because there are still so many issues of racism and bias. But if black reporters are unhappy doing it and don't see the relevance, they won't do a good job. Reporters and writers are more effective when they are assigned what they really want to cover, and if black journalists don't want to report and write black stories, they have the right to choose and should not be restricted. But at Style, my team and I certainly didn't feel that way; we wanted to write black stories.

In the 1970s Style was part of the changing landscape of American culture. It was exciting. It was a whole new world to be able to hire a diverse group of reporters and see their different perspectives impact the newspaper. We let black culture take its rightful place as part of American culture. We expanded the mainstream media to appeal to a broader, more diverse audience. This collaboration was invigorating, and I felt proud to be part of that work. But now that transition had been accomplished, and I was no longer writing about issues that I believed concerned most African Americans. I was unsure of the next step. Little did I know that the career changes I had already undergone from the straight reporting I had done in the early sixties to the features, criticism, profiles, and personal-perspective writing and editing in Style during the seventies was preparing me for my most challenging job yet at the newspaper. In the 1980s, I would move back to the paper's Metropolitan section and become the paper's first black female columnist.

Voice for the Voiceless: The Column and National Association of Black Journalists Years, 1979–1997

While working as a columnist for *The Washington Post*, I modeled at a community fund-raising event in Washington, D.C., in 1983. *(Courtesy of the Dorothy Butler Gilliam personal collection)*

Smiling, at the top of my game, in 1991 when as a columnist for *The Washington Post* and chair of the board of the Institute for Journalism Education, I ran for vice president for print of the National Association of Black Journalists. *(Courtesy of the Dorothy Butler Gilliam personal collection)*

With Milton Coleman and Robert Kaiser of *The Washington Post*, while I was campaigning for president of the National Association of Black Journalists in 1993. *(Used with Permission of Milton Coleman and Robert Kaiser)*

My prayer group got me through! From Washington, D.C., they visited me in New York City while I was a fellow at the Gannett Media Center in 1991. From left, Lavarne Hines Harrison, Grace Wiggins, Pamela McKee, Leilah Telford, Ann Powell, Laura Dixon, and Patricia Press. Not pictured are Evelyn Brewster, Berneice Harleston, Margaret Childs, and Charlotte Douglass. *(Courtesy of the Dorothy Butler Gilliam personal collection)*

I am second from left, second row, at an event sponsored for journalists in the mid-1990s by the American Society of News Editors, an ally to the Institute for Journalism Education and the National Association of Black Journalists in our efforts for diversity. *(Used with Permission of American Society of News Editors)*

Unhappy and growing tired of being a "straw boss" because now I was not searching for talented new reporters, I wrote a memo to Ben Bradlee proposing that he make me editor of *Potomac* and allow me to reshape it. It was an audacious proposal from a black woman journalist at a white newspaper, but as an assistant editor in Style for seven years, I thought my experience had prepared me for a leadership position. However, I harbored no illusions that my request would be readily granted.

Weeks passed, and I heard no response. Finally, I decided to talk to him about it and made an appointment with his secretary for a meeting. I had to go through the huge main newsroom to his office on the north wall to see him. I felt nervous, even a little frightened, as I walked past the small glass-fronted offices on the right and the rows of desks stacked with paper and occupied predominantly by white reporters on my left. The noise of the newsroom was a low hum of voices, but all was quiet as I entered Bradlee's office, which was filled with light from many windows.

Many changes had occurred for him and the newspaper since our luncheon seven years earlier. Watergate had made the newspaper a household name across the world. Bradlee, its driving force, was a hero of *All the President's Men*, the hit movie that followed. He was now the world's most celebrated editor.

Despite the pride I felt in the paper's achievements, I felt added pressure and tension when I entered the beige brick building on 15th Street and sensed the strain in other reporters. Daily newspapers are fundamentally self-centered, driven by the stress of daily deadlines. In addition, Watergate had attracted some of the best journalists in the nation, who wanted to work under Bradlee, intensifying the newspaper's inner tensions as these mostly white and mostly men came "bearing the best of college degrees and the fiercest of ambitions," as David Halberstam later characterized them in *The Powers That Be*. Part of the pressure stemmed from Bradlee's desire for creative tension to emanate from his newsroom as writers and editors produced what Bob Woodward used to call "holy shit" stories. Still, the newsroom had pretty much settled down from the acclaim and damnation it had received for its role in disclosing the Watergate scandal and bringing down Richard Nixon's presidency.

Bradlee greeted me warmly, and I told him, somewhat nervously, I had come for an answer to my memorandum of several weeks before. He looked puzzled and told me he didn't recall seeing it so it must have gone astray. I told him my proposal. He didn't appear shocked but rather matter-of-factly responded that the paper was not prepared to make any changes in the magazine at this time. He said Mrs. Graham also wanted to keep *Parade*, the nationally syndicated, largely picture magazine, because she wanted something in the Sunday paper "for people who moved their lips when they read." I didn't comment on that statement but silently reflected on the fact that such attitudes of superiority were why so many black Washingtonians still thought of *The Washington Post* as a white newspaper in a black city. I withheld comment on that as well, but I wanted to help change such perceptions.

Then, Bradlee asked if I had anything else in mind that might interest me. I didn't have a Plan B in mind, but after reflecting for a moment, I told him I could be interested in writing a column in the Metro section. I knew that columnists were people who by instinct, training, and something deep in their hearts and spirits had been able to rise to the top of a very competitive profession. Columnists held highly prized positions at *The Washington Post*. Columns were not handed out lightly, and at that time you could have counted the number of African Americans in the nation who were columnists for large white daily newspapers on one hand.

Bradlee countered that I should first leave Style and relocate to the Metro section, where I could begin to find and write some feature stories and prove myself to the Metro section editors, Woodward, who was then editor of the Metropolitan section, and Herbert Denton Jr., the paper's first African American city editor. "When—and if—they think you are ready, you might get a column," Bradlee said.

I went back to my desk in Style feeling somewhat triumphant, having not gotten what I asked for but instead an unanticipated opportunity to prove myself in a new way. The nervousness was gone as I returned to my desk. I may have even strutted a little. I was eager to start my new job in the Metropolitan section and to prove I was worthy of a column. So many pressing issues were affecting our city and the nation and were not always covered as well as I would have liked. I thought I could bring an added perspective that was missing from the pages of The Washington Post. As a columnist who set my own agenda, I would be able to shine a light on the challenges and accomplishments of black people. As a Southerner who had lived through the hell of segregation and a District resident since 1961, I had firsthand knowledge of some of the community's problems. I had been one of the "Negroes" who turned "black" in society during the 1960s.

As soon as I got back to Metro, where I had started as a reporter, I began thinking about people-oriented features I could write as a journalist. Particularly concerned about black youth, I looked at what was happening in Washington's black neighborhoods, with their wealth of unheard voices. I settled on someone from my own neighborhood, the racially and economically diverse Mount Pleasant area, and wrote one of my first stories about a man I had interviewed a decade earlier, George Spriggs, "A Man Called Lamb." He was a living example of what was happening to so many young black men as the 1970s came to an end and Ronald Reagan was about to be president. I came to see that our work in Style, editing and writing about black culture, had fed and contributed to the popular interest in African Americans in the 1970s among whites, it did not accrue to the benefit of the larger black population.

This is partly how I told Spriggs's story on June 3, 1979:

Lamb had been a big man then. Life held out a better promise for him. He was gentle, and he was a model for younger kids....A decade later, he said hoarsely, "So many of the guys from then are dead—mostly drugs. I probably would be too if it hadn't been for the program."

I interviewed the man who started the program he talked about with a $75,000 grant from the Labor Department for a pilot Community Action Training School (CATS). It was to raise the racial consciousness of youths who for years had been made to feel inferior. Lacey Streeter, a former Settlement house worker and others, foresaw having the youths organize their communities to work together for change, before eventually entering entry-level jobs. "Some of them were so brilliant we would begin talking about a concept, and they would just grasp it instantly," said Streeter.

They learned black history, but also how the Board of Trade affected the city. They took trips to Harlem to visit Adam Clayton Powell's church and to Cleveland to see the first black mayor of a big city, Carl Stokes. They visited writer Amiri Baraka but also the Newark water commissioner. They prodded Stokes about his political machine and campaign contributions, and the water commissioner about rates in poor neighborhoods. They read the daily newspapers end to end. "We tried to get the dudes off the corners; show them they could do something besides get high," Lamb explained. "It changed my life. I noticed things I never noticed before."

In my column, I concluded:

CATS became the basis for a revived Neighborhood Development Youth Program, and they worked 12-hour days. Then critics of anti-poverty programs questioned their accomplishments and program leaders were forced to spend more time fighting for their program's existence than attaining its goals. The poverty programs, though a brilliant idea, eventually died in a battle without honor.

I wrote success stories about high achievers like Karen Stevenson who grew up in a quiet middle-class neighborhood and became the nation's first African American woman to become a Rhodes Scholar, one of the most prestigious honors open to young scholars in the English-speaking world. (Nine African American men had been so honored.) She was partly a product of the much-criticized D.C. public school system but enrolled in a New England prep school after eighth grade.

The key to Karen's achievements was her mother, Clara Stevenson, a divorcee who moved to D.C. from Texas with Karen and her sister in the early 1960s and later earned a doctorate and became a clinical psychologist for the public schools. She set rules for her girls, such as no television watching from Monday through Thursday, got them library cards in second grade, watched the schools, and monitored her children's homework constantly.

Seeing Karen was not being challenged to reach her full potential, she got her into a preparatory school with five hundred students in Watertown, Connecticut, in 1971, the first year the school admitted girls. Although some gifted Blacks who attended exclusive prep schools met racism, wealth, and class disparities, Karen was able to fit in and be comfortable. "A lot of my mother's friends were black, white, everything," she said, calling her mother her role model. "We grew up with a sense of no limitations," Karen added.

The editors and the public seemed to receive these stories well, and I started a series of features, spread over several years, capturing the life of Julius (Big Red) Holt, a student at Cardoza High School who overcame poverty and turned his life around through sports and the mentorship of teachers. After Big Red graduated from high school, I followed him through his time in Iowa, where he went to study and play football at Ellsworth Community College on a football scholarship in hopes of being ready to enter a major college within a year and a half. He reached that goal, and I followed him to Tucson, where he had enrolled in the University of Arizona hoping it would be a step toward playing in the major leagues. The dream of becoming a pro too often became a nightmare for many inner-city boys who think pro sports are their ticket to riches. It is a one-in-a-million dream, but Big Red also placed a high priority on getting his college degree. Pondering those odds, Big Red told me, "I say I may be one of those guys that make it. It's tough. It makes you want to work harder. I don't crowd out the fact that it could be me—that one in a million that gets the chance to make it. I work on things that make me get better." Big Red graduated from college and made it to the majors for a short time, but it was his education that secured his future. He became a social worker, married, and raised a family. In 2016, he called me from his home in Arizona and said the columns had helped him become the man he is today. I was very gratified.

Meanwhile, the work of IJE moved ahead, slowly making inroads. The eleven-week "boot camp" writing program spun off a full editing program in 1980 at the journalism school at the University of Arizona, Tucson, under the direction of Frank O. Sotomayor. Joining us were Jackie Jones, then of *Newsday*; Angela P. Dodson of *The Louisville Courier Journal* and later *The New York Times*; Robert A. Webb and Cheryl Eaves of *The Washington Post*; William Connolly of *The New York Times*; and Richard Holden and Addie Rimmer of *The Wall Street Journal*. Graduates often went on to become high-ranking editors at newspapers.

We worked hard to find the academic partners, as well as media executives, to achieve this important aspect of training for diversity. These efforts made the universities look good, nudged the executives toward our mutual diversity goals, and gave everyone a stake in the success of reporting, editing, and management training. Well done, for the time being, I thought. IJE was turning up the heat, while applauding the quiet, sometimes-visible efforts of our media supporters. We who worked on the ground floor of the diversity battle watched the practices of our allies. Allen Neuharth, the chairman of Gannett and founder of *USA Today*, was one we all applauded. He bought into the argument that black professionals could succeed at any level of newspaper leadership. When Gannett was trying to blend these principles into its newsrooms, Neuharth tied hiring minorities to financial incentives for the managers. In the 1970s, he and John Quinn, the founding editor of *USA Today*, encouraged the hiring of minority journalists at the chain's local papers and hired Fletcher Clarke, Michael Days, Richard Prince, Doug Lyons, and Jim Mitchell.

Gannett had a chain of small-town papers, and minority journalists were spread out among them. The creation of *USA Today* in September 1982 delivered a concrete example of giving minorities and women a chance at developing new skills and advancing to executive positions. It amused me that some of the *USA Today* observers thought the experiment wouldn't last. Ben Bradlee watched its impact very closely. *USA Today* expanded the use of short, tight stories and colorful photographs and graphics. Distributed nationally, the paper was initially meant for the business traveler, but soon, it found a new audience: a younger generation who wanted capsules of news. There was a trend toward sound bites, and they satisfied many people's appetite for news. *USA Today* also did many prize-winning, in-depth investigations.

After I worked a few months in Metro, Woodward and Denton told Bradlee they thought I was ready to handle a regular column. I would be the first black woman columnist at the paper. I would join fellow Metro columnists Richard Cohen and Judy Mann and would appear twice a week. The most famous African American columnist, my brilliant friend William Raspberry, appeared on the prestigious page opposite the editorial page and was already being syndicated across the nation. Writing a column was important to me because when I looked out on the landscape of America, I perceived that what the majority of Blacks were thinking about was no longer being covered, as the new conservatism emerged in the country. A paper covers what is going on; columnists delve down deep into the community. With a column, I could on a twice-weekly basis emphasize important issues in the African American community. I could also break free of some of the constraints of objective reporting.

The Washington Post was a powerhouse newspaper and, along with *The New York Times*, one of the most respected in the nation. Its location in the nation's capital and its international fame for the Watergate story added to its prestige, power, and influence. As a columnist on the Metro page, I first continued raising issues by finding a "typical person" and writing about that person's situation and how local and national issues affected him or her and others in the community. I mainly selected black persons because they were so often overlooked and my aim was to help the black community see how policies were affecting it then or would in the future.

That was the preferred way of the editors of the Metro section. But as I segued to straight opinion columns, some editors were often alarmed. "Your people columns are fine," one told me, "but those opinion columns.... Whoa!"

That response reflected one of the first challenges I had to face when I started writing opinion columns—the reality of addressing a dual audience. Washington, D.C., was mostly black when I began writing my column, but like the staff of the newspaper, the majority of readers of *The Washington Post* were white, with a history of often-unacknowledged white privilege and a different set of experiences and suppositions. Even as a columnist who didn't have to clear ideas with an editor before I wrote, many days I had to call special friends not in the media and vent to them about criticism I received, and embrace their support to keep on keeping on. I could relate to the stories of many journalists of color who lamented having to prove their worth every day to skeptical editors who didn't believe they were qualified. Many had to mute their voices when their story ideas were discarded.

I had a keen sense of the black struggle and the importance of justice. I believed strongly in democracy, but knew ours did not give equal protection to black Americans. I wanted to contribute to the success of democracy by raising critical issues I didn't see white columnists addressing. I knew I had to look for material to share my perspectives in a variety of places in the news, in books, and among educators, business persons, and multicultural and multiracial experts. I also found sources among "the voiceless"— ordinary folks left out of regular news coverage. I hoped to give them visibility. I worried about some young black women's seeming lack of self-esteem because I knew racism made many black people hate themselves. So, after the hit movie comedy *10* set off a media frenzy in 1979 about the actress Bo Derek's cornrows, the tightly braided, sometimes-beaded hair style that Africans had used for centuries, I jumped in. I knew the adoption of cornrows as a fashion fad, with little consideration for their potent cultural meaning, denigrated and denied black history.

Bo's success set off a rush by some trendier white women to have their hair done in the expensive ($300 to $500), time-consuming (four to fourteen hours) style. Some people were increasingly calling the style the Bo Braid, and many black women and sensitive white women were irate. So, when I boarded the bus to ride home from work one evening and overheard a young black woman say to her seatmate, "I see you're wearing Bo Derek's hairstyle," I wrote black women a poem in my column in hopes of raising their self-esteem. It read in part:

> Cornrows don't belong to no Bo Derek.
> They belong to women selling yams beneath a sweating sun in Senegal.
> They belong to H Street, Northeast
> And to Auburn Avenue in Atlanta.
> They belong to the blues of Jimmie Rushing
> And to the frenetic energy of John Coltrane.
> They belong to the women in Howard University dorms
> And working mothers styling their little girls' hair on Saturday to last all week.
> They belong to Stevie Wonder and Valerie Simpson.
> They belong to you.

Black mothers often cornrowed their children's hair themselves, but among the first famous black women to wear this style publicly were the actress Cicely Tyson and the singer Nina Simone, who wore it on stage in the early 1960s. Some black women criticized the entertainers, saying they were portraying a negative image of African Americans by exposing their natural, unstraightened hair at a time when most black women were pressing naturally kinky hair with hot combs to make it straight or using the chemical relaxer products that were then relatively new. Others adopted cornrows as a symbol of black identity.

Later, in the explosion of black consciousness that erupted with such force, black women across America, including me, went natural, adopting the Afro style to demonstrate black pride. It was a hard-won struggle.

After Ronald Reagan won the presidency in 1980 in an election landslide, I wrote many columns about the New Right. What angered me most about the Reagan presidency was how the black underclass was shelved, put on the back burner by policies that at best ignored them and at worst dismantled the progress that been made in communities across the country. On November 8, in "Carter was Drowned in a Right-Wing Tide," I wrote, "The voting booth represents one of the ultimate freedoms of expression, a place where the average man and woman can declare gut feelings out of sight and sound of potentially disapproving eyes and ears. The voters must have known what they were doing....And the outcome of the election should not really come as a surprise. The conservatism that triumphed...has been dramatically on the rise for many months. 'We knew there were Archie Bunkers out there,' an alarmed friend told me. 'But we didn't know there were that many.' Now we know."

I also wanted to keep the realities of our city, the nonofficial Washington, before the new administration as in "Mr. Reagan, Say Hello to the H Street Strip." H Street was one of the three corridors in Washington left in ruins after the black rebellion following the murder of Martin Luther King Jr. On the streets that branched off from H Street, jobless persons and poor families with children who were badly educated and poorly housed were suffering. I suggested he remind Congress, "H Street is only a holler from the Capitol and frustrated, hopeless people holler real loud."

As part of my work, I was able to meet and observe important civil rights leaders and personalities. In 1981, I went to Atlanta when the Martin Luther King Jr. Center for Nonviolent Social Change moved into the Martin Luther King Jr. National Historic Site on Auburn Avenue, and I interviewed Coretta Scott King and spent time with her. I was impressed with her courage as she continued to carry the banner for her husband, which she did for the remainder of her life. At Congressional Black Caucus events each year, I often saw and then got to know Representative John Lewis. Later, I traveled with a group from the District, Maryland, and Virginia on his annual civil rights tour of the South. I interviewed Jesse Jackson often throughout his presidential campaigns in 1984 and 1988.

I had been buoyed for a decade by contemporary black women's emerging in spectacular ways and wanted to continue my focus on their incipient progress. The years between the mid-1950s and mid-1980s had brought sweeping changes into the lives of many black women. Black women had made spectacular contributions in literature. Maya Angelou published her first book, *I Know Why the Caged Bird Sings*, in 1969. Toni Morrison's first book, *The Bluest Eye*, came out in 1970. Alice Walker won the 1983 Pulitzer Prize for Fiction for *The Color Purple*. These accomplishments came in the mainstream, not isolated in a segregated America, and I saw myself reflected. It had a healing effect on me, and I wanted to share it with my readers. These books had touched me deeply because in my academic history I hadn't read about many who were like me. I highlighted the book *All the Women Are White, All the Blacks Are Men, but Some of Us Are Brave: Black Women's Studies*, edited by Akasha (Gloria T.) Hull, Patricia Bell-Scott, and Barbara Smith, which called for a feminist, pro-woman perspective acknowledging sexual, race, and class oppression in black women's lives.

In 1986, after interviewing fifty achievers, my colleague Jacqueline Trescott and I wrote a series entitled "The New Black Woman" that *The Washington Post* published on the front page. Describing black women, we wrote, "Driven by the aspirations instilled by their families and lured by the widening opportunities of a desegregating America, they had sped through doors opened by the civil rights movement, the women's movement and a generally rising economy to forge new careers, new attitudes and new influence." Many were working in places where only white males had worked. I followed black women's emergence in politics and other places in society because I felt if I didn't comment, nobody else at the newspaper would and that this was why I had this platform.

I deeply admired older black organizations like the National Council of Negro Women (NCNW), which had fought for women and civil rights for decades, and I especially respected and admired its president, Dr. Dorothy Irene Height, who succeeded the great Mary McLeod Bethune. I flew on the same flight with Height to Kenya when the International Women's Convention was held in Nairobi in 1985 and got to know her well. She was untiring and driven. I admired her mind and spirit, as well as her beautiful array of hats. I saw her numerous times in D.C. when she headed the NCNW.

I covered new organizations like the Women's Vote projects and Marian Wright Edelman's Children's Defense Fund, for which Hillary Rodham Clinton once worked, which were developing and competing for political power.

The early 1980s were a time of great change, and I regretted one column when I was still learning that trying to speak to a black audience in a white medium could be problematic. In a piece called, "Coming Out of Closet Is Tougher for Blacks," in July 1980, I named and quoted a young black poet who had first announced publicly that she was a lesbian at a feminist conference the previous year. Reading her poems at the Market Gallery on Capitol Hill, she said, "Throughout our history in this land, homosexuality in the black community has been considered the ultimate taboo. I will tell you this decision [to go public] has been without a doubt one of the most crucial in my life and one of the most definitive."

Since she spoke at a public event, I wrote about her, using the column to encourage the conservative African American community to show more kindness and tolerance to the differences in sexual orientation in our city and nation. I ended by quoting the poet Ethelbert Miller, a heterosexual, who had lectured on homosexual themes in black literature: "By understanding them," he said, "we learn more about what it is to be human, about the full range of black experience."

I later learned the young woman was devastated to see her name in *The Washington Post*. I was wrong, insensitive to the fact that sharing with hundreds of thousands of readers was different from addressing a feminist convention or an enlightened audience at an art gallery. I deeply regretted hurting the young woman and complicating her life. I didn't sleep well for a long time after I learned how upset she was. Perhaps today's widespread acceptance of all diversity in America will ease her pain.

One of my personal challenges during the early days of column writing, before I left Sam, was how to balance my job, family, and home. I used to joke that I carved up my time like a chef slicing a roast beef at lunchtime. I researched, interviewed people for, and wrote two columns a week, met deadlines, attended meetings, and composed talks. I tried to support my husband's upwardly spiraling art career, help raise our children, who ranged in ages by then from mid- to late teens, and supervise our home. The demands on my time were real, not a joke, and they finally caught up with me.

After an unusually busy day on Good Friday in 1980, when we had fifteen artists visiting from out of town for lunch, I had rushed to the office to tinker with my Saturday column and polish off the one for Monday's paper. The next day, I became ill with flu-like symptoms and spent a couple of days in bed. A friend suggested I needed to go to the doctor, and Sam took me to the Group Health Association. The doctors there at first thought it was the flu but suggested that I needed to go to the hospital for further evaluation. It turned out that fibrous scar tissue from a decade-old surgery had wedged its wicked way into my small intestine, obstructing the passage of food and drink. I later underwent surgery. I was off from work for five weeks, and the paper ran a line saying I was ill and the column would resume when I returned.

I had a lot to learn about self-care in the midst of towering responsibilities. Being sick and getting well made me swallow my pride and ask for help—I needed friends and relatives as never before. It made me realize how fortunate I was to have health insurance and a liberal leave policy when millions have neither. It made me want to write about the plight of the poor even more. Meanwhile, I saw my family anew and savored life's gifts. Sickness was hell, but wellness was a great feeling. I was pleased to get back to work after my illness and found the newsroom was as drama-ridden as ever.

As a columnist, I was autonomous, not having to clear my ideas with editors. But I was physically in the same huge, open news-room with reporters and editors. It was there that I saw more of Milton Coleman, a black reporter who had come to the paper in 1976, while I was still in the Style section. He covered local politics and government and was every inch the tough reporter who used his skills, background, and race to his advantage and succeeded

Denton as the new city editor in 1980 after Denton became a foreign correspondent.

Coleman made his mark early in Mayor Barry's first term, in 1979. When a late-February snowstorm closed the city for a day, with many streets impassable, the problem was exacerbated by poor snow removal. Barry invited Coleman to ride with him on a tour of the city. Everything is under control, Barry said as his chauffeured car drove down major arteries that were passable. "It's not a crisis," the mayor remarked. Coleman pressed him about people digging out cars only to have plows block them again.

"How would they get to work?" Coleman asked him.

Barry responded, "Take a bus."

Coleman said, "Buses aren't running."

"Well, Milton, they can walk," Barry retorted sharply.

Reporting the conversation on the front page of *The Washington Post* just the way the mayor had spoken touched off an early firestorm against Barry, who was cast as hard-hearted. Some black Washingtonians criticized Coleman for putting the mayor in a bad light. But I knew he was just being a hard-hitting journalist.

Another newcomer to *The Washington Post* was twenty-six-year-old Janet Cooke. She was hired as a reporter and placed on the District Weekly, which was often the first place young black city reporters were placed and which Cooke later called a ghetto. These reporters were primarily general assignment reporters. I was friendly with her but didn't know her well and was shocked when she wrote an "enterprise" story entitled "Jimmy's World," about an eight-year-old boy named Jimmy addicted to heroin, in the fall of 1980. An "enterprise" story is one initiated by the reporter as opposed to being assigned by an editor. The black community was up in arms, horrified! Police launched a search across the city for the boy, and Mayor Barry declared Jimmy was in treatment and known to city officials. His office later withdrew the statement, the police stopped their dragnet, calling the story a fraud. People inside and outside *The Washington Post* cast doubt on the story. The tension inside the newsroom was thick. My colleague Courtland Milloy was sure the story was a hoax, and a copy editor supposedly had warned colleagues the story wasn't true. Nevertheless, *The Washington Post* nominated her for the 1981 Pulitzer Prize, and she won the coveted national award the next spring. But the story and her career unraveled shortly after the announcement, when her former editors at *The Toledo Blade* noticed discrepancies in her biography. It took more than eleven hours of grilling by several top editors, including Coleman, the city editor, to get her to admit she had made up the story. *The Washington Post* returned the Pulitzer Prize. Baffled by what motivated her, I worried this incredible incident would overturn the work journalists of color were doing to increase diversity in the media. I wrote a hard-hitting column on April 18, 1981 that began

JANET COOKE is a brilliant, cunning mastermind and she happens to be black.

She committed the perfect crime. It was too perfect, in fact.

She concocted a story that fooled almost all of the people, a tale that was so compelling that it spun this community on its ear as has no local story that I can remember and shone light on a serious problem. It catapulted her journalistic career toward the stars. That height—the Pulitzer Prize—eventually was her downfall. If she had not won the prize, for years to come Washingtonians—the believers and the scoffers—would have talked about "Jimmy's World"—and Janet Cooke.

In 1996, *Washington Post* media writer Howard Kurtz wrote about Cooke when she resurfaced in an attempt to try to resurrect her writing career. Kurtz described her as the "author of the most notorious journalistic hoax in modern history [now] working in a Kalamazoo, Mich., department store for $6 an hour." Cooke got her former boyfriend Mike Sager to write a sympathetic article about her for GQ magazine, in which she said she had become an inveterate liar as a child to appease her tough and stingy father and later to get the things she wanted in life. Sager's story ignited a bidding war in Hollywood for a movie about her that never materialized. Bradlee told editors at a convention that she had never apologized to him or the newspaper. I eventually felt sorry for this badly impaired woman and hoped she would have an opportunity for redemption and restoration, which every human being deserves—but probably not as a journalist.

At the time, the Janet Cooke episode was especially exasperating because I felt in constant battle in the column with stereotypes of black families. "Jimmy's World" perpetuated the false labels. I often used the column to teach the history of some stereotypes about black families and to explain why they were so disproportionately impoverished compared to white families. I examined how in the 1960s, Daniel P. Moynihan's widely publicized report "The Negro Family: A Case for National Action" had cited figures on illegitimacy, broken homes, crime, and narcotics addiction to conclude that black poverty stemmed from a weak family structure, not institutionalized racism. His solution was benign neglect. Among African American social critics, Albert Murray called Moynihan's report "a notorious example of the use of the social science survey as a propaganda vehicle to promote a negative image of black life in the United States" and the "stuff of which the folklore of white supremacy is made."

In the summer of 1982, Ken Auletta's book The Underclass looked at street criminals, hustlers, long-term welfare recipients, and the homeless, drawing on the academic debate over poverty. He concluded vaguely that some members of the "underclass" would benefit from attempts to help them more than others and those on the bottom are to be helped one at a time. Both men denied any effect of institutionalized racism and white privilege, which the country had practiced for centuries.

A black professor, James Turner of Cornell University, called this the pathogenic model—the vicious notion that Blacks are afflicted with some kind of pathology that modern socioeconomic medicine can't cure. I agreed with Turner when he said the essential issue with Auletta, as with Moynihan, was that many white social scientists define black reality as lifestyle and behavior and overlook the second dimension, "the structural disadvantage put on black people by the American economic system which keeps many at the bottom."

I agreed with the sociologists that America has always shown this preference to view reality filtered through the prism of its own cultural values, which tended to include institutionalized racism. America is more comfortable that way. White scholars tend to forget where Blacks began: as descendants of people enslaved for 250 years who hadn't received any reparations—not even the promised forty acres and a mule—and were subjected to a century of Jim Crow laws supporting segregation in jobs and housing. Such scholars prefer to look at where Blacks are now—and then dub them deviants because they are not on par with white norms. I agreed with the black social scientists and fumed at the blindness of white writers who failed to talk about the elephant in the living room.

Despite criticism from other editors, readers, and reporters, Ben Bradlee gave me fairly free rein and only once in the entire nineteen years I worked under him called me into his office to question an opinion column. It was for a column I wrote when members of the Ku Klux Klan marched in Washington in late November 1982. I was so outraged that I defended the rioting that erupted in protest.

I knew the lynchings, murders, and hatred against black people the Klan perpetrated. I had seen the faces of people in Mississippi who had lived with the lynching trees and in fear of these hooded cowards.

Here's some of what I wrote in a column headlined, "Outrage":

> The 36 Klansmen who showed up to rally here on Saturday looked impotent when you consider the Klan's vaunted history of lynching and violence. But the counter protesters, many times the minuscule numbers of the Klan, sent a message of strong resolve: certain vulgarities, such as the appearance of the KKK, just won't be tolerated in the nation's capital.
>
> It is unfortunate that the anti-Klan demonstrators became angry when they were denied a confrontation with the white-sheeted purveyors of hate and subsequently vented their fury on the most available symbol—police authority. But it should be remembered that the crowd was orderly until its members were denied what they considered was their right to confront the Klan. Before that time, the protest was carried out in the orderly mode of the '60s civil rights movement, with speeches and singing and banners.
>
> The looting did no credit to the anti-Klan movement....But it would be a mistake, I think, to let the looting and police battling detract from the central theme of the day: The masses were outraged at the Klan's presence and would not let the Klansmen flaunt it in their faces.

The rioters' destruction of private property was not defensible. *Washington Post* readers were outraged at my position. I'm sure Bradlee got many calls criticizing me, but he was cool. He said if he had seen the column in advance, he would have asked me to rethink it because he thought my stance was ill considered. I sat across from him when he politely chewed me out but gave no memorable response.

★   ★   ★

In a reorganization of the newsroom, columnists were given offices, and in July 1982, I received a prized possession I had not sought but appreciated. I was able to move from a desk in the middle of the vast, open, desk-filled space to a small, glass-enclosed office. Despite an occasional longing for the newsroom bustle at deadline time, it brought several unexpected benefits. My little office provided the privacy to tap into my own thoughts, uninterrupted by the fragments of ideas, stories, conversations, and gossip that fly about in newsrooms, and I could better interview experts, discuss ideas with sources, and develop columns.

During this embryonic stage of my column-writing years I separated from Sam, becoming an independent woman in 1982. As I reached midlife, separating from my husband after a twenty-year marriage, when all our daughters were in college or soon would be, my career at *The Washington Post* was going well, although I was neither the best writer nor the smartest person in the newsroom. I had participated in and been affected by the great revolutions of the 1960s, 1970s, and 1980s—in civil rights, women's liberation, and technology. They were causing earthquakes in the cultural, social, economic, educational, and civic life of all Americans. And in the religious/spiritual sphere, too. No doubt the Civil Rights Movement affected me most deeply. Growing up in the segregated South, I had swallowed some of the mentally toxic Kool-Aid of white America about black inferiority, although the teachings of my family, church, community, black schools, and colleges and the Negro press substantially diluted that toxicity. Some of the lies I had ingested were countered by the victory of the brave men and women I personally encountered in the civil rights revolution. Intellectually, I appreciated the black church in which I had come of age, and I loved the Rev. Dr. Martin Luther King Jr. Yet I still avoided traditional religion, although even in this "up" period of my life, I felt a spiritual yearning.

The women's movement surprisingly became a spiritual well-spring within me. I appreciated and benefitted from the leadership of the brilliant Gloria Steinem and other white feminists but didn't identify as a feminist because racism was my priority. Racial discrimination impacted males and females. Black men had been special targets of hundreds of years of oppression, and I could not shut out their need for liberation, although I recognized that, as great as the Civil Rights Movement was, it hadn't addressed black male sexism. I read Alice Walker's 1983 essay collection *In Search of Our Mothers' Gardens*. Walker's term "womanism" better reflected my beliefs than "feminism" because it was more inclusive. Walker embraces the category of black women who have always worked and whose goals differed from those of white women. When theologians like Delores S. Williams, whom I met when we both worked as young reporters at *The Louisville Defender* in the early 1950s, R. Ruth Barton, Raquel St. Clair and Renita Weems developed a spiritual dimension to "womanism," I began to experience a spiritual epiphany. Theirs was an approach to ethics, theology, and life rooted in the experiences of African American women, expanding the black theology formulated by James Cone.

In my column, it was important to me to show ordinary people in the city with their goals for their lives, their families, and the city. People like Joyce Taylor: When she learned that the two young children of a family friend needed a home, she didn't just talk about it, she did something. Acting quickly to take the children into her own three-bedroom Hyattsville apartment, the divorced mother of a seventeen-year-old son also went to court to become their legal guardian. I wrote:

> Such acts of Good Samaritan caring are extraordinary in today's world where self-glorification reigns and concern for others is sadly

lacking. Moreover, how many people, having raised their own children, would be willing to take on the responsibility of raising two girls, ages 3 and 6? But such considerations never entered the mind of Taylor, 40, a telephone operator in the newsroom at *The Washington Post*. "I honestly didn't think about it twice," said Taylor. "I know how kids suffer in this city. Somebody had to take those children who would really care about them. It was that simple."

And I wanted to show people like Dr. John Lewis McAdoo, whom I wrote about in May 1987 in "From Shame to Triumph":

The audience before which he stood, the TRI-Services National Institute of Dyslexia, had just awarded him the Margaret Byrd Rawson achievement prize given annually to dyslexic adults for outstanding accomplishments. As the audience at the awards dinner applauded briskly, some people were moved to tears for the first black recipient of that award. But for McAdoo, an authority on the family and an associate professor at the University of Maryland School of Social Work in Baltimore, the honor for which he had been nominated by a friend had another meaning. "By saying this in public...it's saying that in spite of this you can still be somebody." Indeed, getting to be "somebody" was no easy task for McAdoo. Growing up in Detroit, McAdoo was placed in a class for mentally retarded students because he could not read. Luckily for McAdoo, the class for retarded children was taught by a "very patient" special-education teacher who recognized that he was not retarded. There were not many children in the class, so she had time to teach McAdoo to read. And McAdoo had a secret weapon: his mother. She became paralyzed when he was 7 years old but was nonetheless determined to raise her children. She encouraged him to do his best despite his frustration. "She could sense when I was down, and she would sing and tell me stories or send me to

the store to buy her a murder mystery. I never came back with the
same book twice."

McAdoo's father worked two jobs to care for the family and pay
his wife's hospital bills. McAdoo received a bachelor's degree from
Eastern Michigan University and a master's in social work and a
doctorate in educational psychology from the University of Michigan. He and his wife, Harriett McAdoo, a professor at the Howard
University School of Social Work, have four children; each of their
three boys has inherited some elements of McAdoo's dyslexia. The
couple has worked diligently with the children at home, monitored
their school behavior and found experts to help them. The three
oldest children either attend college or are recent graduates. Since
moving to the District from Columbia a few years ago, McAdoo
said, he has found the city's facilities for working with dyslexic
children deficient as he has sought help for his youngest son,
David, 14.

I tried to look for solutions and hope in my columns and wrote
one prompted by a telephone call from a woman I knew who was
angry:

The black middle class has failed the poor, she began. "Teachers,
social workers, ministers, doctors, lawyers, you name it."

"I'm blaming us for failing to transmit to the poor the same psychological attitude that our parents, teachers and ministers transmitted to us—the message that, in spite of discrimination, we can
accomplish things and we are responsible for our actions," she said.

It was the message that had carried us in the past, when we
were alone and scorned and ignored. But it had been forgotten, by
the middle class as well as the poor, in the past 20 years, forgotten as many took advantage of long, long overdue help from the
government.

"We need to rekindle that attitude now more than ever," she said.

We made a date to talk about her feelings in detail. In the meantime, I reflected on the now classic reports and statistical analyses that were already depressingly familiar.

Take the case of black children as outlined in Marian Wright Edelman's book, "Portrait of Inequality." Millions of them, all crippled by faltering self-confidence, by discouragement, by despair, by rage, growing up in deplorable housing and the basest poverty, fighting themselves and ill health and poor education. Seemingly helpless.

When we finally sat down together, I mentioned the Edelman statistics. I pointed out to her they existed because of government assistance that had helped to lift some black children out of poverty in the late '60s, help that was transferred to other segments of the population in the '70s.

The social programs helped some, I said, but not enough. We had needed more. Now, it seemed, the programs that remained, such as Head Start, maternal and child health care and vocational education, faced substantial cuts.

How could this be the fault of the black middle class?

"Maybe now we can see that some of those social programs were good and bad," she said. "They transmitted the notion to the poor that their total salvation would come from outside themselves. They didn't transmit the idea that along with the welfare check came the responsibility for trying to move off the welfare rolls."

Now, I'm a big believer in black self-help, but I've always felt it must be combined with broad, thoughtful leadership and well-planned strategies from both the public and private sectors. But what with the public sector help apparently drying up, I had to admit it was looking more and more as if the only ones left to help the blacks were the blacks themselves.

She had a prescription. Middle class blacks, she argued, must actively become role models for the poor. It was, she said, not only the good and proper thing for us to do, but our responsibility as well.

We could begin in the workplace, she said. That's because the majority of black professionals work with other black people. We could fight the psychologically devastating message—"You can't achieve"—that has been routinely passed along to the poor with many of the public programs.

Black professionals, she said, could be communicating, "You can achieve."

Instead of "You are a people forever crippled," the professionals, by example and intent, should be communicating, "You are capable, not crippled."

Instead of, "You aren't good enough to make it," they should be communicating, "You are good enough, you do have the ability, you can succeed."

The black social worker who arranges for a check can also deliver a message of responsibility to those who will hear. School teachers can teach reading and pride at the same time to those who will listen. Doctors can deliver babies on Medicare and also birth control information. Ministers can undergird their pie-in-the-sky sermons with some gritty here-and-now advice.

In these hard times of shrinking opportunity and shrinking commitment to justice, black self-help can be mobilized in constructive and deeply meaningful ways. For, while the heat must never be taken off government to be fair and just and compassionate and to help, the private sector must not simply shrug and write off the Republican era as a lost four years.

There is a real danger in that attitude. If middle class blacks refuse this responsibility, they may end up as just empty window dressing—alone, caught between a society whose record of concern for blacks is at best open to question and a bedrock of poor blacks who scorn them as turncoats.

The message—pride, if you will—means not only pride in who we are but pride in what we do.

It is a message we should have never forgotten.

I was happy to see African Americans across the nation and supporters of other races rising in positive new ways. Representative John Conyers of Michigan had introduced a bill in Congress in 1979 to make the birthday of Martin Luther King Jr. a federal holiday and shortly afterward, Stevie Wonder released a song that swept America, "Happy Birthday," in support of the holiday. I wrote supporting columns, as on January 18, 1982, when thousands marched on the mall to honor Dr. King's birthday and urge Congress to make it a national holiday. President Reagan, not surprisingly, did not support the idea. Senator Jesse Helms insisted King had sympathized with Communists as a reason not to create the holiday, threatened a filibuster, and tried to open King's sealed FBI files. With a view toward upcoming elections, Reagan signed the bill on November 2, 1983, and King was granted an honor that had previously belonged only to George Washington and Abraham Lincoln.

As a black columnist, I took a position on so many different issues, and it was quite a responsibility. It was a high-wire act, and I was well aware there was a great diversity of opinions within the black community, but I saw my job as trying to set the debate, not just follow the crowd. In letters and phone calls, some readers told me I was too liberal and others complained I was not sufficiently conservative.

Some told me I moralized too much, as in the column that ignited a minor firestorm because I criticized Marvin Gaye for his song "Sexual Healing," released in 1982. "As an artist, he is tops," I wrote, "but the sex mania message on that record is about as subtle as hardcore porn." Some black men and women accused me of being a Goody Two-shoes. However, I knew that in 1979 in Washington, 55.6 percent of the nearly ten thousand babies born were born to unmarried women. About half of those babies were born to teenagers who hadn't set out to become mothers. I countered the criticism by writing a column to young men telling them to shoulder their responsibilities. I also wanted to show that single mothers were not just statistics but real people, as I wrote in "A Bootstrap Christmas Story" in December 1985:

Her name conjures up the image of a carefree French girl strolling along the Seine, but Lizette Buie, a stick of a woman, is, at 23, three times a mother. She enters the Christmas fantasyland that is the Hecht Co.'s new downtown flagship store with her children, a bit stiffly and soft-voiced. But when she calls out to the children to "Wait!" at the top of a down escalator, they stop at once.

To some people, a former teen-aged mother who has developed the strength to become a successful parent may seem an unlikely woman to applaud for growth and change, when we hear so much about the dismal statistics of D.C.'s teen-aged mothers. But in her mind, Lizette Buie is much, much more than a statistic.

Dressed in jeans, a blue jean jacket and sweatshirt with "Senators" emblazoned on the front, she strolls with confidence into the dignified store, past verdant green trees looped gracefully with glowing colors and luscious ornaments. With her children, she walks along carpeted, curving shopping bays.

It's a confidence Buie did not always have. After becoming pregnant at 16, Buie dropped out of high school and was, by 19, a confused mother of two. When she walked into the Center for Youth Services (CYS), a local nonprofit agency offering psychiatric counseling, employment and educational services and training, she was bitter and hostile. But with the supportive counseling of CYS, at 921

Pennsylvania Ave. SE, she passed her high school equivalency test. "Amidst all her conflicts—and she had many," said CYS Director Myra Wesley King, "There has always been a quest for improvement and a desire for her kids to do better—in terms of their physical care and exposing them to education and activities."

It was important to chronicle African American advancements and challenges, as in a column, "Blacks as Entrepreneurs," in November 1985 about Roderick K. Gaines:

In his 14 years with Trans World Airlines, Gaines went from ticket agent to vice president of a district that generated $135 million annually. Three years ago, Gaines chose to abandon corporate America and become an entrepreneur. He now is developing a variety of products and, according to him, he is not alone in this trend. "Black people are at an interesting point of their history," he says. "They now know their futures are not wedded to white corporations, and the opportunities are not there, either." Gaines, addressing a panel on capital formation, mentioned his reason for leaving the corporate world almost in an aside. "I was looking for growth opportunity, for more to do with my talent and energy," he says. "So I was willing to give up material security for the opportunity to grow." That sentiment turned out to be one of the recurrent informal themes of a minority business associations conference. In one sense, this trend results from a growing understanding of one of the realities of corporate America:

Only the luckiest few blacks who make it into middle management in the first place can ever hope to rise to a level beyond assistant vice president or perhaps vice president.

I also took on the mainstream media when I felt it was appropriate or necessary to do so. For example, I bemoaned lingering issues that divided people in the greater Washington community and across America in late 1980, in "Violent Crime du Jour Is a Wrong Approach":

> The [Washington] Star's new front-page feature entitled "Today's Violent Local Crime"—usually a thumbnail sketch of some grisly rape, beating or murder—strikes me as not only cheap and sensational but also potentially further divisive to the already taut social fabric in this town.
>
> This way of portraying crime has a terribly negative effect on the tone of the whole metropolitan area, and especially the city, and it feeds the fear, terror and paranoia that people already have. It plays to the kind of alienation that divides a city and Lord knows, we have paranoia enough. One confirmed anti-handgun resident speaks now of carrying a giant flashlight—in effect, a club—when strolling the streets of his quiet neighborhood.

The Washington Star, a long-running afternoon newspaper and competitor to *The Washington Post*, closed its doors for the last time in 1981. I regretted seeing it die as I believed it was better for readers for the town to have two daily newspapers.

I also wrote about the importance of training minority journalists like Luis J. Rodriguez for U.S. newsrooms. He decided he wanted to be a reporter after a Latino reporter, Ruben Salazar, was killed covering his people's suffering. Through the Summer Program for Minority Journalists, he achieved his goal. Rodriguez said, "This program has given us a way to begin to do something for our community within a newspaper environment."

I felt it was crucial to have more African American decision makers and managers in television news. In the mid-1980s, of the 762 commercial television stations in the country, only three had black general managers and only three had black station managers. I kept that issue before the public.

One huge incident at *The Washington Post*, in September 1986, left me terribly conflicted. *The Washington Post* was picketed several days by groups of community protesters including some outstanding black citizens and representatives of black and white organizations. They vehemently objected to the first issue of the redesigned *Washington Post* magazine, which featured a long story on New York rap singer Joseph (Just Ice) Williams, who was charged with the murder of a Washington area drug dealer. The community wanted the paper to recall the magazine because it chose to focus on a stereotypical, negative depiction of Blacks.

My struggle was that I cared about both the community and the newspaper. My heart sank when I saw the story because it sent out distorted messages, and in my column I quoted one protester who expressed my views exactly when she said, "Our kids don't need to believe the way you get publicity is antisocial behavior."

Because I knew how important journalists of color were to the community, I often wrote about the internal struggles of the excellent ones like J. C. Hayward and Maureen Bunyan when they had behind-the-scenes challenges with contracts at their stations. I objected once when a local show was canceled to make way for a national one, *The Oprah Winfrey Show*.

At *The Washington Post*, more younger minority reporters were being hired and promoted, and I was happy to see a new generation of journalists emerging. One of the bright lights who impressed me right away was Gwen Ifill, who came to *The Washington Post* in 1984. She was promoted quickly to the national staff, the most prestigious section. Ifill was later hired away from *The Washington Post* by *The New York Times* and honed her extraordinary talent covering the Jesse Jackson presidential campaign in 1984.

Jesse Jackson's presidential run was historic, controversial, and riddled with questions of meaning. The first African American man to run for president, he was preceded by Representative

Shirley Chisholm, a New York Democrat who was the first black presidential aspirant and first female of any race to toss her hat into the ring. Jackson awakened the slumbering black vote. For the first time, African Americans could see themselves mattering in the political sphere.

I was surprised when *The Washington Post*'s Milton Coleman reported that Jackson had privately referred to Jews as "hymies"—an old slur—and to New York City as "Hymietown." It was a horrible and racist statement that did not at all reflect widespread attitudes of Blacks toward Jews. Controversy arose as to whether Jackson had said it, over Coleman's role in making the remark public, and over black reporters' obligations to report on black politicians. Some African Americans questioned whether a black journalist should have "snitched" on a revered black leader. I certainly thought black journalists should report fair and balanced stories on black newsmakers, but I also knew some reporters did not report on the after-hours peccadillos of U.S. presidents. Should black journalists report on off-the-record comments of black politicians, holding them to a higher standard?

Coleman later wrote an article for Outlook, *The Washington Post*'s Opinion section, and then gave an interview to *The American Journalism Review*. He said he was talking directly to Jackson, though the rules of the conversation were unclear. Many black reporters thought it was a betrayal and others thought it was breaking journalism rules. Coleman would later become a sensitive, wise man in the newsroom and beyond, one to whom I would turn for career advice.

In 1985, IJE expanded its training efforts once again and introduced a management program at Northwestern University under the leadership of the industrious Ellis Cose. With IJE's full plate of programs and challenges, I became chair of the board in 1985.

From the beginning, IJE had a multiracial board and was recruiting and training Asian Americans, Hispanic Americans, and Native Americans, as well as African Americans. Our founders included two white journalists, Aarons, who was Jewish, and Stovall, a son of the South, and they had tremendous impact in those early days. As a woman from the segregated South, I must admit I was slow to embrace the concept of a multiethnic society. However, I came to know the risks other journalists were taking and how they dealt with diversity issues. Somehow, this education and realization became a breakthrough in how I viewed diversity and the issues all racial and ethnic groups shared. They were what we had in common, even while each group celebrated its distinctions and culture.

Ellis Cose, president of IJE from 1983 to 1986, introduced new research on mobility within the industry and published it as an article in 1985 entitled "The Quiet Crisis: Minority Journalists and Newsroom Opportunity." Cose found reporters' numbers were barely moving. What was equally disturbing was that 40 percent of working journalists said they didn't see promotions in their future and were planning to leave the business. "Blacks were leaving at a faster rate than whites, and there was enormous frustration about seriously thinking about management careers," said Cose. Simmering in different parts of the country were actions that made people leave the business and others go to court. We all watched the developments in the lawsuit that four black journalists had filed against *The New York Daily News*. The case went to court in 1987. The reporters' lawyers argued that their race had prevented any advances in their careers. The decision was that *The Daily News* had discriminated.

Another study pinpointed lack of retention as a serious barrier to advancement. Senior editors were white and male. Cose proposed that IJE offer a management fellowship and for the first time, white women and men attended the resulting IJE program so they also could see the need for diversity and put those practices into their newsrooms. I confess I was initially uneasy about the inclusion of white journalists. I thought we were moving away from our fundamentals. Montiel, a staunch board member, was one of my guides to the reordered priorities. The idea of having more diverse newsrooms was to have more content that was accurate with white professionals and journalists of color learning side by side. Overall, one thousand people participated in IJE's residential programs. The institute's reporting program closed in 1990, with a twenty-year record and 275 graduates. One of the reasons for the shutdown was that individual newspapers had started their own training programs, based on our model.

With our gains and setbacks, sometimes I felt journalists of color were fighting the fight alone. But I was wrong. Out there, people were monitoring the fits and starts in the industry and, particularly, its treatment of minorities reporting and making the news. San Francisco State University started the Center for Integration/Improvement of Journalism, which had a media-monitoring component. Certainly, I cheered when in 1990 Eddie N. Williams, the president of the Joint Center for Political and Economic Studies, raised an alarm. Seeing all the political implications of a lack of diversity in the media, he called for another Kerner Commission.

The time was right for me to go outside the newsroom and reflect on the fight for diversity. The entire media was undergoing tremendous change. Newspapers were on the brink of a new era, losing some readers and uncertain about what the newspaper of the future would look like. Events were moving fast. In 1991, I received a fellowship at the Gannett Center for Media Studies at Columbia University. A book on diversity in the media had been my goal, but I soon realized I had better channel my own ideas through direct action. A book wouldn't do it. Annoyance with media leaders who came to the forums in New York pushed me to think harder about my own role. Some who had the power to green light a more diverse media were negative and showed a blatant lack of interest in diversity; they displayed irritation toward me, one of two African Americans in the fellows group, for bringing up the subject. When I raised diversity, it was as if I had brought a skunk into the room. Their primary interest was the Internet, which was then called the Information Superhighway. One of the fellows was developing what would become the iPad. Many were involved in technology, and one was writing a book. There appeared to be little interest in diversity.

Several factors cemented my next moves. Dr. Alexander Lowen, a psychiatrist, urged me to think about how to effect change. The irrepressible Sheila Brooks, a former television journalist who started her own production company, suggested I run for an NABJ office. Then I had a long conversation with NABJ president Tom Morgan of *The New York Times*, a colleague and advisor, who urged me to run for vice president for print of NABJ. Tom said learning the organization and the players was a solid first step, and I would be creating a record of activism. It was wise counsel. I certainly hadn't been silent, having served as a founding member of the IJE board since 1977 and then IJE board chair since 1985, all while judiciously agitating for diversity in my own newsroom.

I turned my activism to the NABJ, running for and winning the office of vice president for print in 1991, and then the job of president of NABJ in 1993. Some who had been in NABJ since the very beginnings in 1975, raised questions about my commitment. Most knew my name and my body of work, but I had been on the outskirts of NABJ, concentrating on IJE. Some thought I was riding on my reputation but hadn't paid my dues inside the NABJ circles. Tom had warned me about these hazards. All the objections only made me vow to work even harder. I wanted to give the organization the benefit of my thirty years of experience as a pioneering journalist and survivor of many battles in civil rights, reporting, and leadership. I saw my role in NABJ as a two-way street; I would both share my experience with others and achieve my own personal growth.

NABJ had its challenges and internal debates. One question was whether the media should sponsor our events. Would media dollars temper our ability to criticize their records on race issues, or was it a natural revenue stream? It was my challenge to let the broader media know that diversity was an important ethical and financial issue. I also wanted to know the views of NABJ members. As vice president for print, I supervised a report on African American journalists' views about the civil unrest in Los Angeles that followed the police beating of Rodney King. Right before my election as president in 1993, I coordinated a survey and issued a report entitled "Muted Voices: Frustration and Fear in the Newsroom." Wanda Lloyd, then a top editor at *USA Today*, worked with her statisticians compiling the numbers of black journalists who were so frustrated that they were in actual pain during the day and plotted to walk out on their jobs. One striking result was on the question of whether white managers thought Blacks were less likely to be considered for career advancement. The white managers didn't see race as an obstacle, with only 2 percent saying it was a problem; 73 percent of black respondents said the obstacle was real. That study, which included statistics and narratives, became a blueprint to understanding why black journalists were frustrated and leaving the field, creating retention problems for media companies. We presented the findings at NABJ's Houston convention that summer and received coverage from the local papers. Pushing for inclusion of African Americans into mainstream media remained at the forefront of NABJ's mission, and mine. In a way, my career was coming full circle—learning from mentors, like L. Alex Wilson and Simeon Booker from the black press, becoming a mentor myself, and now representing all my black colleagues in the media on a national platform. I wanted to be armed with data.

At NABJ, I was deeply committed to reaching out to the younger members, who hadn't been through the battles of my pioneering generation. I wanted to be a bridge for them, as my mentors in the Negro press had been for me. During the campaign, a Young Professionals for Gilliam group popped up. I was pleased and somewhat amused at that. Retha Hill, a pioneering online editor for *The Washington Post*, had organized the group. Hill later became vice president for content for BET Interactive, the online affiliate of Black Entertainment Television, and joined the journalism faculty at Arizona State University in 2007.

I served as NABJ president from 1993 to 1995. It wasn't easy. Outside the organization, diversity gains were slow. ASNE reported in 1994 that 10.9 percent of the country's journalists were minorities. It wasn't proportionality, but many publishers and editors praised that benchmark, which had increased from 4 percent in 1978. We were far, far from proportionally represented in the media. In 1994, there were only twenty ranking editors or executive editors of color at 1,600 newspapers. (In 1998, the ASNE board renewed its commitment but acknowledged a slower pace than expected and adjusted the goal to the year 2025. In 2015, the ASNE census found 12.76 percent of newsroom employees were minorities. Surely, a forty-seven-year plan was achievable!)

While serving at NABJ, I also had a personal loss. Bob Maynard died from prostate cancer in 1993. Following his years at *The Washington Post*, his laboratory had been *The Oakland Tribune*, which he bought in 1983, a landmark purchase. *The Tribune* became the first African American–owned major metropolitan newspaper. The paper earned national praise and a Pulitzer for its coverage of the 1989 earthquake in the Bay Area. Bob built the most diverse newsroom in the country. He sold *The Tribune* in 1992, the year before he died. Even with the demands of running a newspaper and during the worst days of his illness, Bob was so dedicated to our goals that we had IJE meetings in his Oakland home. He had continued to travel for our diversity work. I fondly remember our dinners in Washington gave him the opportunity to do some people watching. He always had a good story. When he died at age fifty-six, it was a profound loss for the industry. Media diversity lost a champion with his death, and I lost a friend and confidant. We renamed IJE the Robert C. Maynard Institute for Journalism Education (MIJE) in his honor.

As NABJ president, I knew I needed my own "kitchen cabinet" to advise me on the details of leadership, help me maximize my good points, and protect me from my weaknesses. Wanda Lloyd advised me to get help organizing my time and my office. She brought an extremely helpful executive coach, Emily Barnes, into my life. I also asked Donald Graham, *The Washington Post* publisher, if he would meet with me regularly and give me an old pro's advice, as well as financial support. He agreed, and we went to lunch on a regular basis. On taking office, my overarching goal was getting ready for the Unity Convention in 1994 in Atlanta, a joint gathering with the Hispanic, Asian, and Native American journalist organizations. The conference had been approved before my tenure. Unity was the brainchild of Will Sutton, a past president of NABJ, and Juan Gonzalez, a past president of the National Association of Hispanic Journalists (NAHJ), who had come up with the idea while working at rival newspapers in Philadelphia. Sutton later became the deputy managing editor at *The News & Observer* in Raleigh, North Carolina, and editor of *The Gary Post-Tribune* in Indiana. After leaving Philadelphia, Gonzalez wrote a prize-winning column for many years at *The New York Daily News* and was an anchor for *Democracy Now!*, on the Pacifica network.

It was extremely important that this first summit, which would be under the microscope for many reasons, be successful. The joint effort was initially controversial, especially within NABJ. Sidmel Estes-Sumpter, the first female NABJ president and my predecessor, as well as an outspoken leader and Emmy Award–winning producer at WAGA-TV, was skeptical about the multi-cultural meeting. Even though NABJ was the largest contingent, she argued that the power of black journalists might be diluted, and others took her view seriously. She felt that black people were losing out as diversity efforts increasingly focused on Hispanics. At the time, the NABJ was a stronger organization than NAHJ. Deep cultural conflicts surfaced. The other organizations raised questions. The Native American journalists, for instance, objected to the meeting location in Atlanta because the city's baseball team, the Atlanta Braves, perpetuated negative stereotypes of Native Americans. Some of the other journalists objected to the location because Atlanta was internationally known as the "black capital."

My stand was that we were all underrepresented, the media was covering no one's community adequately, we should work together on what we had in common, and there was room for all of us under the media canopy. My role was mediator, handling personality conflicts and legitimate objections among Unity's leadership.

With all sides still not agreeing, I urged all the organization heads to sit down together before our memberships saw how divided we were. With an emergency grant from the McCormick Foundation, we attended a weekend retreat, with Dr. Ronald Brown, a highly respected African American consultant, as the facilitator. The Atlanta chapter, with Sidmel coordinating, took the lead, and we put the public survival of the organizations above our squabbles. In the end, Sidmel, who lived and worked in Atlanta, organized a memorable and historic meeting.

The 1994 Unity Convention was a vast billboard for diversity. Six thousand members of the media attended Unity in 1994, many leaving with new allies. Common ground, indeed. Quieting the critics who thought diversity applied only to black journalists was one of my goals. Gayle Pollard-Terry, a former reporter and editorial writer for *The Boston Globe, The Miami Herald,* and *The Los Angeles Times,* recalled my role. "You spoke about diversity being like the colors of the crayons in the big box. You led that battle in the face of members who thought diversity should only include black people. Some thought Hispanics, Asians, Native Americans and gays were taking advantage of what Black Americans had fought for without having a sense of solidarity," she said, in words that humbled me and reminded me how much I had grown from the days when I had believed diversity meant only Blacks.

Three of the four presidents of the Unity organizations were employed by *The Washington Post* newspaper or other Post holdings. Evelyn Hsu, president of the Asian American Journalists Association, and I worked at *The Washington Post.* Evelyn was also a member of the MIJE board and served as co-director with Martin G. Reynolds of the Maynard Institute. Diane Alverio, president of NAHJ, was a reporter for WFSB-TV in Connecticut, then owned by the Post-Newsweek stations. The fourth was Paul DeMain, president of the Native American Journalists Association, who worked for *News from Indian Country.*

At Unity, we hosted an exciting panel entitled "The Journalists of the Future." We all had our eyes on the impact of technology and were figuring out the role of journalists. Leonard Downie Jr., the managing editor of *The Washington Post;* Joel Dreyfuss, who had been a reporter for several publications, in addition to *The*

Washington Post, and editor of high-tech magazines, acknowledged that websites were another way to get the stories out. But at what cost? The audience wondered if their jobs were at stake. Downie said more jobs were being created and in-depth reporting wasn't disappearing. Prescient, Dreyfuss agreed that the emerging technology would make it easy to distribute new types of information and would expand the vision of journalists, but it was also creating a hazardous line between reporting and opinion.

Unity had life, and other meetings followed. Mark Trahant, former editor of the editorial page of *The Seattle Post-Intelligencer* and former IJE board chair, who is a Native American, reminded me that I wanted to start an archive of Unity's history so no one would reinvent programs. Successful conventions under the Unity banner were held in 1999 in Seattle; 2004 in Washington, D.C.; and 2008 in Chicago. What we learned from the Unity format was that the industry representatives, particularly the recruiters, took the effort seriously. The joint presence of the different groups created a stir within the newspaper and broadcast industries. From the journalist attendees' perspectives, they could meet more of their peers from around the country and listen to their views in workshops about concerns they all shared. We certainly had laid the groundwork. Gone were the days when black reporters for the black press sat at a segregated table at court hearings!

Eventually Unity leaders discontinued their partnerships over governance and financial matters. However, in 2016 NABJ and NAHJ joined forces for a joint convention in Washington, D.C.

Hardly had the debates about the value and successes of Unity died down, when I was confronted with a furor that erupted around a former journalist in Philadelphia, Mumia Abu-Jamal, during the second year of my NABJ presidency. A radio journalist, Abu-Jamal had been a founding member of the Philadelphia Association of Black Journalists. He had been charged with the murder of a white police officer, William Faulkner, and condemned to death after a controversial trial. It was a national news story, and people debated what had occurred on a street at four a.m. when Abu-Jamal had come upon the scene as his brother, William Cook, was being arrested by Faulkner. The prosecution said— and the jury believed—that Abu-Jamal ran up behind Faulkner and shot him. After Faulkner fell to the ground, prosecutors said, Abu-Jamal shot him three more times in the face. As he collapsed, Faulkner spun around and shot Abu-Jamal in the chest, they said. Abu-Jamal's lawyers said his trial was a travesty of justice. They said his court-appointed attorney had been ill-prepared and had taken the case reluctantly and that the court had allocated only $150 to the defense for the investigation before the trial. Presiding over the trial was Judge Albert Sabo, a former member of the Fraternal Order of Police who, according to the NAACP Legal Defense and Education Fund, has put more people on death row than any other sitting American judge.

The last days of my NABJ presidency in 1995 were almost sidelined by the uproar over my executive decision to write in support of a new trial in my *Washington Post* column. Some in NABJ were furious, believing any level of advocacy was inappropriate for a journalism group. My training at Columbia related to objective reporting had been combined with thirty years of reporting, writing, and editing. I had experienced the brutal days of the Civil Rights Movement and many other wrongs. I held journalistic standards in high esteem, but I was a journalist because I wanted to effect change. I felt that while objective reporting was important individually, as a journalism *organization*, we had power and could take a stand. A fellow NABJ member's life was at stake. I felt strongly that NABJ should send someone to the pretrial hearing and keep the membership informed. I contacted Don Williamson, then the editor of *The NABJ Journal*, to cover the hearing about a new trial and report back to the board. I paid his way through my NABJ presidential funds.

Among the membership, some worried that NABJ decisions on this controversial issue would put their jobs and organizations in jeopardy. Others thought I was pushing the whole organization to call for a new trial. As questions about my decisions became more intense, we held a preconvention board meeting in Philadelphia. The board decided not to take a stand on a new trial for Abu-Jamal, and several board members wanted to reprimand and censure me for authorizing the money for Williamson to attend the hearing. The reprimands didn't pass, but the time leading up to the convention was very tough. Abu-Jamal supporters picketed the NABJ convention. More than two decades later, at this writing, he is in prison and in declining health.

I never regretted my actions, but the Abu-Jamal incident helped me know I needed a prayer community. I had left behind the deep-faith community that my father had led during my growing up years. When Pamela L. McKee, former employee in the Clinton White House, employed at the time at *The Washington Post* as a temporary worker, invited me to a brunch at her home, the emotional part of faith that I needed so much was rekindled.

When I got there, a group of mostly Caribbean women were sitting on the floor of her living room talking about God. They shared concrete needs God had met and talked about things God had done. Their conversation made faith so tangible, so real. One woman talked about how her daughter was healed of cancer in the leg; she lost part of her leg, but God cured the cancer. I went back to the kitchen and asked Pamela, "Would you call some of these women together to explain to me what they are talking about?" She later invited those women and others to all come to her home with Bibles, and she started a prayer group. Pamela actually became my prayer partner. Having been a preacher's kid, growing up in the church, it felt like I was digging deeper into something that had started a long time before. It felt good. It felt comfortable. I could relate what was happening in my life to our spiritual talk at our prayer groups.

Faith had not actively figured in my work at The Washington Post. I was not writing about faith. Somewhere in the back of my head was a sense of foreboding about including faith in my columns or in my reporting, though I don't think it was explicitly forbidden by anyone. I would sometimes feature a well-known black minister or write about how I had spent Easter when I was a kid. I even wrote about my father's faith legacy, but I never explicitly included faith. I did not think faith was part of my life anymore, not necessarily guiding my life in any way. But the difficulties at NABJ brought me to my knees, and the prayer group—simply called The Group—became a sustaining part of my life, which would eventually lead me full circle back to my roots of faith.

Writing my column twice a week continued to be my main focus. Readers gave me a lot of feedback. I received dozens and dozens of letters. My perspectives angered some readers, many self-identifying as white, who challenged my positions and those of other African Americans I quoted. Their response ranged from a brief "You're an asshole," handwritten on a sheet from a tablet and postmarked Virginia, to frequent messages left on my telephone calling me the "N" word. In a neatly typed letter, a married woman from a Michigan suburb who had seen me on television, questioned if I knew what I was doing "repeating the tiresome litany of so-called victimization of women and minorities" and asked, "Do you not see that your reinforcement of portrayals of women and minorities as victims is just that, a self-fulfilling prophecy?" She declared, "You're a 'lightweight.'" I was charged by a reader with having a "biased, racist" viewpoint. I was told that I was supersensitive. "Lighten up," one reader said. Still another said I was "not facing black inadequacies."

In the mid-1980s, a syndicate picked up my twice-weekly column, and it ran in *The Philadelphia Daily News* and other papers for a brief time. I pondered whether it might be more widely distributed. I asked Vernon Jordan, whom I knew from various events, to lunch to give me advice about how to go from being a local to a national columnist. I wanted someone wise who could help me plan a strategy. To my surprise, he told me bluntly that I "had to be more conservative" to build a national following. That was not an option for me. My parents, community, church, black history professors like Lincoln University's Dr. Lorenzo Green, and the ancestors had put too much into me for me to adapt my views to fit the changing tide.

The decade of the 1980s had seen an increase in the number of black columnists, and I was thrilled that diversity in that part of the craft was growing. By 1992, more than forty black columnists worked at daily newspapers across America, and a group of seventeen of us gathered at Harvard University in December of that year to discuss the state of our craft and our place in it. Two of the most outstanding ones, DeWayne Wickham, columnist for *USA Today* and other Gannett-owned newspapers, and Les Payne, assistant managing editor for national and foreign news at *Newsday* and a columnist for the Los Angeles Times Syndicate, were behind the first official meeting of this group. Both Wickham and Payne were also founders and past presidents of the NABJ.

Those attending included Courtland Milloy and Donna Britt, both my colleagues at *The Washington Post*; Mark August of *The Tampa Tribune*; Wayne Dawkins of *The Courier Post* at Camden/ Cherry Hill, New Jersey; Gregory Freeman of *The St. Louis Post-Dispatch*; Derrick Jackson of *The Boston Globe*; Wiley Hall of *The*

Baltimore Sun; Sherman Miller of the black press and *The Wilmington News Journal*; Lorraine Montre of *The St. Louis Post-Dispatch*; Richard Prince of *The Rochester Democrat and Chronicle*; Kevin Blackistone of *The Dallas Morning News*; Betty Baye of *The Louisville Courier Journal*; Peggy Peterman of *The St. Petersburg Times*; and Norman Lockman of *The News Journal* in Wilmington, Delaware.

We organized formally as the Trotter Group, named for William Monroe Trotter, the great black editor of *The Boston Guardian*, a black publication. What spurred the meeting was presidential candidate and Arkansas governor Bill Clinton's campaign promise to Wickham and Derrick Jackson to end mistreatment of thousands of Haitian refugees being held at the U.S. Naval Base at Guantanamo Bay, Cuba. In his call to us, Wickham had invoked the words of H. L. Mencken: "The Negro leader of today is not free. He must look to white men for his very existence, and in consequence he has to waste a lot of his energy trying to think white. What the Negroes need is leaders who can and will think black." Wickham added: "Those who accepted the call to meet at Harvard understand that the craft of journalism is in dire need of black columnists who can and will think black."

As a black columnist whom readers and colleagues have often accused of only thinking black and focusing too much on race, I went to the meeting with joy in my step. I was happy to greet newcomers to the ranks and appreciated that our numbers were growing. Les Payne discussed the challenge of writing for dual audiences—writing for a predominantly white readership in a dominant society that has different assumptions and a different orientation and are likely to draw different conclusions from the same set of facts.

As black columnists, we had to construct, define, analyze, and dedicate our voices as an instrument for change, racial fairness, and empowerment. Our challenge was to "form a counterforce to the white viewpoint in the media," as A. J. Liebling once wrote. We were to encourage, empower, and develop the black viewpoint in the media so we could be proactive, not simply react to events.

A session on censorship reminded me of the subtle ways my disturbing columns were seemingly "hidden"—moved from the front of the section and placed on page 3 or, occasionally, deep inside the section.

The Trotter Group went on to interview President Bill Clinton twice, Vice President Al Gore, Secretaries of State Madeleine Albright, Colin Powell, and Condoleezza Rice, and former Zambian president Kenneth Kaunda. It has sent its members on fact-finding missions to Cuba and Grenada. I was pleased that new voices were emerging to shine a light on black struggles and triumphs, and I happily took part in Trotter Group activities when I could get away from the demands of my column.

My column-writing years were both some of the most rewarding and the most problematic of my life. I was forced to grow spiritually and emotionally. Despite the bold stances I took in my columns, I was at times at a spiritual low point, suffering mild depression, for which I saw a counselor. I wanted to change the world but I was still craving sweets and eating compulsively to help me cope with painful emotions. My life had become unmanageable, my weight ballooned yet again. I wondered if I would ever conquer the food challenges I'd battled since Daddy's last days. Then, my old friend Merle Goldberg from Columbia told me about an anonymous, free fellowship with people of different races, genders, atheists, agnostics, and religious folks. I was willing to take the prescribed steps to recover and I did. I went to my first meeting of the fellowship program for compulsive eaters three blocks from the newspaper and was shocked to see twelve skinny white women talking about their feelings and eating issues.

As I went to similar meetings of the fellowship in various parts of the metropolitan area, I found more diversity and learned that "retained hate is overweight." When I tapped into this anger against white people and was able to articulate it, I was eventually spurred to admit that I was powerless over a lot of things: food, people, places, events, emotions, racism, white supremacists, all of it! Continuing racism and the effect of it on my people is very, very painful for me. I gained insight into how I used food to deal with painful emotions. For example, I had made this journal entry in 1990, still fleeing from my feelings: "I eat chocolate as I watch Africa on television." I admitted my powerlessness and came back to conscious contact with God, a power greater than myself, who restored my sanity.

Through Pam and my prayer circle, I had started a daily routine of prayer and meditation, which continues to the present day. Still, something was missing in my life. In 1996, on New Year's Eve, I found myself in a small A.M.E. church on upper 14th Street N.W. where I knew no one. I wept and wept and wept. I knew then I needed to better rule and reign in my life. I knew being a part of a church was the place to learn how to do it. I returned to the A.M.E. Church partly because of the teachings of my father and my early church upbringing.

I remembered the talk about the importance of love. God is love. They hadn't been denying that oppression existed, but they taught that hate is harmful to the hater. My friend Margaret Springer, who became my sister-in-law, reminded me of our junior high school commute to the segregated school. We had to pass through a neighborhood where white kids lived, and they would throw rocks at us. It was so hard not to retaliate, but Margaret helped me recall the words our school teachers and our Sunday school teachers gave us to deal with it: "Do not hate them because that will diminish *us*." The humiliation I had felt when

I first joined *The Washington Post* when many of my colleagues wouldn't speak to me, the rejection and invisibility that I felt—these I hadn't let turn to hate. Somewhere within me I inherently knew that to hate would harm me. And now I knew that what was inherent was something spiritual, faith that I'd been given in those old A.M.E. churches. I needed a better understanding of who I was in God's larger plan, and guidance in all aspects of my life—relationships with family, friends, finances, and health. I wanted to be a blessing to others. From growing up in a church, I knew loving people would always be on my right and left to support me when I was weak. And I could do the same for someone else.

Despite this resolve, I did not join the little church I found myself in that night. I continued healing emotionally and spiritually, finding comfort in the words of one of my former ministers who said that sometimes years of stepping away from traditional religion can be very helpful. We returners can be much more devout than people who stay the whole time, because we're not so religiously minded that we're no earthly good. The following year, I decided to pull up to the table of Metropolitan A.M.E. Church at 1518 M Street N.W. for my ongoing spiritual nourishment and development. Metropolitan was located around the corner from *The Washington Post*. I occasionally saw the pastor, the Rev. William P. DeVeaux, as he jogged around the neighborhood. He often stopped to chat, and when he learned I was the daughter of an A.M.E. minister, invited me to his church. I joined Metropolitan A.M.E. Church in 1997, as I was winding down my column-writing career, uncertain about the future, and desiring a closer walk with God. There I learned forgiveness, peace with God, access by faith to God's grace, joy, triumph in troubles, and more about God's love. I also found the spirit of my ancestors in the people there. I learned as a child that Richard Allen had founded the denomination during the height of slavery, in 1787, to protest segregated worship at a white Methodist Church in Philadelphia. That history had meant little to me over the decades during which I had stepped away from the denomination, but what I learned on my return was the denomination had provided anti-slavery leadership in the nineteenth century, harboring those who had run away from the bondage of slavery. Metropolitan's history reflected the strength of African Americans locally and nationally who came together to help themselves, and the Washington church was a local and national church, called the National Cathedral of African Methodism. Deliberately built in proximity to the Capitol, Supreme Court, and White House, Metropolitan's mission was worship, liberation service and justice, and speaking truth to power. It affirmed me because at its inception, formerly enslaved African Americans built the church through which A.M.E. leaders showed white Americans that Blacks were not chattel and Blacks defined themselves as people of talent, helping each other to develop schools and businesses. Metropolitan A.M.E. had been a forum for dazzling oratory by Frederick Douglass (whose funeral in 1895 took place in its sanctuary), Paul Laurence Dunbar, Mary McLeod Bethune, and many others. U.S. presidents have spoken or worshipped there from President Taft in 1910 to, more recently, Jimmy Carter, Bill Clinton, and Barack Obama.

After I joined the church, one of the first familiar faces I saw was that of Gwen Ifill, the journalist I had first met in 1984 when she had come to work at *The Washington Post* and who went on to become a beloved anchor for PBS. I had already been at the paper fifteen years then and saw Gwen as part of the new breed—a younger generation of journalists working on the national staff, covering politics. She would go on to be one of the most successful female journalists in history. Seeing Gwen gave me comfort I had made a good choice in Metropolitan. We both had learned to speak truth to power in our work. I hadn't known before that we had something else in common. We were both daughters of ministers in the A.M.E. Church.

I continued to write my column, and church fellowship eased one problem I had faced, like so many other emerging African American women: isolation in white corporations. Some black women's response to this experience was to come together, fortify themselves with pats on the back and good food, and then head back out into worlds of business, journalism, and finance that were not so welcoming. Some of the women I got to know were executives on the business side of *The Washington Post*, which handled advertising, marketing, and financial matters. Ours was an unusual alliance because of the firewall between the editorial and business departments, to avoid conflicts of interest. However, I met some of them through my volunteer work while helping to diversify the media, and we would socialize outside of work.

Years before, after reading Terry McMillan's hit novel about a group of women friends, *Waiting to Exhale*, in 1992, my friends Gloria Norman, Leonade Jones, Candice Bryant, and Joyce Richardson from the business side were eager to see the film. We called ourselves the Sagittarius group. In 1996, we went together and afterward went to a nearby café so I could interview them for my column. One of them, Joyce Richardson, a highly placed Post executive, recalled its impact on her. "It was a theater full of black women," Richardson told me in a conversation recently. "Never saw that kind of audience before or since. I hated to see the movie end. We laughed, we wiped away tears, and loved the soundtrack of the film. We all knew someone who could fit the roles of those women, and sometimes it was us! Just like the friendship of the characters Gloria, Robin, Savannah, and Bernadine, our get-togethers lifted us up when we were down, helped us network, gave us shoulders to lean on, advice when we needed it, and a safe place to share the good or bad times," she said. "Each of us could connect with the issues that these women had in one way or another. Lord knows (that like the characters in the novel), we were searching for our Mr. Right while trying to build successful careers and find our little piece of happiness in the world. I particularly connected with Loretta Devine's character, a plump single mother raising a son. I was rooting for the love affair that finally came to fruition for her with Gregory Hines's character. It's funny because just as Gloria found romance with her next-door neighbor, so did I some nine years later." Richardson continued: "Like the women in the movie, our paths often took us in different directions, but we were a group of strong women who liked to strut our independence and who knew that we could always count on each other for support; that when you got knocked down by an unworthy man, or your career wasn't going exactly as you planned, you planted a big smile on your face and just picked yourself up and kept moving, frequently with a glass of champagne."

In the fall of 1996, I sat at the John F. Kennedy School's Institute of Politics (IOP), part of Harvard University, as an IOP fellow, and thought about reporting as teaching, editing as guidance. That was the hands-on work I had done to bring more talent into the journalistic pipeline. I wanted to do more. The fellowship gave me time to absorb how the world looked from other perspectives. I was the only journalist in the group. The other members were five politicians. Yes, I carried the standard for all the media! I entitled a weekly session I was required to lead "Redefining the News." It was my attempt to examine issues that would make the news more diverse. I brought in speakers who epitomized that and embodied the issues.

(Oh, how I wish I had had a crystal ball! Technology was revving up to change so many things about the news business. I had seen the newspaper business go from hot type, which I had learned in my journalism course at Lincoln University, to the awesome electronic systems housed on the lower floors of *The Washington Post*, and I could never have predicted I would see the digital age, nor foretold Jeff Bezos's ownership of *The Washington Post*. Bezos is the founder/ owner of Amazon, and his acquisition symbolizes a completely new era for *The Washington Post*. It is probably the only newspaper in America that actually increased its staff in 2017. Because they produce video and other nonpaper news elements, Bezos's ownership has meant a revitalized newspaper, in many respects.)

IOP gave me an opportunity to look at my own journey, my place in the business. I started to think the column had run its course. I searched for the messages behind the comments I would hear from *The Washington Post* editors when they said, "All you ever write about is race." I felt a deep pain. My response was, "What's wrong with that?" But I realized the need to look for an alternative. It was time to do something else.

One of the wise men I turned to was Milton Coleman. He was a striking presence in *The Washington Post* newsroom from his days as a reporter to his role as city editor and Metropolitan editor to deputy managing editor. He knew the city and the reputation of *The Washington Post* from the positive and negative sides. Milton also knew from my work with the Maynard Institute and the NABJ that diversity, the push for more minority reporters and voices, was always part of my conversation. And he recognized restlessness within me and the desire for change by top management. He had moved around newsrooms and up *The Washington Post* editing ranks and later gained industry leadership as the president of the American Society of News Editors, in 2010. So, my dilemma didn't surprise him.

What Milton suggested was that I look at the region's high school newspapers, a traditional stepping stone to a journalism career. Almost everyone I knew in journalism had worked for their school newspaper, yearbook, or some other publication that had kindled their interest in reporting. As I began looking into it, I was surprised to find out that the D.C. high schools had not produced any newspapers in 1997. The suburban schools weren't much better. This trend seemed to have started in the 1990s.

Frankly, I was outraged at this lack. Editing the school newspaper had always been a badge of achievement for high school students. The congregants at Youngs Chapel A.M.E. saw that byline as an achievement, and were so proud of me. Black newspapers were at a pinnacle of success at that time. My community's excitement for me spurred me on to a career in journalism. I wanted to provide teens this same opportunity. School administrators around the country were always fighting with the school-newspaper staffs over coverage and direction. Some school papers were even censored. Now, it seemed support for the newspapers was just as tenuous as support for other extracurricular activities. Correcting this would be my new mission.

But I moved cautiously. I attended a retreat, organized by Emily Barnes, one of my go-to advisers. She was and still is an executive coach and leadership-development specialist. Joining me were two other women who were at a crossroads in their public and private life. Each of us talked about our challenge in our life or career. I said I saw the handwriting on the wall, the end of my column. Barnes advised me to do the column until my editors asked me to do otherwise, to listen to advice I was getting from others, and to pursue other options.

My prayer group said to jump.

Before I went to IOP an editor at *The Washington Post* had asked me, "Is there anything else you want to do at *The Post*?" After I returned and researched the high schools, Milton, Leonard Downie Jr., the executive editor of *The Washington Post*, and I agreed that the column would end at the conclusion of the year, and I would start a new project at *The Washington Post*. I didn't take the jolting loss of my column with equanimity at first, but I came to see it as a fulfillment of my destiny and an opportunity to give back to the industry.

I announced the end of my column in December 1997. No longer would I have a high-profile byline. After almost forty years, that proved to be an adjustment. But, with faith, I learned a new skill—to go beyond pride of self. I wrote my last two columns, looking back and then explaining what I would be doing next:

DECEMBER 13, 1997, SATURDAY, FINAL EDITION

Looking Back Before Moving On

I was an insecure, 16-year-old college freshman when I became hooked on journalism. Hired to do secretarial work after classes at the black weekly Louisville Defender, the editor asked me one day to substitute for a sick reporter. My budding journalistic interest was concretized that day, and I never returned to secretarial work.

That was more than 35 years ago. It's time to graduate from daily journalism and begin a new phase in the profession. Ending this current labor of love—writing a regular column for the past 18 years—ties the loop on one circle of my career. It is a bittersweet time, which few previous experiences in my life can match.

You, dear reader, have been the object of my most intense professional relationship. I regarded it as a sacred trust. So in my two final columns, I want to share some of my journey, an African American woman's progress against the odds.

Undergirding my early journey in the racially segregated South were my parents, teachers and community. They taught me the three R's and basic values.

I came of age during two revolutions—civil rights for African Americans and liberation for women. As one of the first black women to break into the predominantly white, male-controlled media, I lived through those same revolutions in the newsroom.

Washington was little more than a sleepy Southern town when I came here to take my first daily newspaper job in the 1960s, having served my apprenticeship in the black press and having graduated from the Columbia University Graduate School of Journalism. I joined only two other blacks among scores of white reporters at The Post.

Retired Post reporter and editor Elsie Carper, who is white, remembered taking me out to lunch one day. The only place we could be assured of service was Sholl's, then located at 19th and K streets NW. We black reporters—Wallace Terry, Luther Jackson Jr. and I—had trouble getting cabs to pick us up in front of The Post building and after assignments. We endured the crotchety editor who ignored black murders, which he called "cheap deaths" and colleagues who expected us to fail.

Routinely, fellow reporters avoided speaking to me on the street, averting their eyes or meeting my smile and hello with a stony stare. A few exceptionally warm and welcoming persons, such as city editor Ben Gilbert and his wife, Maureen, took away some of the sting of the broader rejection that tugged relentlessly at my self-esteem. I fought to write good stories and tried not to complain about professional or personal obstacles that I felt could be interpreted as whining to mask incompetence. Only occasionally was I moved to tears of frustration as the deadline neared and another cab rolled by.

One of my most unforgettable assignments was covering James Meredith's entry into the University of Mississippi. My white Post colleague stayed at the Sand and Sea Motel while I stayed in private homes and even in a funeral home one night.

Twenty-five years ago, most newspaperwomen worked on women's pages—a fate I considered equal to death. By this time,

I had married, and we had begun our family. Absent flex-time and other perks of women's liberation, my husband and I decided I should spend more time with our three daughters. I became one of the first wave of blacks hired in television, working part time for Channel 5 as colleagues helped crack the color line, such as the late Max Robinson, who was the first black to anchor a local news program here.

The stimulus partly was the burning cities and urban riots of the '60s and '70s. A presidential commission said the media had to hire and promote more blacks because its mostly segregated coverage was helping create two separate, unequal societies.

Yet, print remained my first love and I was happy to be rehired seven years later by Ben Bradlee as an assistant editor in The Post's Style section. Thanks to the women's movement, I was able as a young mother to work part time. More blacks and women were on board and the newsroom felt warmer and friendlier.

I had left a good newspaper. When I returned—with Katharine Graham's and Bradlee's leadership, with Watergate and the Pentagon Papers—it was becoming a great one.

Restless with editing after a few years, I approached Bradlee in 1979 with a list of several possible new assignments, including a column. "We had nobody talking for that segment of our audience," he once told an author. "We were becoming aware of shortcomings in local coverage, but none of us were as prescient as we should have been." To this day, I'm grateful to The Post for the opportunity to find my voice, to grow and develop as a writer and thinker.

One of the early challenges of column writing was having my work taken seriously. I wanted to gain the respect of people of all colors, of oppressed people, as well as senators or congressmen. I wanted the black man to think I'd finally "got it" by articulating his reality, or to express for the older church lady feelings she couldn't find words for on a heavy issue.

As this city has gone through its political transformations, much of it, unfortunately, focused on Mayor Marion Barry, I've tried to be fair. I praised him when he did well. I also was the first to demand that he resign in 1990, even before The Post editorial board did so. I've also criticized The Post coverage, when, for example, I felt the paper based stories about Barry's drug use and womanizing on hearsay and rumor.

It's been important to hold on to the sense of who I am, to respect my community, to be a voice for the underdog and to be a self-respecting African American woman. This wasn't easy in a media industry that rewards black conservatives and black reporters who hold their communities' problems up to view without so much as a nod to the context of racism and poverty in which pathology flourishes.

I've tried to approach issues and problems with an eye to the basic humanity that unites us all—writing not only as an African American woman, but also as a middle-class, longtime resident who loves this city, and as a mother. I've tried to relate to every level of society with boldness and honesty, take the lumps and the kudos, even as I've grown personally and professionally.

Writing more than 1,500 columns over 18 years is growing up in public. It's a tough and vulnerable position. It's also been a rewarding, victorious journey.

DECEMBER 20, 1997, SATURDAY, FINAL EDITION

The Next Stage in The Journey

A journalist's job, at its best, is one of the world's finest. We get paid to investigate the right and wrong of people and events, divide truth from lie, occupy a vaunted front-row seat on history, and even write its first rough draft. We fall short daily of achieving those noble ideals; yet they continue to motivate the most serious of us. At its peak, the newspaper business can also be fun.

Writing a regular column has been a rare privilege. As I make a transition to a new phase of journalism here at The Washington Post, I'll still be on the same road—just taking a different path. I'll be putting what I've learned as a reporter, editor, columnist and career professional to a fresh use—working to help The Post develop young journalists in the Washington area. Leaving the daily newspaper isn't easy, but the transition is a natural progression—the continuation of a much larger journey.

From fairly early on in my career, I have combined work at this newspaper with fairly intense volunteer activity to increase racial diversity in the wider news industry. As one of the first African American women to break into the predominantly white male-controlled media, I knew firsthand the importance of hiring and promoting more minorities and women.

Newsrooms that do not reflect America's diversity do their readers an injustice. They fail to tell the stories of all of its citizens, they give readers a distorted image of themselves and they grossly twist the reality of minority groups.

Twenty years ago, my then-Post colleague Robert C. Maynard asked me to be part of a fledgling venture to help train African Americans, Hispanics, Asian Americans and Native Americans for reporting careers. I jumped at the opportunity. When we incorporated as the Institute for Journalism Education, I became one of the founding directors and served as board chair from 1985 to 1993.

In that role, I helped conceptualize and operate programs in reporting and in the training of editors and managers that helped prepare and place hundreds of journalists of color in jobs on the nation's newspapers. When Maynard died a few years ago, we renamed the nonprofit organization in his honor. Based in California, it continues to operate across the nation.

That work led to a decision to run for president of the 3,000-member National Association of Black Journalists. As its head from 1993 to 1995, I was part of a team that put on the historic Unity convention in 1994, which brought together 7,000 journalists of color to advance racial diversity in media. I'm grateful to this newspaper for supporting me in those efforts, as well as for approving my more formal diversity tutelage during a 1991 sabbatical at the Freedom Forum in New York City and at Harvard University's Institute of Politics in the fall of 1996.

Retaining and promoting people of color in the newspaper industry continues to be a problem. Nationwide, 88 percent of newspaper journalists are white. The Post has dramatically increased its diversity from my early days, yet it is clear that newspapers need to get involved much earlier in the education process in order to guide bright young people—especially minority students—toward the newspaper business.

Therefore, I took seriously an idea the paper's top editors proposed a few months ago—to generate a newsroom-driven, long-term initiative to help produce young local talent, some of which may show up in Post newsrooms in the next few years.

The multifaceted program aims to place the newspaper in a more visible position in key high school and college journalism programs and to increase the pool of potential hires. By recognizing and nurturing local talent through several developmental programs, the paper will help individuals and communities, even as its efforts help the larger profession and potentially increase its own ranks of minorities.

Two initiatives connected to high schools kicked off in September, as a prelude to the more comprehensive program. The Post received a Freedom Forum/American Society of Newspaper

Editors matching grant to partner with H.D. Woodson High School in Northeast Washington.

We considered three Washington area high school programs as possible partners and chose Woodson for a couple of reasons. It had good talent, a lot of potential and a dedicated journalism adviser and English teacher, Charmaine Turner, who told us that few D.C. public schools had published newspapers last year.

The Post has replaced Woodson's outdated computers, supplied photographic equipment and, with the aid of some 40 Post reporters and editors who volunteered, helped the students revive their newspaper, the Insider.

In addition to Woodson, The Post is also printing high school newspapers for Montgomery Blair High School in Silver Spring and Suitland High School as part of this early initiative.

We're also going to work with area college journalism programs, starting with the University of Maryland and Howard University, to develop a unique comprehensive program and educational partnership. We're going to get Washington Post professionals into the classrooms at these universities and plug outstanding high school journalists into a summer boot camp at the University of Maryland.

A special initiative for Hispanic students, a partnership with the Urban Journalism workshop and a Washington Post journalism scholarship program complete the opening thrust of the project.

Signing on to head this project as director of young journalists' development in the newsroom personnel office, I'll still be on the same road—serving people.

Next summer, I'll also be teaching journalism at Rhodes University in Cape Town, South Africa, as part of the Knight International Press Fellowship Program.

I sincerely thank everyone who has taken the time to read my efforts over the years. I love you all and...I'll see you on the hustings.

Last Years at *The Washington Post*: Is There Anything Else You Want to Do? 1998–2003

I served on the selection committee of the fifteenth annual Herbert H. Denton Jr. Memorial Scholarship for high school students. Winners are shown at the dinner on June 24, 2005, with Donald Graham, *The Washington Post* CEO and chairman of the board (rear, second from right), and Milton Coleman, deputy managing editor of *The Washington Post* (top left). *(Used with Permission of the Denton Scholarship)*

With Frank Sesno, director of
George Washington University
School of Media and Public
Affairs, which supported the
founding of the Prime Movers
Media Program to promote
media training for Washington,
D.C.–area high school students.
*(Used with Permission of Frank
Sesno)*

I was proud to be one of the judges who selected Akua Walker as the 1998
winner of the Herbert H. Denton Jr. Memorial Scholarship. Donald Graham
awarded the scholarship annually to students of color for more than twenty-five
years. At the dinner honoring Akua is Milton Coleman, deputy managing editor of *The Washington Post* (far left), and Graham, *The Washington Post* CEO and
chairman of the board (far right). Akua Walker is flanked by me and her mother,
Abena Walker, an educator and writer. *(Courtesy of the Dorothy Butler Gilliam
personal collection)*

Four times during my career, I had to clean out the cobwebs of my brain, which was filled with interviews, speeches, encounters with the famous and the ordinary, and decide what to do with the next phase of my career. I had loved reporting, from my embryonic days in the all-important black press to my color barrier–breaking ones at *The Washington Post*. I had enjoyed the years freelancing when I was a young wife and mother. I had been passionate about editing *The Washington Post* Style section and helping define the importance of black culture in the 1970s and 1980s when it had a renaissance in the output of poets, film-makers, painters, and actors. And I loved my column, reaching out to all levels of the region's residents, from the corner grocer and dance-school teacher to the politicians who shaped the city's new government in the first years of self-rule.

As I looked back over my years as journalist—reporter, editor, and columnist—I saw a new path. What had gratified me most was participating in the struggle to diversify the news media, grooming young reporters. I was most pleased by my activism through advocacy and training to create and foster a diverse work force in the media, and was happy I'd be continuing those efforts. I had made the decision after much conversation and self-reflection. All my advisers recognized that involvement with my adopted city was so important to me, that it went way beyond being a journalist and mentor; it also included intense involvement with my family and my church. What I was tapping into was the vibrant tradition of giving and giving back in the black community and reaching out to a younger generation. My church, the A.M.E. denomination, had certainly shown that involvement in building, giving, and sharing. Few obstacles had stopped those forefathers and foremothers, who faced violence and segregation and developed a special philanthropy even when their earnings allowed them just to get by and no more.

By starting the Young Journalists Development Program at *The Washington Post*, I hoped to give young people the gifts and tools to make it in the media, tell their own stories, and make them hopeful for the future. Their generation has some things mine did not have. But some things we had are only now being rediscovered. For example, elements of the African Diaspora are infused with science fiction and fantasy in pop-culture sensations, shattering preconceived notions of history and race. Something similar but less well-known happened in the 1980s and 1990s when black theologians began to fight lies with their corrected historiography, reading and thinking about the Bible through the African American experience. We must teach our youth that they must speak out on their issues, and they can do that through the media. We need to affirm that they deserve to be heard, that their voices can make change. Teaching this message is more than speaking it to our youth; we need to train them, impart skills. (I was impressed as I watched the giant march led by the Parkland, Florida, high school students in March 2018. They are part of the change for their generation, as I was part of mine. The cold, icy finger of racism is still apparent, but their issues are gun control, the banning of assault weapons, and addressing the increase of violence among high school students.)

With Milton's leadership, and executive editor Leonard Downie Jr.'s support, we devised a program to help high schools without newspapers. For the *Washington Post* Young Journalist Development Program to get newspapers started and prospering, I needed to reach out to my colleagues for participation. My work with the schools was facilitated by Milton Coleman's relationship with top officials, who approved of the project. We had enthusiastic support from *The Washington Post* newsroom, beginning with

Downie and Robert G. Kaiser, who was then the managing editor, as well as the business side, with Graham; Boisfeuillet (Bo) Jones Jr., then vice chair of the Post Company; and Theodore C. Lutz, the vice president of communications. No one at *The Washington Post* had extra time on their hands, but they made time. When David Broder, the dean of political reporters, and Bob Woodward, one of the most famous reporters of all time, volunteered, I felt our message was reaching all levels.

This new venture was just the right answer to the questions I had about my own direction. As a columnist, you are an isolated member of the staff. You are apart from the excitement of daily reporting, and, far too often, reacting to an issue. Several steps removed was often the position of the columnist. But the journalist program gave me the interaction that I had been missing. I was out in the schools, meeting teachers and administrators, getting to know students. I had to deal with the human side of teenagers, with all their personal pressures and family circumstances. Their issues didn't disappear just because we showed up with the promise of a fun project.

In addition to harsh poverty in some areas, a crack-cocaine epidemic was ravaging the poorest neighborhoods. Drug-related violence added to this disaster. But I had great help. Because the program enlisted volunteers from the newsroom, from copy editors to reporters, I got to know people with whom I had had only cursory conversations. There was nothing like riding back and forth to a high school, watching the expressions and listening to the questions of the teenagers, and wrestling over story drafts for creating bonds.

I contacted District schools directly. Most of the schools were enthusiastic. The first year, we recruited staff and students from Woodson Senior High School, in Northeast D.C., and added two other schools. In the year 2000, other schools in *The Washington Post* circulation area became part of the program. By 2007, we had sixty-five active schools.

We all learned lessons. Milton Coleman remembered discussing sports coverage with the school counselor at Woodson. "I asked her who was writing the stories about the football team. She said the players were. And then she asked, 'Is that wrong, Mr. Coleman?' I told her that was unacceptable," he recalled, citing the basic rules of ethics and writing that the students needed to learn.

Developing an online presence for our work with WashPost .com was an early effort in the online publishing world. One of the challenges we had was getting the high school students interested in the media. Throughout most of the twentieth century, and even earlier, many African Americans distrusted the white media. Black people had established newspapers to tell their point of view, going back to Frederick Douglass's *North Star*. We relied on black newspaper chains for straightforward reporting, including *The Atlanta Daily World, The Chicago Defender, The Amsterdam News, The Pittsburgh Courier, The Washington Informer,* and the *Afro-American* newspaper group. Those of us who didn't live in the major cities had our own delivery system. The Pullman porters, the African American men who worked on the railroad, gladly passed the papers from stop to stop. As we read their stories, we knew there were black reporters and photographers who had put their lives in danger to tell them. Washington had not been immune from this news segregation. Black citizens believed the media ignored the deaths of black people. The media ignored the good news, they thought, such as school achievements, the creation of businesses and charitable organizations.

The Washington Post was considered the big white paper downtown. At times when black reporters went into predominantly black neighborhoods, some chastised them for representing the white media and even regarded them as messengers carrying white perspectives and asking their editors' questions, not their own. These were perceptions we black journalists had to counter. Added to this was a vacuum of information about how the media worked because the students got their news in small bits on the music radio channels they favored. Or they were getting snippets from the family television while they did homework or had dinner. We needed to put newspapers in their hands, and to build trust. We had to help young people, as well as their teachers and families, understand the reporters' role.

While the start-ups were challenging, we found students who grasped the importance of news coverage and emerged as talented writers. When Dakarai I. Aarons was about fifteen, working on the newspaper at Duval High School in Lanham, Maryland, he told me he wanted to be a journalist. Then the Urban Journalism Program, a weekend workshop started by local NABJ members and supported by *The Washington Post*, National Public Radio, and the Associated Press, became an option for him. Eventually, Aarons became the coordinator for students interested in the workshop. He came along at a time when the ranks of professional minority reporters were growing but nowhere near the percentages a city like Washington should have. Aarons reflected on that: "The programs were instrumental in showing that there were media professionals that looked like us, and you could have a career. We could see the people on television, but we didn't know the people beyond the bylines," he said. "So, meeting and talking to journalists was very important."

Finding out there were choices was another eye-opener. The Annandale school paper received a technology grant from *The Washington Post*. The school installed a system that helped improve the design, layout, and production of the paper. Aarons loved writing and plunged into reporting about teens and AIDS/HIV education. He also joined his fellow junior reporters and went to the White House, interviewing people on the visitors' line about the possible impeachment of Bill Clinton, which was then a top news story.

This is what we wanted: an eager student, who enjoyed reporting, and used the opportunity to further his education and dream about a career. Based on the strength of his high school clippings, Aarons attended the University of Nebraska and got to work on the campus newspaper when he was a first-semester freshman. That combination of school and reporting led to an interest in education reporting. Working at *The Commercial Appeal* was his first full-time job, and then he went on to *Education Week*. "I wanted to do more in-depth stories, and beat reporters didn't have that time," he said.

I had worried about diversity in the newsroom for so long and didn't know if the post–Civil Rights and post–Affirmative Action cohort still believed diversity was important. But Aarons was active in asking the Education Writers Association about diversity in their workplace and coverage. Inequality in the schools was the most under-covered story, the responders to the survey replied. Aarons then joined an education-advocacy group but admitted he missed the daily reporting when a big story was breaking.

Aarons has moved on to become communications manager/education at the Chan Zuckerberg Initiative. He is from a generation I am so pleased to have encouraged.

One student who found her way to journalism through the *Washington Post* Young Journalists Development Program was Luz Lazo. A high school student at Bell Vocational High School, she had moved with her family from El Salvador to Washington. I met her at her school when she was thirteen. Not only was she dealing with a new culture and language in the United States but she was also learning to navigate the environs of her Columbia Heights neighborhood and exploring the rules of reporting in her elective journalism class. That's where I entered her life, speaking at a job fair at the school with my colleague Sylvia Moreno, a *Washington Post* reporter. Lazo became the executive editor of the Bell newspaper. One of her pressing concerns was whether she could afford college and get established as a working adult. She was in the States on a visa with protective status and was ineligible for government education grants. What she found through the Young Journalists was the encouragement to go after scholarships and work-study programs. We got *The Washington Post* to pay two semesters of her tuition at American University, and she worked to save the rest. "You always made me feel I could do it. I didn't have confidence," recalled Lazo. "I was young. I spoke with an accent. I was from a different culture. You didn't see that. You made sure I had opportunities." What Lazo also found through Young Journalists were group mentors. Sylvia and I were there for all sorts of consultations. But also, Milton Coleman and Luis Estrada, then a reporter with *The Washington Post*, were major factors in her development.

Because of her financial needs, Lazo didn't take the traditional route—coveted internships at other papers out of town—to a newsroom job at *The Washington Post*. She needed to stay home and help her family when she could. While in college she worked as a copy aide and a news aide at *The Washington Post*, assisting reporters and editors, answering phones, running errands, and making calls. Later, she freelanced for a special page called Kids Post. Through a special internship at American University, she worked at the NBC affiliate television station in Washington. Her earnings went to her tuition. When *The Washington Post* bought *El Tiempo Latino* in 2004, she joined the staff as a full-time reporter, writing in Spanish. Then, assisted by the *Washington Post* Young Journalists Development Program, she attended a National Association of Hispanic Journalists conference. *The Richmond Times-Dispatch* hired her, and she spent almost four years covering local government and education. Then Moreno called her about a fellowship *The Washington Post* was starting with American University, in which the reporter worked at *The Washington Post* and earned a graduate degree from American. Lazo got the fellowship, and when it ended, she worked on contract for *The Washington Post* and then came on full-time in 2013. How wonderful not only to watch her progress but also to see someone who believes in the value of diversity in the newsroom. Lazo says hearing all the speeches at NAHJ and seeing the presence in the newsroom of minorities helped cement that perspective.

Throughout the country, other newspapers and colleges were starting weekend sessions and summer intensive programs. The local NABJ chapters, helped by volunteers, became an important part of the pipeline to get young people interested in reporting, and hopefully, joining our ranks. Each year, at the annual convention, NABJ hosts a training program with aspiring college reporters.

When it was time for me to formally retire from *The Washington Post*, I had spent six years with the Young Journalists, from 1998 through 2003 and I was succeeded by Athelia Knight, a fine journalist who later taught at Georgetown University. *The Washington Post* had helped me take that next journey and I felt sincere gratitude. As a send-off, the Graham family gave me a rooftop party with a calypso band. My Louisville family and my daughters attended. Several executives spoke about me as a preacher's daughter. It seemed to indicate something that had enhanced my work at *The Washington Post*. Bradlee was one of the speakers and joked, "I noticed you put all the white boys first to speak." He is a picturesque speaker, and looked out at the exceedingly diverse audience and said, "We would not have had this kind of audience here if it hadn't been for Dorothy."

Epilogue

When I retired from *The Washington Post*, I was ready to use journalism education to address "diversity fatigue" in the media. One of my contacts at George Washington University (GWU) suggested I come there and nominated me in 2003 as a Maurice Shapiro fellow. I spent the first year designing the format and fund-raising for a journalism-training program with local high schools, under the administration of GWU School of Media and Public Affairs. The Prime Movers Media at GWU launched in the fall of 2004 and spread to Philadelphia. Getting minority aspirants ready for the real world of news gathering continued to be one of my challenges and satisfactions, even in retirement.

The long-range goal was to make the Prime Movers program national, with partnerships between colleges and high schools. The White House Correspondents Association provided valuable resources. Beginning in the fall of 2011, the association arranged for Prime Movers' high school students to attend a White House press briefing and tour the White House. That opened the world for so many of our young people. The association did a video about our program featuring our students' work, and showed it at their annual dinner. Seeing their work on the screen was, to them, almost a miracle and brought them national attention, since C-Span broadcast the dinner. I sat in the audience, deeply gratified. The next year, in 2012, 43 percent of the high school participants said they were considering a career in the media and by the following year, we had reached four thousand students in D.C. and Philadelphia. (Unfortunately Prime Movers, D.C., closed its doors in 2013 after ten years, due to decisions by the D.C. school officials. But, happily, the program in Philadelphia survived a $304 million budget shortfall and teacher layoffs, due to media and funding partners, including Temple University.)

In those tumultuous times, teachers wanted to help but had questions. Their concerns are instructive for everyone working to resolve diversity fatigue in the media. How were they going to fit teaching journalism into their work days, and what resources and support would they have, given that about 40 percent of the seventeen thousand high schools in the country didn't have student media? We encouraged them to let the students cover serious topics that affected them, and the young people didn't hesitate to do so. They tackled the homicide rate in Philadelphia, the resignation of the school superintendent, race relations in America, and cyberbullying. We worked to find them partners like Temple.

Ten years after it started, the program was still going, bringing together students at the National Constitution Center for the annual year-end closing program. One team from the Benjamin Franklin High School attended and reported on the draft of the National Football League in their city in 2017. Every time students wrote a story, received positive feedback, and learned a skill, their joy and increasing self-esteem gave me a boundless satisfaction.

I am grateful to have had the opportunity to work in the mainstream media and to work with innovative programs to train young journalists and add diversity to the country's newsrooms. What has been most rewarding in my sixty-year career is training high school students in underserved communities.

People call me a pioneer. When I think back to those days covering the integration of Central High School in Little Rock in 1957 and the final years of my career, making a way for young people to succeed in the field, I feel fortunate to have been a journalist, blessed to be a witness and an activist for diversity in the media. My own opportunities have resulted from a strong faith in God, through whom I was able to deal with anger and resentment and be courageous against giant societal odds. The experiences of my generation helped to pave the way for opportunities for future generations.

Today there are many strong minority mentors and role models in the media, but still not nearly enough. The media is different now than when I walked into *The Washington Post* newsroom in 1961, but there is more work to do. The excuse I heard from white editors when I began my career in journalism, "We can't find anyone qualified," is, unfortunately, still voiced in the media today. I knew it was not true then, and with many others, I responded with action, using the tools I had, believing all the while that racial equality, diversity, and inclusion are worth fighting for.

At the height of our diversity movement the proportion of men and women of color in the media was over 30 percent. The numbers have dropped, and we have lost ground at a time when inclusion is more important than ever (see Appendix 1). Newspaper opportunities are continuing to shrink, with mergers and layoffs reducing jobs. However, recent reports show that the percentage of women and people of color in local television newsrooms and in TV news management are at the highest levels ever measured by the RTDNA/Hofstra University newsroom survey. But Bob Papper, professor emeritus at Hofstra University, added that "while the minority population in the U.S. has risen 12.4 points in the last twenty-eight years, the minority workforce in TV news is up just seven." At a time when the nation is more diverse than ever, the media overall is sliding backward where diversity is concerned. Most painful for me is that increasing numbers of minorities believe the media doesn't accurately report on their communities.

Encouraging, however, is that some digital-age journalists are getting diversity right and in this new era, even the word "diversity" is sometimes being challenged. BuzzFeed offered an interesting definition of diversity in an email from its editor-in-chief Ben Smith to staff in 2014: "BuzzFeed's working definition of diversity is this: enough people of a particular group that no one person has to represent the supposed viewpoint of their group—whether ethnicity, gender, sexual orientation, religion, gender identity, socioeconomic background, or disability. And if the group is a small one we should never expect one person to be the 'diverse' reporter or writer, or to speak for anyone other than themselves."

We are nearly a score of years into what I call "New Century journalism." *The Washington Post,* under Jeff Bezos's ownership is one of the few daily newspapers that has done any significant hiring in the last year or two. We are witnessing the emergence of readers who have new habits due to the rise of social media. I have espoused the importance of giving young people of color voices in the media and have been thrilled to see so many of them use social media to good effect. Black Lives Matter and other important movements that may turn out to be the equivalent of the Civil Rights Movement are due to young people's adept use of social media. The media is now in the process of developing what its future is going to be. Media and technology are partners like never before. Media is more important today than ever despite the internet, despite social media, despite all of the new ways for exchanging information. Regardless of the technology, questions and challenges remain to end white superiority and low black self-esteem.

The current attacks on the media are very dangerous. American democracy, while flawed, as I experienced growing up during segregation, has nevertheless been a touchstone around the world.

A president who attacks freedom of the press—even if tweeted and erased the next day—has a very destabilizing effect on our democracy and throughout the world.

I am very proud of how far African Americans have come, although I still see fear of people of color in the white community. While white fear has definitely changed since I began my career, I would like to say to whites, "Don't be afraid of the African American voice, be an ally. Racial equality, diversity, and inclusion benefit you."

Acknowledgments

This book has a long trajectory—more than seventy-five years. I am grateful for the help of many colleagues, professionals, friends, and family in completing this work. I am thankful to *The Washington Post*, which made available photographs, columns, and articles I wrote over a thirty-three-year career. I am deeply indebted to my Center Street/Hachette Book Group editor, Adrienne Ingrum, who guided the overall development of the book and pushed me to share with readers the full range of emotions and experiences that helped shape my life. Hers was the firm hand, sharp intelligence, and compassionate heart I needed. I would also like to thank other staff at Hachette including Grace Tweedy Johnson, an assistant editor, Dorothea Halliday, copy editor, Mari Okuda and other members of its production team, and my publicist, Laini Brown.

I also appreciate Angela P. Dodson, an editor and writer, who helped outline the book and guide me before I secured the contract with Hachette, was steadfast while I completed it, and researched and compiled Appendices 2, 3, and 4. I am grateful also for friend and former colleague at *The Washington Post* Jacqueline Trescott, who helped stimulate my memory about events, people, and places at the newspaper. She also interviewed people with whom I interacted at the National Association of Black Journalists, Maynard Institute, the Young Journalists Development Program, and Prime Movers Media Program, helping me accurately reconstruct the impact of those events, movements, and organizations in which I was a leader.

I want to sincerely thank my daughters, Stephanie, Melissa, and Leah Gilliam, who contributed in various ways to the completion of this book, most notably to the family chapter.

I am deeply grateful to my Louisville family, to my sister, Evelyn Butler Campbell, ninety-two, who shared memories about our growing up years, as did Margaret Butler, my sister-in-law. Special appreciation is extended to my nephew Blair Davis Butler, the family patriarch, who oversees the care of my sister and the old friend with whom she lives, Mary Burton. Their loving and steady care gave me the freedom I needed to focus and complete the book.

A strong team of professionals was crucial to completing the book. The services of Lynne Suzette Price, Esq., ranged from helping execute my contract to negotiating with *The Washington Post*. Charles Morris of SKM Business Solutions was persistent in securing the licenses for the photographs. Blue Boy Imaging in Washington, D.C., helped with cleaning, scanning, and obtaining high-resolution photographs. Betty Anne Williams double-checked facts. Evelyn Hsu of the Maynard Institute gave valuable support, as did Katanga Johnson, an NABJ intern at Thomson-Reuters in Washington, D.C. Thank you all for your invaluable assistance!

Most of all, I glory in God's sustaining power aiding me in producing this work. I am grateful for spiritual guidance and support from Rev. Drs. Natasha Jamison Gadson, D. Gadsden, Ronald E. Braxton, and William H. Lamar IV.

Appendix 1

Fifty Years of Success and Setbacks in Media Diversity

Jacqueline Trescott

Publication of *Trailblazer*, almost two decades into the twenty-first century, is an opportunity to look at the long and troubled walk toward diversity in the news industry. Dorothy Butler Gilliam's memoir is testimony that the media industry has been pushed to include diversity in employees, newsmakers, and storytelling for at least fifty years. All sectors have seen progress. But the efforts to diversify demand to be rekindled and are even more important now. Numbers and visibility of minorities have increased, but without consistency.

The media is dramatically changing, the delivery of our news has been upended, and new voices emerge in endless mobile forms. While all involved seek balance—creatively and financially—we must also urgently reshape our quest for diversity.

Most of the media hung its head at the 1968 report of the Kerner Commission, stung by the rebuke from that presidential panel. The critical words were received, promises were made and efforts by IJE, NABJ, NAHJ, the Native American Journalists Association, the Asian American Journalists Association, and other organizations were supported.

So, How Far Have We Actually Come?

The credible argument after the Kerner Commission Report was that the target proportion of media employment should equal a group's percentage of the population.

In 2015 the U.S. population stood at 321.4 million. Those who identified themselves as black to the U.S. Census were 46.3 million. That's 14.4 percent of the country's population. The total for all who identified themselves as people of color—all groups combined who did not identify as non-Hispanic white—were 127.9 million. That's 39.8 percent of the country's population.

2015 American Society of News Editors Annual Survey of Journalists of Color in Newspaper and Online Newsrooms

U.S. population	321.4 million
Black/African American population	46.3 million (14.4% of total population)
ASNE Black/African Americans in newsrooms	1,560 (4.74% of newsroom employees)
People of Color population	127.9 million (39.8% of total population)
ASNE People of Color in newsrooms	4,200 (12.76% of newsroom employees)

Few leaders in newsrooms argue openly against diversity. An investigation by the *International Business Times* in 2015 found that although few numbers were available, editors vowed diversity was important.

These numbers followed an already-troubling trend for Blacks in media in the preceding decade. In 2010, the ASNE report found that from 2001 to 2010 the number of African Americans in mainstream newsrooms had dropped 34 percent, although Native Americans, Latinos, and Asian Americans all had some increase in percentages. The exception was African American journalists.

Diversity in Legacy Media versus Online Media in New-Century Journalism

Diversity leadership in legacy media—traditional print outlets—became hard to find, reported the ASNE summary in 2015. *The New York Times* newsroom staff was only 19 percent nonwhite professionals. At *USA Today*, the proportion was also 19 percent.

In what was a turbulent year of layoffs and voluntary changes, 2017, the ASNE survey found that minority employment in newsrooms slipped slightly to 16.6 percent, however, an exception to the downturn came from new media. Online news outlets became a popular goal for entrepreneurship and hiring; employment of people of color in those organizations was reported at 24.3 percent. In 2015, BuzzFeed editorial employees were 22.9 percent minority.

The world's transition to digital media in the early 2000s affected the livelihoods of all journalists. While trying to solve its own resultant turmoil, the news business was rocked by recession, struggled with new ways of delivering the news, and lost valuable reporters through age, layoffs, and frustration. The diversity census [ASNE] showed the departure of experienced and valued journalists who left for other fields, frustrated at the lack of advancement and the shifts in how the news was covered.

Distrust of the Media by Communities of Color

The American Press Institute and the Associated Press–NORC Center for Public Affairs Research reported in 2014 that only

25 percent of African Americans and 33 percent of Hispanics believed the media was accurate when it came to stories about those minorities.

Changing Habits of the Readership

News audiences, especially younger ones, have turned to mobile consumption, whether online editions of legacy newspapers or Facebook or other digital sources.

The American Press Institute in 2015 found African Americans and Hispanics between ages eighteen and thirty-four favored Instagram and YouTube for their news, as well as Facebook.

A survey by the Pew Research Center backed up finding of the electronic preferences. It found young African Americans, like their white counterparts, are using their cell phones to get news and follow news on Facebook, but they are more invested in Twitter and Instagram: 40 percent of African Americans between eighteen and twenty-nine used Twitter; 34 percent of Hispanics and 38 percent of Blacks used Instagram, compared to 21 percent of whites, according to a 2015 report by the Pew Research Center.

Pipelines for Fresh, Diverse Talent Exist

A study by The Columbia Journalism Review found minority participation in journalism or communications program enrollment was 24.2 percent. Those who graduated were 21.4 percent of the class. But, the analysis found, the job market had several hurdles. The minority graduates didn't have experience on campus newspapers, often couldn't take advantage of unpaid internships, and didn't have connections in the industry. Alex T. Williams, the author of the 2015 Columbia Journalism Review report, concluded, "They're just invisible because they aren't getting job interviews."

What Is Needed to Fight Diversity Fatigue

Media organizations must not wait until a street war, a police shooting, or protest becomes news to recruit minority reporters to cover the story.

Minority reporters who have invested in their education and preparation should be given a chance to cover their communities in times of distress and times of calm. Reporters with the interest to cover communities of color outside the explosive times should be able to bring their insight to all stories—every day, every story. That will be the solution to these ongoing diversity efforts.

In both legacy media and the new world of instantly delivered news, young reporters and editors must inherit the high standards of previous generations.

Media leaders must rethink how to cover the policies of a White House administration that openly targets a free press. President Donald Trump, and many of his staff, speak of fake news and alternative facts, maliciously undermining the free press. The Trump team started this attack in the 2016 campaign and accelerated it when the administration became the official government in 2017.

Jacqueline Trescott, an award-winning writer and editor based in Washington, D.C., has been involved in the training of young journalists and a participant in the fight for diversity in newsrooms for nearly fifty years.

She spent most of her journalism career as a reporter in two newsrooms: The Washington Star *and* The Washington Post. *During her thirty-six-year career at* The Washington Post, *she covered the national arts institutions, such as the Smithsonian Institution and the John F. Kennedy Center for the Performing Arts. Her work included feature profiles, daily news stories, and investigative pieces. Her work was honored with prizes from the Investigative Editors and Reporters Association, the Society of*

Professional Journalists and other journalism groups. She was also elected to the Hall of Fame of the National Association of Black Journalists in 2015.

In addition, she worked in the diversity field as a director and instructor of the multiethnic Summer Program for Minority Journalists, a founding program of the Maynard Institute for Journalism Education.

Appendix 2

A Black Press Time Line and Current African American Newspapers

Angela P. Dodson

1827

The Rev. Peter Williams Jr. and other free black men in New York City founded *Freedom's Journal*, the first African American owned and operated newspaper in the United States. A weekly, it was edited by the Rev. Samuel Cornish and John B. Russwurm.

1829

Samuel Cornish renamed *Freedom's Journal* as *The Rights of All*.

1837

Samuel Cornish edited *The Colored American*, formerly *The Weekly Advocate*.

1843

Martin R. Delaney began publishing *The Mystery* in Pittsburgh, Pennsylvania.

1847

Frederick Douglass began publishing *The North Star* in Rochester, New York.

1852

Mary Ann Shadd Cary published *The Provincial Freeman* (Windsor, Canada), to advocate that black Americans relocate to Canada after the passage of the Fugitive Slave Act.

The Alienated American was published by William Howard Day in Cleveland, Ohio.

The A.M.E. Church established *The Christian Recorder* as the denomination's official organ.

1855

The Mirror of the Times became the first black paper in California, published in San Francisco by Melvin Gibbs.

1859

Thomas Hamilton published *The Anglo-African* magazine in New York City.

Frederick Douglass published *Douglass Monthly* in Rochester, New York.

1864

Dr. Louis Charles Roudanez founded *The New Orleans Tribune*, the first black daily newspaper in the United States, published in French and English.

1866

Pinckney Benton Stewart Pinchback, Reconstruction-era governor of Louisiana, published *The New Orleans Louisianan*, the first black semiweekly.

1878

Richard DeBaptiste published *The Conservator*, later owned by Ferdinand Barnett and Ida B. Wells.

1879

John James Neimore established *The California Owl*.

1880

T. Thomas Fortune became editor of *The Rumor* (later called *The New York Globe*).

1883

Henry Clay Smith and his partners established *The Cleveland Gazette*.

1884

T. Thomas Fortune became publisher of *The New York Freeman* (later called *The New York Age*)
Christopher J. Perry founded *The Philadelphia Tribune*.

1885

The A.M.E. Zion Church established *The Star of Zion*, edited by John Dancy.

1888

Edward Elder Cooper founded *The Indianapolis Freeman*, the first illustrated African American journal.

1889

Ida B. Wells and her partners published *The Memphis Free Speech*.

1892

John Henry Murphy Sr., founded *The Afro-American* in Baltimore.

1894

Josephine St. Pierre Ruffin published *The Woman's Era*, the first national newspaper written for and by African American women and the official organ of the National Association of Colored Women.
George P. Stewart and William H. Port began *The Indianapolis Recorder* as a church bulletin.

1900

John Bass founded *The Topeka Plaindealer*.

1901

William Monroe Trotter established *The Boston Guardian.*

1905

Robert S. Abbott launched *The Chicago Defender* as "The World's Greatest Weekly."

1907

Edwin Harleston established *The Pittsburgh Courier,* which became the most widely circulated black newspaper with a national circulation of almost 200,000.

1909

James H. Anderson established *The Amsterdam News* as a weekly in New York City.

1910

P. B. Young Sr. purchased *The Norfolk Journal and Guide,* formerly the organ of a fraternal order, and built it into a major newspaper. The National Association for the Advancement of Colored People was founded and began publishing *The Crisis* magazine, edited by W. E. B. Du Bois.

1912

Joseph Edward Mitchell founded *The St. Louis Argus.*
Charlotta A. Bass (née Spears) and her husband assumed control of *The California Owl* and renamed it *The California Eagle.*

1915

Roscoe Dungee founded *The Oklahoma Black Dispatch* in Oklahoma City.

1916

Dr. Carter G. Woodson founded *The Journal of Negro History,* later *The Journal of African American History.*

1917
A. Philip Randolph and Chandler Owen published *The Messenger.*

1918
Marcus Garvey established *The Negro World.*

1919
Chester A. Franklin founded *The Call* in Kansas City, Missouri.
Joseph D. Bibb established *The Chicago Whip.*

1923
The Urban League established *Opportunity: A Journal of Negro Life*
as its official organ under the editorship of Charles S. Johnson.

1925
Constant C. Dejoie founded *The Louisiana Weekly.*
Anthony Overton founded *The Chicago Bee.*

1926
Harlem Renaissance literati published one edition of *Fire!!*, an
African American literary magazine before it ceased publication.

1927
Robert Jervay established *The Cape Fear Journal* in North Carolina
(later *The Wilmington Journal*).

1928
William Alexander Scott published *The Atlanta Daily World,*
which became the first successful black daily newspaper.
A. N. Johnson, Nathan Young, and Nathaniel Sweets began *The
St. Louis American.*

1930
Robert S. Abbott founded *Abbott's Monthly: A Magazine That's
Different.*

1931

Forrest White Woodard founded *The Philadelphia Independent.*

1933

Leon Washington founded *The Los Angeles Sentinel.*

1942

John H. Johnson founded *The Negro Digest*, later renamed *Black World*, as an African American magazine.

1945

John H. Johnson founded *Ebony*, a monthly news and lifestyle magazine for African Americans.

1951

John H. Johnson founded *JET*, "the Weekly Negro News Magazine."

1960

Malcolm X founded *Mr. Muhammad Speaks*, later *Muhammad Speaks.*

1967

The Black Panther Party began publishing a newspaper, *The Black Panther*, based in Oakland, California, and distributed nationally by members.

1970

Edward Lewis, Clarence O. Smith, Cecil Hollingsworth, and Jonathan Blount founded *Essence* as a lifestyle magazine focused on black women.

Earl G. Graves Sr. founded *Black Enterprise*, a monthly business magazine for African Americans.

1982

Ragan Henry, the first African American to own a network affiliated television station, founded *The National Leader*, the

first national African American newspaper. Claude Lewis, a
Philadelphia journalist, was the founding editor.

1989

Wilmer C. Ames created and published *Emerge* as a monthly news
magazine for African Americans.

1992

Quincy Jones, the music producer, and Time Warner launched *Vibe*,
a hip-hop/R&B magazine aimed at young, urban audiences.

1993

Heart & Soul, a wellness and lifestyle magazine for black women,
was first published as part of a joint venture between Reginald
Ware and Rodale Press and was later owned by BET and
Vanguarde Media. Edwin A. Avent purchased it in 2004 and
sold it to Brown Curry Detry Taylor & Associates, LLC, in
2012. BET also launched a lifestyle magazine, *BET Weekend*.

1998

William E. Cox Sr., Adrienne Ingrum, and Susan McHenry
founded *Black Issues Book Review*, a bimonthly published in
New York City. It featured book reviews and articles about
African American authors, books, and publishing.

2000

Vanguarde Media announced the launch of *Savoy*, a general-interest
lifestyle magazine targeting an upscale African American
audience, edited by Roy S. Johnson.

2008

Henry Louis Gates Jr., the Harvard professor, and Donald E.
Graham, chairman of the Washington Post Company, founded
The Root, an Afrocentric online magazine. It was owned by

Graham Holdings Company through its online subsidiary, The Slate Group.

2009

NBC launched TheGrio.com, a website with news, opinion, entertainment, and video content targeted to African Americans and edited by David Wilson.

2016

ESPN launched The Undefeated website with the goal of becoming "the premier platform for exploring the intersections of race, sports and culture," edited by Kevin Merida, former managing editor of *The Washington Post*.

Sources: *The Black Press: Soldiers without Swords, http://www.pbs.org /blackpress/news_bios/index.html; Black Press Research Collective, blackpressresearchcollective.org*

Current African American Newspapers

The National Newspaper Publishers Association (NNPA) represents more than two hundred black newspapers in the United States and the Virgin Islands, with a combined readership of 20 million. NNPA listed the following current members on its website, https:// nnpa.org/current-members/(accessed September 25, 2018):

Alabama
Birmingham Times
Greene County Democrat
Mobile Beacon-Citizen
Speakin' Out News

Arizona
Arizona Informant

California
Bakersfield News Observer
Black Voice News
The California Advocate
California Voice
L.A. Focus Newspaper
L.A. Watts Times

Los Angeles Sentinel
Oakland Post
Our Weekly
Pasadena San Gabriel Valley–
  Latino Journal
Precinct Reporter
Sacramento Observer
San Bernardino American News
San Diego Voice & Viewpoint
San Francisco Sun Reporter
Tri-County Sentry
Wave Community Newspapers

Colorado
Denver Weekly News

Connecticut
Inner-City Newspaper

District of Columbia
Afro-American–Washington
District Chronicles
Walls Communications
Washington Informer

Florida
Capital Outlook
Daytona Times
Florida Courier
Florida Sentinel Bulletin
Florida Star
Florida Sun
Jacksonville Free Press
The Miami Times

Orlando Advocate
Pensacola Voice
South Florida Times
The Weekly Challenger
Westside Gazette

Georgia
Atlanta Daily World
Atlanta Inquirer
Atlanta Tribune the
  Magazine
Atlanta Voice
Columbus Times
CrossRoadsNews
Macon Courier
Metro Courier
Savannah Herald
Savannah Tribune
Southwest Georgian–Albany

Illinois
Chatham-Southeast Citizen
Chicago Crusader
Chicago Defender
Chicago Standard
Chicago Weekend
Final Call
Hyde Park Citizen
Muslim Journal
South End Citizen
South Suburban Standard
The Times Weekly
Windy City Word

Indiana
Frost Illustrated
Gary Crusader
Indiana Herald
Indianapolis Recorder

Kentucky
Louisville Defender

Louisiana
Alexandria News Weekly
Data News Weekly
Louisiana Weekly
New Orleans Tribune
Shreveport Sun

Maryland
The Afro-American–Baltimore
The Baltimore Times

Michigan
Grand Rapids Times
Michigan Chronicle
Michigan Citizen
Michigan Front Page
Telegram Newspaper

Minnesota
Insight News
Minneapolis Spokesman Reporter

Mississippi
Jackson Advocate
Mississippi Link

Missouri
East St. Louis Monitor
Kansas City Call
St. Louis American
St. Louis Metro Sentinel

Nebraska
Omaha Star

New Jersey
New Jersey City News
Jersey City Daily Challenge
South Jersey Journal

New York
Afro American Times
Buffalo Criterion
Challenge Group
Harlem News Group
Hudson Valley Press
New American of New York
The New York Amsterdam News
New York Beacon
New York Carib News
New York Daily Challenge
Westchester County Press

North Carolina
Carolina Peacemaker
The Carolina Times
The Carolinian
The Charlotte Post
The County News
Greater Diversity News

Wilmington Journal

Winston-Salem Chronicle

Ohio

The Buckeye Review

Call & Post–Cleveland

Call & Post–Columbus

The Cincinnati Herald

The Communicator News

Dayton Defender

The Reporter–Akron

Toledo Journal

Oklahoma

The Black Chronicle

The Tulsa Oklahoma Eagle

Oregon

Portland Observer

Portland Skanner

Pennsylvania

New Pittsburgh Courier

The Philadelphia Observer

The Philadelphia Tribune

South Carolina

The Charleston Chronicle

Community Times

South Carolina Black News

Tennessee

Memphis Silver Star News

Nashville Pride

The Christian Recorder

The Tennessee Tribune

Tri-State Defender

Texas

African American News & Issues–
Dallas

African American News & Issues–
Houston

African American News & Issues–
San Antonio

African News Digest

Dallas Examiner

Dallas Post Tribune

The Dallas Weekly

East Texas Review

Garland Journal

Houston Defender

Houston Forward Times

Houston Style Magazine

The Houston Sun

A King Size View

La Vida News—The Black
Voice—NOKOA, the
Observer

North Dallas Gazette

San Antonio Observer

Southwest Digest

The Villager

Texas Metro News

Virginia

Politic365

New Journal and Guide

Richmond Free Press

The Legacy Newspaper

Washington

Metro Home Maker

Seattle Medium

Seattle Skanner

Tacoma True Citizen

Wisconsin

The Madison Times Weekly

Milwaukee Community Journal

Milwaukee Courier

Milwaukee Times Weekly

Source: The National Newspaper
Publishers Association,
https://nnpa.org/current-members/

Appendix 3

First Wave of Black Columnists Working at Daily Newspapers

Angela P. Dodson

The following is a list, arranged by city, of African American columnists active in the early 1990s, when the Trotter Group formed:

Atlanta
Cynthia Tucker, *The Atlanta Journal-Constitution*

Baltimore
Wiley Hall and Gregory Kane, *The Baltimore Sun*

Bergen, New Jersey
Lawrence Aaron, *The Bergen Record*

Boston
Leonard Greene, *The Boston Herald*
Derrick Jackson and Larry Whiteside, *The Boston Globe*

Buffalo
Rod Watson, *The Buffalo News*

Camden/Cherry Hill, New Jersey
Wayne Dawkins, *The Courier-Post*

Charlotte, North Carolina
Mary Curtis, *The Charlotte Observer*

Chicago
Vernon Jarrett and Mary Mitchell, *Chicago Sun-Times*
Clarence Page, *Chicago Tribune*

Dallas
Kevin Blackistone, *The Dallas Morning News*

Detroit
Rochelle Riley, *The Detroit Free Press*

Fort Worth, Texas
Nichelle Hoskins, *Fort Worth Star-Telegram*

Hackensack, New Jersey
Lisa Baird, *The Record*

Hampton Roads, Virginia
Roger Chesley and Will LaVeist, *The Virginian-Pilot*

Hartford
Stan Simpson, *The Hartford Courant*

Houston
James Campbell, *Houston Chronicle*

Jacksonville
Tonyaa Weathersbee, *The Florida Times-Union*

Kansas City, Missouri
Lewis Diuguid, *The Kansas City Star*

Las Vegas
Barbara Robinson, *Las Vegas Review-Journal*

Louisville, Kentucky
Betty Baye, *The Courier Journal*

Los Angeles
Erin Aubry Kaplan, *The L.A. Weekly*

Miami/Fort Lauderdale
Leonard Pitts, *The Miami Herald*

Milwaukee
Eugene Kane, Tannette Johnson-Elie, and Gregory Stanford, *The Milwaukee Journal Sentinel*

Nashville
Dwight Lewis, *The Tennessean*

New York City
Earl Caldwell, Errol Louis, and E. R. Shipp, *The New York Daily News*
Bob Herbert, *The New York Times*
Les Payne and Sheryl McCarthy, *Newsday*

Oakland
Brenda Payton, *The Oakland Tribune*

Philadelphia
Elmer Smith and Jenice Armstrong, *The Daily News*
Annette John-Hall, Acel Moore, and Claude Lewis, *The Philadelphia Inquirer*

Pittsburgh
Tony Norman, *Pittsburgh Post-Gazette*

Raleigh, North Carolina
Barry Saunders, *The News & Observer*

Richmond
Michael Williams, *The Richmond Times-Dispatch*

Rochester, New York
Richard Prince, *The Democrat and Chronicle*

San Antonio
Cary Clack, *The San Antonio Express News*

San Jose, California
Loretta Green, *The Mercury News*

St. Louis
Bryan Burwell, Gregory Freeman, and Lorraine Montre,
    The St. Louis Post-Dispatch

St. Petersburg, Florida
Peggy Peterman, *The St. Petersburg Times*

Seattle
Jerry Large and Don Williamson, *The Seattle Times*

Tampa, Florida
Mark August, *The Tampa Tribune*

Wilmington, Delaware
Norman Lockman and Sherman Miller, *The Wilmington News
    Journal*

Washington, D.C.
Donna Britt, Dorothy Butler Gilliam, Colbert I. King, Courtland
    Milloy, William Raspberry, Michael Wilbon, *The Washington
    Post*
Adrienne Washington, *The Washington Times*
Joe Davidson, *The Wall Street Journal*
Barbara Reynolds and DeWayne Wickham, *USA Today*

Sources:
Wayne Dawkins, Rugged Waters: Black Journalists Swim in the
    Mainstream *(August Press, 2003);*
Wayne Dawkins, Black Voices in Commentary: The Trotter Group
    (August Press, 2006);
additional research by Wayne Dawkins and Angela P. Dodson

Appendix 4

Founders of the National Association of Black Journalists

Angela P. Dodson

On December 12, 1975, black journalists met at the Sheraton Park Hotel in Washington, D.C. (later named the Marriott Wardman Park), to discuss their mutual concerns and to consider forming a national organization. Forty-four men and women signed a list affirming support for formalizing the organization, and they are known as the founders of the National Association of Black Journalists. Here are their names and job affiliations at the time.

Norma Adams-Wade, *The Dallas Morning News*
Carole Bartel, *CORE* magazine
Edward Blackwell, *The Milwaukee Journal*
Reginald Bryant, *Black Perspective on the News*
Maureen Bunyan, WTOP-TV (Washington, D.C.)
Crispin Campbell, WNET-TV (New York City)
Charlie Cobb, WHUR (Washington, D.C.)
Marilyn Darling, WHYY-TV (Wilmington, Delaware)
Leon Dash, *The Washington Post*
Joe Davidson, *The Philadelphia Bulletin*

Allison J. Davis, WBZ-TV (Boston)

Paul Delaney, *The New York Times*

William Dilday, WLBT-TV (Jackson, Mississippi)

Sandra Rosen Dillard, *The Denver Post*

Joel Dreyfuss, *The Washington Post*

Sam Ford, WCCO-TV (Minneapolis)

David Gibson, Mutual Black Network

Sandra Gilliam-Beale, WHIO-TV (Dayton, Ohio)

Bob Greenlee, *New Haven Register*

Martha Griffin, National Public Radio

Derwood Hall, WSOC-TV (Charlotte, North Carolina)

Bob Hayes, *San Francisco Examiner*

Vernon Jarrett, *Chicago Tribune*

Mal Johnson, Cox Broadcasting

Toni Jones, *The Detroit Free Press*

H. Chuku Lee, Africa Journal Ltd.

Claude Lewis, *The Philadelphia Bulletin*

Sandra Dawson Long, *The News Journal* (Wilmington, Delaware)

Pluria Marshall, freelancer

Acel Moore, *The Philadelphia Inquirer*

Luix Overbea, *The Christian Science Monitor*

Les Payne, *Newsday*

Alex Poinsett, *Ebony*

Claudia Polley, NBC News

Richard Rambeau, Project Bait (Detroit)

W. Curtis Riddle, *The Louisville Courier-Journal*

Max Robinson, WTOP-TV (Washington, D.C.)

Charlotte Roy, *The Detroit Free Press*

Vince Sanders, National Black Network

Chuck Stone, *The Philadelphia Daily News*

Jeannye Thornton, *U.S. News & World Report*

Francis Ward, *The Los Angeles Times*

John C. White, *The Washington Star*
DeWayne Wickham, *The Baltimore Sun*

Note: Paul Brock was a convener of the meeting, but there was debate over the role of nonjournalists and they were excluded from membership. Brock became the founding NABJ executive director.

Notes

Coming to The Washington Post, 1961

Chalmers M. Roberts, *The Washington Post: The First 100 Years* (Houghton Mifflin Harcourt, 1977).

Ben W. Gilbert, "Toward a Color-Blind Newspaper: Race Relations and the 'Washington Post,'" *Washington History* 5, no. 2 (1993): 4–27.

"University of Georgia Desegregated (Jan)," *Civil Rights Movement—History and Timeline, 1961*, accessed January 19, 2018. http://www.crmvet.org /tim/timhis61.htm#1961uga.

"Rock Hill SC, 'Jail-No-Bail' Sit-Ins (Feb–Mar)," *Civil Rights Movement— History and Timeline, 1961*, accessed January 19, 2018.

"Tougaloo Nine and Jackson State Protest (Mar)," *Civil Rights Movement— History and Timeline, 1961*, accessed January 19, 2018.

"Burning Bus in Anniston, AL," *Civil Rights Movement—History and Timeline, 1961*, accessed January 19, 2018.

"Freedom Rides Roll across the South," *Civil Rights Movement—History & Timeline, 1961*, accessed January 19, 2018.

"Rock Hill SC, 'Jail-No-Bail' Sit-Ins."

"Desegregate Route 40 Project (Aug–Dec)," *Civil Rights Movement—History and Timeline, 1961*, accessed January 19, 2018.

Roberts, *The Washington Post*, 320.

Ibid., 348.

David Halberstam, *The Powers That Be* (University of Illinois Press, 1975), 376.

Simeon Booker and Carol McCabe Booker, *Shocking the Conscience: A Reporter's Account of the Civil Rights Movement* (University Press of Mississippi, 2013), 44.

Roberts, *The Washington Post*, 359.

Ibid., 294.

Ibid., 328.

Dorothy Gilliam, "Court to Weigh Fate of Boy Who Acts Like a Dog," *The Washington Post*, November 1, 1962.

Booker and Booker, *Shocking the Conscience*, 45.

Ben Bradlee, *A Good Life: Newspapering and Other Adventures* (Simon & Schuster, 1995), 269.

Assignment: Mississippi, 1962

William Doyle, *An American Insurrection: James Meredith and the Battle of Oxford, Mississippi, 1962* (Anchor, 2003). (Originally published by Doubleday in 2001 as *An American Insurrection: The Battle of Oxford, Mississippi, 1962*.)

Roberts, *The Washington Post*, 328.

Ibid., 328.

Ibid., 330.

Doyle, *An American Insurrection*, 283.

Gene Roberts and Hank Klibanoff, *The Race Beat: The Press, the Civil Rights Struggle, and the Awakening of a Nation* (Vintage, 2008), 150.

Moses Newson, "Mississippi Rebels," *The Afro-American*, September 29, 1962.

Booker and Booker, *Shocking the Conscience*, 66.

Carl Rowan, *South of Freedom* (Knopf, 1954).

Carl Rowan, *Breaking Barriers: A Memoir* (Perennial, 1991).

Doyle, *An American Insurrection*, 283.

Dorothy Gilliam, "Mississippi Negroes Happily Stunned by Meredith," *The Washington Post*, October 6, 1962.

Dorothy Gilliam, "Mississippi Mood: Hope and Fear," *The Washington Post*, October 14, 1962.

Medgar Evers, *The Autobiography of Medgar Evers: A Hero's Life and Legacy Revealed through His Writings, Letters, and Speeches* (Civitas Books, 2005), 7.

Roberts and Klibanoff, *The Race Beat*, 150.

Dorothy Gilliam, "First Lady Plays Santa to 'Village,'" *The Washington Post*, December 14, 1962.

Growing Up a Preacher's Kid, 1936–1961

African Methodist Episcopal Church, "Our History," African Methodist Episcopal Church, accessed January 20, 2018, https://www.ame-church.com/our-church/our-history/.

"Music Beale Street Memphis United States of America Tennessee Elvis Presley," Alamy Ltd., 2018, accessed January 20, 2018, http://

www.alamy.com/stock-photo-music-beale-street-memphis-united
-states-of-america-tennessee-elvis-6858412.html.

William Christopher Handy, "Beale Street Blues" (Pace & Handy Music, 1916).

Bruce M. Tyler, *Louisville in World War II* (Arcadia Publishing, 2005), back cover.

Mervin Aubespin, Kenneth Clay, and J. Blaine Hudson, *Two Centuries of Black Louisville: A Photographic History* (Butler Books, 2011).

Delores Carpenter and Rev. Nolan E. Williams, eds., *African American Heritage Hymnal* (GIA Publications, 2001), 494.

Carter G. Woodson, *The Mis-Education of the Negro* (Washington, D.C.: Associated Publishers, 1969), xxxiii. (Originally published in 1933.)

Aubespin, Clay, and Hudson, *Two Centuries of Black Louisville.*

Donald Bogle, *Toms, Coons, Mulattoes, Mammies, and Bucks: An Interpretive History of Blacks in American Films* (Viking, 1973).

"Tom Mboya: The Charismatic Pan-Africanist, Freedom Fighter, and the Greatest," *Trip Down Memory Lane*, accessed January 20, 2018, https://kwekudee-tripdownmemorylane.blogspot.com/2013/12/tom-mboya-charismatic-pan-africanist.html.

Being Mrs. Sam Gilliam, 1962–1982

African Methodist Episcopal Church, *The Doctrines and Discipline of the African Methodist Episcopal Church* (University of North Carolina Press, 2001), 219.

Ursuline Sisters of Louisville, "Ursuline College," Ursuline Sisters of Louisville, accessed January 20, 2018, http://www.ursulinesisterslouisville.org/ursuline_college.php.

All Souls Unitarian Church, "All Souls Archives and History," All Souls Church Unitarian, accessed January 20, 2018, http://www.all-souls.org/archives.

Jonathan Binstock, *Sam Gilliam: A Retrospective* (University of California Press, 2005), 19.

Return to The Washington Post: The Style Years and Founding the Institute for Journalism Education, 1972–1979

Joshunda Sanders, *How Racism and Sexism Killed Traditional Media: Why the Future of Journalism Depends on Women and People of Color* (Santa Barbara: Praeger, 2015), 14.

Roberts, *The Washington Post*, 426.

Ibid., 428.

Ibid., 389.

Ibid., 427.

Ibid., 429.

Ibid., 438.

Ibid., 379.

Ben W. Gilbert, *Ten Blocks from the White House: Anatomy of the Washington Riots of 1968* (Pall Mall Press, 1969), 3.

Maureen Beasley, *Women of the Washington Press: Politics, Prejudice, and Persistence* (Evanston: Northwestern University Press, 2012), 58.

Gilbert, "Toward a Color-Blind Newspaper," 10.

Halberstam, *The Powers That Be*, 525.

Ibid., 565.

Katharine Graham, *Personal History* (Vintage, 1998), 458.

Henry Louis Gates Jr. and Donald Yacovone, *The African Americans: Many Rivers to Cross* (SmileyBooks, 2013), 251.

Ibid., 242.

Ibid., 254.

B. Alexandria Painia, "Never Forget #004: Eartha Kitt Made Lady Bird Johnson Cry . . . and Got Blackballed for It," The Visibility Project, accessed January 28, 2018, http://www.thevisibilityproject.com/2015/04/09/never-forget-004-eartha-kitt-made-lady-bird-johnson-cry-and-got-black-balled-for-it/.

Harry Jaffe and Tom Sherwood, *Dream City: Race, Power, and the Decline of Washington, D.C.* (Simon & Schuster, 1994), 45.

Ibid., 60.

Ibid., 93.

Interview of Hollie I. West by the author.

Interview of Deborah Heard by the author.

Joel Dreyfuss, "Waltzing with Ben and Sally," *Huffington Post*, accessed January 28, 2018, https://www.huffingtonpost.com/joel-dreyfuss/waltzing-with-ben-and-sal_b_6041026.html.

Interview of Jacqueline Trescott by the author.

Dorothy Gilliam, "The Television Series: Out of Balance with History," *The Washington Post*, January 28, 1977.

Dorothy Gilliam, *Paul Robeson: All-American* (New Republic, 1976), back cover.

Jacqueline Trescott, "Alex Haley: The Author, Astride Fame's Moment . . . ," January 28, 1977, *The Washington Post*, Style section.

Jacqueline Trescott, "The Torment of Fame; Donny Hathaway's Struggle With Success," January 19, 1979, *The Washington Post*, Style section.

Jacqueline Trescott, "The Hemings Affair; The Black Novelist and the 'Sally Hemings' Affair," June 15, 1979, *The Washington Post*, Style section.

Interview of Karen DeWitt by the author.

Voice for the Voiceless: The Column and National Association of Black Journalists Years, 1979–1997

Halberstam, *The Powers That Be*, 711.

Dorothy Gilliam, "Promise of '60s Faded; The Man Called Lamb Recalls Glory of Brief Period That Had a Future; Commentary," *The Washington Post*, June 3, 1979.

Dorothy Gilliam, "Can a 14th Street Kid Make It to Pro Football?" *The Washington Post*, March 9, 1981.

Frank Sotomayor, "The First 30 Years of MIJE: Making Newsrooms Look Like America," Unity Conference, National Association of Black Journalists, accessed January 28, 2018, https://www.mije.org/about/history/.

Dorothy Gilliam, "Cornrows Don't Belong to Bo," *The Washington Post*, February 4, 1980.

Dorothy Gilliam, "Carter Was Drowned in a Right-Wing Tide," *The Washington Post*, November 8, 1980.

Dorothy Gilliam, "Mr. Reagan, Say Hello To the H Street Strip," *The Washington Post*, December 1, 1980.

Jacqueline Trescott, Dorothy Gilliam, and *Washington Post* Staff Writers, "Mold-Breakers in the Mainstream," *The Washington Post*, December 28, 1986.

Dorothy Gilliam, "Coming Out of Closet Is Tougher for Blacks," *The Washington Post*, July 14, 1980.

Interview of Martin Coleman by the author.

Dorothy Gilliam, "Janet Cooke: Journalist Who Happens to Be Black," *The Washington Post*, April 18, 2017.

Ken Auletta, *The Underclass* (Random House, 1982).

Dorothy Gilliam, "Outrage," *The Washington Post*, November 29, 1982.

Alice Walker, *In Search of Our Mothers' Gardens: Womanist Prose* (Harcourt Brace Jovanovich, 1983).

Dorothy Gilliam and *Washington Post* Staff Writers, "An Act of Caring," *The Washington Post*, September 29, 1986.

Dorothy Gilliam, "From Shame to Triumph," *The Washington Post*, May 11, 1987.

Dorothy Gilliam, "A Bootstrap Christmas Story," *The Washington Post*, December 19, 1985.

Dorothy Gilliam, "Values," *The Washington Post*, November 15, 1982.

Dorothy Gilliam, "Blacks as Entrepreneurs," *The Washington Post*, November 4, 1985.

Dorothy Gilliam, "Violent Crime du Jour Is a Wrong Approach," *The Washington Post*, December 20, 1980.

Dorothy Gilliam, "Training Minorities For U.S. News Rooms," *The Washington Post*, September 8, 1980.

Elise Cose, *The Quiet Crisis: Minority Journalists and Newsroom Opportunity* (Institute for Journalism Education, 1985).

Mark Fitzgerald, "Black Columnist, White Papers," *Editor and Publisher*, accessed January 28, 2018, http://www.editorandpublisher.com/news/black-columnists-white-papers-p-12/.

Dorothy Gilliam, "Looking Back before Moving On," *The Washington Post*, December 13, 1997.

Dorothy Gilliam, "The Next Stage in the Journey," *The Washington Post*, December 20, 1997.

Last Years at The Washington Post: Is There Anything Else You Want to Do? 1998–2003

Interview of Athelia Knight by Jacqueline Trescott.

Interview of Milton Coleman by Jacqueline Trescott.

Interviews of Dakarai I. Aarons by Jacqueline Trescott.

Interview of Luz Lazo by Jacqueline Trescott.

Interview of Lois Page by Jacqueline Trescott.

Interview of Saudia Harris Staten by Jacqueline Trescott.

Interview of Yolanda Woodlee by Jacqueline Trescott.

Interview of Maida Odom by Jacqueline Trescott.

Interview of Reginald Moton by Jacqueline Trescott.

Bibliography

Abbott, William F. "Vietnam War Casualties by Race, Ethnicity and National Origin." The American War Library. Accessed January 28, 2018. http://www.americanwarlibrary.com/vietnam/vwc10.htm.

African Methodist Episcopal Church. *The Doctrines and Discipline of the African Methodist Episcopal Church.* University of North Carolina Press, 2001.

All Souls Church Unitarian, "All Souls Archives and History." All Souls Church Unitarian. Accessed January 20, 2018. http://www.all-souls.org/archives.

Asim, G'Ra. "Paul Delaney: Lifetime Achievement Winner." National Association of Black Journalists. Accessed January 28, 2018. http://www.nabj.org/page/PaulDelaney.

Aubespin, Mervin, Kenneth Clay, and J. Blaine Hudson. *Two Centuries of Black Louisville: A Photographic History.* Butler Books, 2011.

Basconi, Mary Alice. "Summer in the City, 1968–74: Columbia University's Minority-Journalist Training Program." *Questia—Journalism History.* Accessed January 28, 2018. https://www.questia.com/library/journal/1P3-15344 52981/summer-in-the-city-1968-74-columbia-university-s.

Beasley, Maureen. *Women of the Washington Press: Politics, Prejudice, and Persistence.* Northwestern University Press, 2012.

Unitarian Universalist Association, "Beliefs & Principles." Unitarian Universalist Association. Accessed January 20, 2018. https://www.uua.org/beliefs/what-we-believe.

Bernstein, Adam. "Gwen Ifill, Who Overcame Barriers as a Black Female Journalist, Dies at 61." *The Washington Post.* Accessed January 20, 2018. https://www.washingtonpost.com/entertainment/tv/gwen-ifill-journalist-who-became-staple-of-public-affairs-tv-shows-dies-at-61/2016/11/14/2ae4c106-aa91-11e6-977a-1030f822fc35_story.html?utm_term=.2c383a683675.

Binstock, Jonathan P. *Sam Gilliam: A Retrospective*. University of California Press, 2005.

Bogle, Donald. *Toms, Coons, Mulattoes, Mammies, and Bucks: An Interpretive History of Blacks in American Films*. Viking, 1973.

Booker, Simeon, and Carol McCabe Booker. *Shocking the Conscience: A Reporter's Account of the Civil Rights Movement*. University Press of Mississippi, 2013.

"Burning Bus in Anniston, AL." *Civil Rights Movement—History and Timeline, 1961*. Accessed January 19, 2018. http://www.crmvet.org/tim/timhis61 .htm#1961uga.

Caldwell, Earl. "Interview with Austin Long Young." Robert C. Maynard Institute for Journalism Education. Accessed January 28, 2018. https:// archive.org/details/caolaam_000064.

Carpenter, Delores, and Rev. Nolan E. Williams, eds. *African American Heritage Hymnal*. GIA Publications, 2001.

Clair, Raquel St. "Womanist Biblical Interpretation." *True to Our Native Land: An African American New Testament Commentary*. Fortress Press, 2007, 54–62.

Cose, Ellis. "Biography of Ellis Cose." EllisCose.com. Accessed January 28, 2018. http://elliscose.com/bio/.

"Desegregate Route 40 Project (Aug–Dec)." *Civil Rights Movement—History and Timeline, 1961*. Accessed January 19, 2018. http://www.crmvet.org /tim/timhis61.htm#1961uga.

Doyle, William. *An American Insurrection: James Meredith and the Battle of Oxford, Mississippi, 1962*. Anchor, 2003. (Originally published by Doubleday in 2001 as *An American Insurrection: The Battle of Oxford, Mississippi, 1962.*)

Dreyfuss, Joel. "Waltzing with Ben and Sally." *Huffington Post*. Accessed January 28, 2018. https://www.huffingtonpost.com/joel-dreyfuss/waltzing -with-ben-and-sal_b_6041026.html.

Duke Ellington. "Sophisticated Lady." Genius Lyrics. Accessed January 20, 2018. https://genius.com/Duke-ellington-sophisticated-lady-lyrics.

"EducationMakers." The HistoryMakers. Accessed January 28, 2018. http:// www.thehistorymakers.org/biography/paul-delaney-41.

Evers, Medgar. "Mississippi Mood: Hope and Fear." *The Washington Post*, October 14, 1962.

Evers, Medgar Wiley. *The Autobiography of Medgar Evers: A Hero's Life and Legacy Revealed through His Writings, Letters, and Speeches*. Civitas Books, 2005.

Fitzgerald, Mark. "Black Columnist, White Papers." *Editor and Publisher.* Accessed January 28, 2018. http://www.editorandpublisher.com/news /black-columnists-white-papers-p-12/.

"Freedom Rides Roll across the South." *Civil Rights Movement—History and Timeline, 1961.* Accessed January 19, 2018. http://www.crmvet.org/tim /timhis61.htm#1961uga.

Gates, Henry Louis, Jr., and Donald Yacovone. *The African Americans: Many Rivers to Cross.* SmileyBooks, 2013.

Gilbert, Ben W. *Ten Blocks from the White House: Anatomy of the Washington Riots of 1968.* Pall Mall Press, 1969.

Gilbert, Ben W. "Toward a Color-Blind Newspaper: Race Relations and the 'Washington Post.'" *Washington History* 5, no. 2, 1993.

Graham, Katharine. *Personal History.* Vintage, 1998.

Halberstam, David. *The Powers That Be.* University of Illinois Press, 1975.

Handy, William Christopher. "Beale Street Blues." Pace & Handy Music, 1916.

Henning Byfield, Anne. "Produced by Strength: Living by Power." True Vine Publishing, 2013.

Jaffe, Harry, and Tom Sherwood. *Dream City: Race, Power, and the Decline of Washington, D.C.* Simon & Schuster, 1994.

La Cruise, Sharon. "Daisy Bates: First Lady of Little Rock." *Independent Lens.* Public Broadcasting Service. PBS.org. Accessed January 20, 2018, www .pbs.org/independentlens/films/daisy-bates-first-lady-little-rock/.

"MediaMakers." The History Makers. Accessed January 28, 2018. http:// www.thehistorymakers.org/biography/milton-coleman.

McEmrys, Aaron. "Engaging the Sacred Wisdom of Our Sisters in the Wilderness: A Unitarian Universalist/Womanist Dialogue." *The Journal of Liberal Religion* 7 (2009): 1–17.

McHenry, Elizabeth. *Forgotten Readers: Recovering the Lost History of African American Literary Societies.* Duke University Press, 2002.

"Metropolitan AME Church, African American Heritage Trail." Cultural Tourism D.C. Accessed January 20, 2018. https://www.culturaltourismdc .org/portal/metropolitan-ame-church-african-american-heritage-trail.

"Music Beale Street Memphis United States of America Tennessee Elvis Presley." Alamy Ltd. 2018. Accessed January 20, 2018. http:// www.alamy.com/stock-photo-music-beale-street-memphis-united -states-of-america-tennessee-elvis-6858412.html.

"Our History." African Methodist Episcopal Church. Accessed January 20, 2018. https://www.ame-church.com/our-church/our-history/.

Painia, B. Alexandria. "Never Forget #004: Eartha Kitt Made Lady Bird Johnson Cry…and Got Blackballed for It." The Visibility Project. Accessed
January 28, 2018. http://www.thevisibilityproject.com/2015/04/09/never
-forget-004-eartha-kitt-made-lady-bird-johnson-cry-and-got
-blackballed-for-it/.

Prince, Richard. "Was Hillary Clinton Asked the Right Question at
the NABJ-NAHJ Convention?" Journal-isms. Posted August 6, 2016.
Accessed January 28, 2018. https://journalisms.theroot.com/was-hillary
-clinton-asked-the-right-questions-at-the-na-1790888807.

"Remembering Jim Vance: Honoring the Life and Career of the Iconic News4
Anchor." NBC4. Accessed January 19, 2018. https://www.nbcwashing
ton.com/news/local/News4-Anchor-Jim-Vance-Dies-at-75-436001373
.html.

Roberts, Chalmers M. The Washington Post: The First 100 Years. Houghton
Mifflin Harcourt, 1977.

Roberts, Gene, and Hank Klibanoff. The Race Beat: The Press, the Civil Rights
Struggle, and the Awakening of a Nation. Vintage, 2008.

"Rock Hill SC, 'Jail-No-Bail' Sit-Ins (Feb–Mar)." Civil Rights Movement—
History and Timeline, 1961. Accessed January 19, 2018. http://www.crmvet
.org/tim/timhis61.htm#1961uga.

Sanders, Joshunda. How Racism and Sexism Killed Traditional Media: Why the
Future of Journalism Depends on Women and People of Color. Praeger, 2015.

Simkin, John. "American History, Watergate, Michele Clark." Spartacus
Educational. Accessed January 28, 2018. http://spartacus-educational
.com/JFKclarkM.htm.

Skyhorse, Brando, and Lisa Page, eds. We Wear the Mask: 15 True Stories of
Passing in America. Beacon Press, 2017.

Sotomayor, Frank. "History of the Maynard Institute—The Beginning:
Making Newsrooms Look Like America." Unity 2008 Conference. 2008.

Sotomayor, Frank. "The First 30 Years of MIJE: Making Newsrooms Look
Like America." Unity Conference, National Association of Black Journalists. Accessed January 28, 2018. https://www.mije.org/about/history/.

"The First Ride (May, 1961)." Civil Rights Movement—History and Timeline,
1961. Accessed January 19, 2018. http://www.crmvet.org/tim/timhis61
.htm#1961uga.

"Tom Mboya: The Charismatic Pan-Africanist, Freedom Fighter, and the
Greatest," Trip Down Memory Lane. Accessed January 20, 2018. https://
kwekudee-tripdownmemorylane.blogspot.com/2013/12/tom-mboya
-charismatic-pan-africanist.html.

"Tougaloo Nine and Jackson State Protest (Mar)." *Civil Rights Movement—History and Timeline, 1961.* Accessed January 19, 2018. http://www.crmvet .org/tim/timhis61.htm#1961uga.

Thurman, Howard. *With Head and Heart: The Autobiography of Howard Thurman.* Houghton Mifflin Harcourt, 1981.

"2017 Deadline Club Hall of Fame." The Deadline Club. Accessed January 28, 2018. http://www.deadlineclub.org/2017-deadline-club-hall-of -fame-2/.

Tyler, Bruce M. *Louisville in World War II.* Arcadia Publishing, 2005.

"University of Georgia Desegregated (Jan)." *Civil Rights Movement—History and Timeline, 1961.* Accessed January 19, 2018. http://www.crmvet.org /tim/timhis61.htm#1961uga.

Ursuline Sisters of Louisville. "Ursuline College." Ursuline Sisters of Louisville. Accessed January 20, 2018. http://www.ursulinesisterslouisville .org/ursuline_college.php.

Walker, Alice. *In Search of Our Mothers' Gardens: Womanist Prose.* Harcourt Brace Jovanovich, 1983.

Williams, Delores. "Womanist Theology." In *Women's Visions: Theological Reflection, Celebration, Action,* ed. Ofelia Ortega. WCC, 1995.

Woodson, Carter G. *The Mis-Education of the Negro.* Ed. Charles H. Wesley and Thelma D. Perry. Washington, D.C.: Associated Publishers, 1969. (Originally published in 1933.)

Index

About the Author

DOROTHY BUTLER GILLIAM has been a journalist for more than six decades. She started in the black press, working in Louisville, Kentucky; Memphis, Tennessee; and Chicago. In 1961, she became the first black woman reporter for *The Washington Post*. She went on to become an editor and a columnist for the paper before retiring in 2003. Throughout her career, she also worked tirelessly to nurture other journalists of color and to diversify newsrooms across the United States.

Ms. Gilliam is a co-founder, former chair, and current board member of the Robert C. Maynard Institute for Journalism Education (MIJE), which has trained thousands of people of color as traditional and multimedia journalists and managers for print, television, and new media. She has taught in MIJE's summer editing and reporting training programs and mentored many journalists over the years.

She is a former president of the National Association of Black Journalists and of the Unity Journalists of Color. She was a leader of the first Unity Convention, held in Atlanta in 1994. An estimated eight thousand journalists of all races and ethnicities attended that groundbreaking conference.

Ms. Gilliam has broad national contacts among journalists of diverse races and cultures, media executives, universities, select school districts, and foundations. In the past dozen years, she has become a national leader in creating pathways for underserved urban high school youth to consider media careers. In her final years at *The Washington Post*, she founded the Young Journalists Development Program and was most recently founder-director of the Prime Movers Media program at George Washington University. This program operated within the school systems of Washington, D.C., and Philadelphia, sending professional journalists and interns from George Washington and Temple Universities into high schools to help students create or revitalize school media. It still operates in Philadelphia city schools. Through this position, Ms. Gilliam made many contacts throughout the nation in scholastic journalism at high schools, colleges, and universities.

Ms. Gilliam is a well-known public speaker who has addressed groups in sizes up to several thousand. She was featured in a well-received 2005 documentary entitled *Freedom's Call*, with photographer Ernest Withers, about their work together as civil rights journalists. She is also featured in two additional documentaries, *Southern Journalists Who Covered the Civil Rights Movement* and *Hope & Fury: MLK, The Movement and The Media* (MSNBC, 2018).

Ms. Gilliam formerly had her own show on BET-Television and in the late 1960s and early 1970s appeared regularly on a daily show called *Panorama*, co-hosted then by Maury Povich. She also appeared regularly on Howard University Television, and *To the Contrary* on the Public Broadcasting Service.

Ms. Gilliam is the author of *Paul Robeson: All American* (1976). Some of her *Washington Post* columns appeared in *She Said What: Interviews with Women Newspaper Columnists* by Maria Braden (2009), and she contributed a chapter to *Skin Deep: Black Women & White Women Write About Race* by Marita Golden and Susan Shreve (1996). She wrote the first three chapters in *The Edge of Change: Women in the 21st Century Press* (2010).

She is a steward emerita of the 1,100-member Metropolitan African Methodist Episcopal Church in Washington, D.C., a role that gives her access to A.M.E. churches across the nation as venues for book signings, sales, and speeches. She is also a member of a prestigious national black fraternal organization, Alpha Kappa Alpha Sorority, Inc. She received Columbia Journalism School's Alumni of the Year Award in 1979 and received the 2010 Lifetime Achievement Award from the Washington Press Club Foundation. She is a member of the Washington, D.C., and Lincoln (Missouri) University Hall of Fame and a national "History Maker"—a contributor to an oral history collection of firsthand accounts of African American leaders. She is a former member of the National Press Club and Leadership Greater Washington.

She has three daughters and three grandchildren.